Currents of Warm Life

Popular Culture in American Higher Education

Currents of Warm Life

Popular Culture in American Higher Education

Compiled and Edited by
Mark Gordon
and
Jack Nachbar

Assisted by
James Von Shilling
and
Michelle Kuebbeler

Bowling Green University Popular Press
Bowling Green, Ohio 43403

Library of Congress Catalog Card No.: 80-80344
ISBN: 0-87972-152-9
    0-87972-153-7

Cover design by Lynn Nachbar

CONTENTS

LIST OF TABLES

Acknowledgments

The authors wish to acknowledge those people who lent their support, guidance and efforts toward the successful completion of this project. Dr. Karin Sandel, for her generosity and assistance in guiding us along the lines of a new research method with which we were unfamiliar, and Dr. Ray Browne for his helpful interviews, suggestions and criticisms and generous support throughout the developlment of the research and writing. Special gratitude must be extended to James Von Schilling for his service and patience as the director of computer operations and Michelle Kuebbeler for her good natured assistance on all parts of the manuscript. Our appreciation to student helpers Carolyn Legg and Nora Bautista for invaluable hours spent gathering materials in the appendices. And finally we thank all those who took time to fill out a laborious survey form and all the contributors to the course syllabus section of this study. Nancy Kula is to be commended for her persistence and expertise in the typing of parts of the script. Finally, our thanks for favors along the way to Pat Browne, Joyce Moore and Rebecca Peters.

Appendices

That which had been negligently trodden under foot by those who were harnessing and provisioning themselves for long journeys into far countries, is suddenly found to be richer than all foreign parts. The literature of the poor, the feelings of the child, the philosophy of the street, the meaning of household life, are the topics of the time. It is a great stride. It is a sign—is it not?—of new vigor when the extremities are made active when currents of warm life run into the hands and the feet. I ask not for the great, the remote, the romantic; what is doing in Italy or Arabia; what is Greek art, or Provencal minstrelsy; I embrace the common, I explore and sit at the feet of the familiar, the low. Give me insight into to-day, and you may have the antique and future worlds. What would we really know the meaning of? The meal in the firkin; the milk in the pan; the ballad in the street; the news of the boat; the glance of the eye; the form and the gait of the body;—show me the ultimate reason of these matters; show me the sublime presence of the highest spiritual cause lurking, as always it does lurk, in these suburbs and extremities of nature; let me see every trifle bristling with the polarity that ranges it instantly on an eternal law; and the shop, the plough, and the ledger referred to the like cause by which light undulates and poets sing;—and the world lies no longer a dull miscellany and lumber-room, but has form and order; there is no trifle, there is no puzzle, but one design unites and animates the farthest pinnacle and the lowest trench.

The American Scholar

Introduction

Popular Culture Studies in America

Although some scholarly involvement with mass society and the popular arts occurred earlier in the 20th century, academic interest in popular culture did not reach a recognizable stage of development in the United States until the early 1960s. The first signs of interest in popular culture can be traced back (at least) to the early 1900s when American intellectuals considered the effects capitalism, technology and industrialization had on beliefs and lifestyles.

Another early scholarly movement related to popular culture studies, known as intellectual history, began in the 1920s. Intellectual historians remained primarily elitist in attitude but they occasionally used popular literature as sources of American thought.[1] This tendency is best expressed by Vernon L. Parrington's *Main Currents in American Thought* (1927). Nevertheless, as Garth Jowett notes, "While these [and other] works did mention (sometimes in detail) the content of American popular culture, they seldom attempted to delve into the relationship between the public and its popular art forms."[2]

Interdisciplinary approaches to American culture began in 1936 with the initiation of the American Civilization program at Harvard.[3] Similar programs developed at other colleges. In 1951, the American Studies Association was founded. Because they attempted to distinguish American culture from European culture, advocates of American Studies claimed it was a creative reaction against the restrictiveness of established disciplines.[4] This thrust allowed some scholars to investigate new dimensions of American life such as folklore and popular culture. Henry Nash Smith, for example, included a chapter on dime novels in *Virgin Land* (1950). Overall, however, American Studies scholars relied on materials from traditional fields, primarily American literature and history.

During the 1960s the academic study of popular culture was finally fully realized. A number of books were directed to mass society and the popular arts. [5] Of greatest significance were the ambitions of scholars such as Russel B. Nye, John G. Cawelti, Marshall Fishwick and Ray B. Browne, all of whom had been working with aspects of popular culture within traditional disciplines for years. Ray Browne felt strongly that popular culture had to be studied in and of itself. As a folklorist and English professor, and as a long-time member of the American Studies Association, Browne knew other scholars and students who wanted to devote more of their energies to the study of popular culture but lacked the means of doing so. His answer was to found the *Journal of Popular Culture* in 1967, and

1

subsequently to organize a Popular Press around it.

According to Browne, the *Journal* was designed to broaden the scope of other academic journals and, more importantly, to step up the activities in the area of popular culture study.[6] The *Journal* sought new scholarly approaches to American and international life. Unlike the American Studies Association-sponsored *American Quarterly,* the *Journal of Popular Culture* placed its primary emphasis upon the culture of the general populace. The Fall 1968 issue of *American Quarterly,* for example, featured articles on Henry David Thoreau, Robert Penn Warren, John Barth and Thorstein Veblin, whereas the *Journal of Popular Culture* in its Fall 1968 number published articles on New Orleans jazz, science fiction, nineteenth century American broadside ballads and pop art. There was some overlap: *AQ* published an article on marriage proposals, and *JPC* published an essay on Herrick and Hawthorne. The difference in emphasis, however, between the two journals was obvious.

Despite controversies and criticism about the *Journal* expressed by those unwilling to accept its thrust, popular culture studies in general have prospered ever since the first issue of the *Journal of Popular Culture* was released. David Mead, English professor at Michigan State University, read that issue and joyously exclaimed to Russel Nye, "I've finally found a journal where I can publish my material!" By the end of 1968 the *Journal* had a promising 500 subscribers. At the same time, colleges were beginning to allow more popular culture courses into their curricula. English departments showed the greatest receptivity, offering courses in science fiction, detective fiction, westerns and other forms of popular literature. Several departments, including English, Speech and Journalism, began offering an unprecedented number of courses in film. A survey conducted by the American Film Institute in 1969 listed a surprising 1,233 film courses at 219 academic institutions—an increase of 84% since 1964.[10] These developments encouraged Ray Browne to make another important move. As Program Chair of the American Studies Association in 1969, he decided to devote a special afternoon session of that year's national ASA meeting to explore the possibility of establishing a national organization known as the Popular Culture Association. Two hundred persons attended the meeting, including Abraham Kaplan, John Seelye, John Cawelti, Marshall Fishwick, Russel Nye and many other notable scholars in American Studies. They discussed the need for a new direction in the study of American mass culture, and before the session ended, plans were made for the creation of this Popular Culture Association.[11]

In 1970 Russel Nye's *The Unembarrassed Muse,* a detailed history and re-evaluation of the popular arts in America, was enthusiastically received by reviewers and scholars. In the meantime, Ray Browne had established at Bowling Green State University the Center for the Study of Popular Culture. A huge collection of popular literature and artifacts was assembled into a special research division of the University library. Two floors above it the BGSU Living Archives was formed along with the Audio Center, headed by William Schurk. In 1971 a Master of Arts program in Popular Culture was added to the English Department at Bowling Green State University. Bowling Green University also became the headquarters for the

Secretary-Treasurer of the Popular Culture Association, though the Presidency moved throughout the country. The first national meeting of the PCA in 1971 at Michigan State University included over 200 professors, graduate and undergraduate students from all regions of the United States.[12]

Popular Culture studies at Bowling Green was moved from English to a separate department in 1973, thereby becoming the first department in the United States devoted exclusively to courses in popular culture. At the same time, however, it was estimated that over 600 college courses in the United States focused exclusively or mainly on popular culture courses, while hundreds of others included heavy use of popular materials under traditional course titles. [13] Subscription to the *Journal of Popular Culture* had risen to over 2,000 by 1973. The success of *JPC* prompted the publication of three more journals closely or loosely associated with the Popular Press: the *Journal of Popular Film* (edited by Michael T. Marsden and Jack Nachbar), *Popular Music and Society* (edited by R. Serge Denisoff, a member of the Sociology Department at Bowling Green State University), and *Popular Culture Methods,* (edited by Sam L. Grogg, Jr., and financed by the Popular Press). The last named is an educational journal distributed at no cost to members of the PCA as an aid to the development of popular culture curricula.

The seventies have held unmeasured growth of popular culture in higher education in the United States. Scores of courses on television have taken their places alongside the film courses that had appeared a decade earlier. Traditional departments of "Speech" changed their names to "Communications" and revised their curricula to include mass media studies as an essential part of their offerings. The serious study of sports, recreation and leisure activities began to be an accepted addition to the courses presented by sociology and physical education departments. During the past few years earlier arguments over the respectability of popular culture courses have shifted to discussions of what methodologies should be employed. Only one other degree program was pushed into existence—a Master's degree program at Morgan State University—but course offerings within traditional departments have grown into the thousands. One of the seventy working sections of the Modern Language Association is Popular Culture, and most of the regional Modern Language Association divisions regularly include programs in the area, as do the national and regional meetings of the American Historical Association, and various other academic associations. The Popular Culture Association has divided into regional subgroups which also meet annually to bring professors and other interested persons together. In 1979 there was the first national meeting of the American Culture Association, an allied group whose interests parallel and extend those of the members of the PCA. Attendance at the 1979 national meeting of the PCA (and ACA) was over 800. Regional PCA meetings in 1979 attracted nearly 1000 participants. There are now more than 5000 subscribers to the various journals (including 1500 to the two-year-old *Journal of American Culture*).[14]

4   Popular Culture Studies in America

The Problem of Direction and Scope

The extent to which popular culture studies have entered the U.S. four-year university and college could in part have been predicted by the growing number of published popular culture books and increasing number of PCA members. It is presumed that with the passing of time increased scholarly interest has resulted in a proliferation of courses. Yet basic questions remain unanswered. What schools offer popular culture courses? What kinds of courses have attracted special academic attention? Because no recent effort has been made to determine the range or taxonomy of popular culture courses on a national scale, not even popular culturists have enough information to confidently answer these questions.

Besides the absence of recorded statistics, there are three interrelated reasons why popular culturists do not know the scope of their field. The first is a problem which has existed since the beginning of the study of mass culture: a lack of philosophical realization of *what* constitutes Popular Culture. During the early days of the Popular Culture Association, Ray Browne convinced other scholars that the definition should be kept loose and open. This, argued Browne, would nurture the young discipline by allowing a maximum number of subjects to be studied. As Browne stated in the *Journal of Popular Culture,* "our concern with methodologies should not obstruct our interest in the primary materials."[15]

A second difficulty with charting the territory of popular culture studies is the distance between discreet boundaries. If the definitions presented by Ray Browne, Russell Nye, and other founders are even partially accepted,[16] they still leave a multitude of cultural aspects which could properly be studied under the heading of Popular Culture. A common tendency is to reduce one's concept of popular culture to a comfortable size, thereby excluding many subjects others would include, such as modern architecture and the psychology of collective behavior. Conversely, some persons overwhelmed by the area covered by the term popular culture are inclined to include courses which traditionally belong to other disciplines, examples being "Philosophy in Utopian Literature" or "Art of Igmar Bergman." This discrepancy, of course, confuses any ideas of scope.

The third and greatest hindrance to knowing where and how many popular culture courses there are is the present scarcity of organized programs in the U.S. Besides Bowling Green, only Morgan State University in Baltimore, Maryland, has a degree program with a Popular Culture title.

Other colleges and universities such as Northeastern Illinois University, Michigan State University, SUNY-Fredonia and the University of Southern Florida have developed excellent popular culture archival resources but as yet have not begun formal degree programs.

A few departments and interdisciplinary projects have been designed to study popular phenomena, but coordinators have chosen more "legitimate" names like "The Center for Comparative Culture Study" at the University of California (Irving).

The vast majority of popular culture courses are consequently offered within traditional departments and are often taught under the guise of standard course topics. One example is a Religion course at Dartmouth College entitled "Religion and Society." It is described in the 1978 *Dartmouth Bulletin* as a course which "focuses upon cult-like groups and popular religious expression in contemporary America."

Thus, the task of locating popular culture courses requires one to look beyond what is suggested merely by the course title. A few more examples taken directly from college bulletins will illustrate the point:

American Studies 350—*Culture and Arts in America*
Popular attitudes towards arts, travel, fashions, craft and industrial productions, recreation. Past used to explain the present.

(University of Hawaii, Manoa)

English 205—*Propaganda Survey and Analysis*
A study of the language, myths, and stereotypes and uses by the mass media (newspapers, magazines, television, advertising, protest songs, etc.) in the propaganda process.

(Iowa State University)

English 33—*Science Fiction*
Speculative fiction in popular culture. Examines science fiction and fantasy as an expression of cultural values.

(Austin College)

Chemistry 10030—*Consumer Chemistry*
Designed for non-science majors. Covers many everyday encounters with chemical problems faced by consumers.

(Kent State University)

These problems have caused internal conflicts among popular culturists over the past decade, and as expected they made the task of gathering course statistics diffcult. Because the problems were treated in the process of conducting the following survey of popular culture courses, however, the result is some resolutions to them as well as a report of the status of popular culture studies in United States higher education.

Structure

The text of this study is divided into four parts. Each succeeding part is intended to be a more specific look at an area of popular culture studies than the one that precedes it. Part one presents the results of a national survey of popular culture courses being offered through 1979 at American four year universities and colleges. Part two attempts to narrow and bring alive the rather abstract data of part one by describing the development of popular culture courses and programs at three specific academic institutions. The third part focuses on specific courses. Instructors from all over the United States were invited to submit course syllabi for possible publication. Those selected were chosen to represent the wide variety of topics and methods being used nationally to present popular culture materials in the classroom. Part four are appendices of specific courses, institutions and respondents to the survey which may be of use to readers who desire more information about popular culture courses being taught close by.

Notes

[1] To be published by Prentice-Hall, p.2.

[2] Jowett, p.2.

[3] Noted by Robert J. Mertz and Michael T. Marsden, "American Culture Studies: A Discipline in Search of itself," *Journal of Popular Culture* IX:2 (Fall 1975), p.462.

[4] Mertz and Marsden, p.461.

[5]A few of the earlier examples are: Norman Jacob, ed., *Culture for the Millions* (New York: Free Press, 1961); Stuart Hall and Paddy Whannel, *The Popular Arts* (New York: Pantheon Press, 1965); and Nicholas Tucker, *Understanding the Mass Media* (Cambridge, Mass: Harvard University Press, 1966). And of course there are the books of Marshall McLuhan.

[6]From interview with Ray Browne, Bowling Green State University, July 11, 1979.

[7]Published examples of negative criticism are best represented by Russell Kirk's, "Anti-Culture at Public Expense," *National Review*, September 23, 1969, p.962.

[8]Reported to Ray Browne by Russell Nye (information from the interview with Ray Browne).

[9]From interview with Ray Browne.

[10]Included in John Cawelti's article, "Popular Culture Programs," *Popular Culture and Curricula*, ed. Ray B. Browne and Ronald J. Ambrosetti (Bowling Green: Popular Press, 1972), p.23.

[11]From interview with Ray Browne.

[12]From interview with Ray Browne.

[13]Browne and Ambrosetti, ed., *Popular Culture and Curricula* (Bowling Green: Popular Press, 1972), from the introduction.

[14]Information available from secretarial records at the Center for the Study of Popular Culture at BGSU.

[15]From the introduction to an in-depth section on "Theories and Methodologies," *Journal of Popular Culture*, IX:2 (Fall 1975).

[16]Essays directed to the problem of definition have appeared in several Popular Press publications. In a textbook for introductory courses in popular culture, *The Popular Culture Reader*, edited by Jack Nachbar, Deborah Weiser, and John L. Wright (1978), three of the most commonly used definitions appear. Ray Browne defined popular culture as "the culture of the people, of all the people, as distinguished from a select, small upper-class group. It is also the dominant culture of minorities, of ethnic, color, social, religious, of financial minorities." (p.12). Russell Nye defines popular culture by the visible product it encompasses, those productions, both artistic and commercial, designed for mass consumption, which appeal to and express the tastes and understanding of the majority of the public, free of minority standards" (p.22). Nachbar and Wright describe popular culture, in the simplest terms, as "mainstream culture—the arts, artifacts, and beliefs shared by large segments of society" (p.5).

PART I

Chapter One:
Research Intentions and Procedures

Aims of the Survey

The purpose of this section is to report the current overall status of popular culture studies at colleges and universities in the United States. It provides the first detailed assessment of the courses and trends which characterize the field. The key questions the research attempts to answer are:

1) What is the approximate number of popular culture courses offered in four-year colleges and universities across the United States?
2) What is the nature of these courses? I. e. what are the most common topics and subjects? What seem to be the most common approaches to popular culture materials?
3) In what departments are the largest numbers of courses found? What departments seem to have shown a special interest in popular culture (and in what specific subjects) over the past decade?
4) What is the approximate student enrollment in popular culture courses (in general and according to specific types of courses)? Also, how frequently do the different types of courses tend to be offered?
5) What years have large numbers of popular culture courses been introduced into curricula? What trends from the early 1970s are falling and what new trends appear to be developing.
6) Is the number of popular culture courses likely to increase, decrease or remain the same in the near future? What are some reasons for these projections?

The information gathered to address these questions is the outcome of a nation-wide survey. The results of this survey, given in Chapter Three, will then be compared to a small piece of related research conducted in 1972 by John Cawelti.[1] This comparison is used to gain some perspective in checking the directions popular culture studies have taken since that early developmental stage. Even though Cawelti's research involved only 36 schools, it represented until now the only survey and breakdown of popular culture courses ever made.

Cawelti found that 21 schools out of the 36 which completed his questionnaire offered courses in some form of popular literature. The second most frequent subject was 20 instances of ethnic subculture courses, mostly

7

Afro-American. There were 17 reported courses in mass media and films; 16 in popular music; and 9 in popular art and architecture. These findings suggest that popular culture courses in 1972 were varied and fairly well balanced in terms of subjects covered.

Because most members of the Popular Culture Association were and still are affiliated with English Departments[2], one would expect popular literature courses to dominate by a greater margin than Cawelti's survey reported. They may have, in fact, since Cawelti's research was so limited as to be possibly misleading. A survey of *Journal of Popular Culture* articles taken in 1972 showed 30% of the articles dealt with popular literature compared with 10.3% in film, 9.9% in popular music, and 5% in popular arts and entertainment.[3] Another survey of the topics delivered at the 1972 Popular Culture Association convention reveals that 23.4% were about popular literature, compared wth 16% about film and the mass media; 14.1% about arts and entertainments; 7.4% about pedagogy and curriculum; and 5.7% about popular music. Only five topics out of a total of 175 delivered (2.9%) were about ethnic subcultures.[4] These supplementary figures show a stronger degree of interest in literature among early popular culturists than Cawelti discovered, and very little interest in ethnic studies. Hence some adjustment in his course breakdown may be in order.

This survey is more than an updating of Cawelti's survey. It includes a more detailed listing of course topics as well as a breakdown of departments in which popular culture courses are offered. Also included are the number of times per year most of the courses are offered and a tabulation of enrollment. The survey utilizes information obtained from questionnaires mailed to a large number of institutions all over the country, making its range significantly broader than Cawelti's.

A departmental breakdown shows, among other things, the extent to which popular culture studies has entered other fields. Estimations in the early 1970s had nearly all courses within English, history, communication and journalism departments.[5] The close link to English and literary analysis has been all too strong according to popular culturists who have also spoken out as critics. In 1972, for example, Bruce Lohof charged that popular culture scholars "have been called... a colloquy of voices, but we remain the prodigal sons of an indulgent English Department."[6]

Lohof's argument is equally true of the present. If he counted the number of professors and presentations at the 1979 PCA meeting, Lohof would find that a startling 296 out of 497 professors in attendance were from English departments (60%) and about one-third of the topics were about some form of popular literature.[7] On the other hand, he would find a comforting 164 newcomers from disciplines other than English, history, communication and journalism, who gave presentations of 150 topics other than literature, mass media, history and the popular arts. One aim of this survey is to assess the degree to which popular culture studies have penetrated into areas beyond English, history, communication and journalism.

Investigative Procedures

It seemed obvious to us that the most reasonable technique for gathering data would be the mailing of questionnaires. The methodology applied was derived from a system of guidelines for mail surveys called the TOTAL DESIGN METHOD (TDM).[8]

The TDM, according to the researcher who founded it, basically involves "the identification of each aspect of the survey process that may affect response quantity or quality and shaping them in a way that will encourage good response."[9] In other words, it is a method which is supposed to produce high and reliable response rates because special attention is given to each procedural step of the survey as it is being conducted.

The TDM was used only in part for this project because of the shortage of personnel, time and money. The one serious deviation, however, was not following up with the standard three additional questionnarire mailings after the first comprehensive one. Time was an essential deterrent and consequently we limited the number of follow up mailings to one.

Sources of Data

Since the data needed for this survey were information about popular culture courses at four-year colleges and universities in the United States it seemed logical to mail the surveys to college professors who could supply this information. Time and budget allowed for the printing of approximately 2,500 five-page questionnaires (including cover letter, instruction sheet, and course forms). The initial mailing sample was set at 1,200 subjects. This permitted the printing of 1,000 revised questionaires for second mailing and a surplus of 300 potential questionnaires for alternative uses.

The next concern was efficient use of these materials. If the subjects would be asked to report courses for an entire university, they would either have be knowledgeable of popular culture studies at that institution or they would have to be willing to take the time to find this information. If this were true, many subjects would not bother to complete the questionnaire or would do it haphazardly. Therefore in constructing a mailing list, the best possible solution would be to have a random sampling of colleges, but to use specific addresses of professors at those colleges who would be likely to cooperate. This strategy is referred to in the TDM as a *specialized population sampling.* It is a more direct means to obtain a particular kind of information and to induce a higher percentage of responses.

The mailing lists from the *Journal of Popular Culture* and the *Journal of Popular Film and Television,* which are available at the Center for the Study of Popular Culture, were sources for specialized sampling. Subscribers to these journals are also likely to be members of the Popular Culture Association*. If anybody at a college could report information about popular culture courses, or would make an effort to get this information, it would be someone connected to the field. Moreover, these persons are well distributed across every state in the country, and they are affiliated with all types of educational institutions. Because American Studies is also an interdisciplinary approach to American Culture, additional mailings were sent to American Studies chairs in the United States.

---

*Yearly membership fees to the PCA include a yearly subscription to the *Journal of Popular Culture,* or vice versa; but this plan does not include the *Journal of Popular Film and Television.*

The questionnaire

The questionnaire was designed according to TDM theoretical guidelines for form and content. Each step is given below. Particular problems with the questionnaire will be discussed in the next section.

A cover letter stated the problem of research and explained how the participation of selected professors could help to solve that problem. Respondents would be rewarded if the subject were successful enough to be published; their names would be included in the publication, and they would be given a copy at reduced price according to printing costs. If for any reasons the selected persons could not complete the questionnaire, they were asked to pass it on to a competent colleague who would complete it. An address and phone number were given for further questions.

Instructions were given in a concise manner on the second page of the questionnaire. Subjects were again reminded of the importance of this research to the development of Popular Culture and were asked to take special time in answering the questionnaire as thoroughly as possible. They were advised to consult a college bulletin if necessary. Basically, subjects were asked to report on popular culture courses along with a few descriptive details about those courses. To help them identify those courses that qualified as popular culture a statement of definition was given. (See instruction sheet of sample questionnaire in Appendix C.)

Most of the information asked for had to be reported subjectively, through open-ended questions. But a limited set of questions was used pertaining only to the specific research intentions. The first question asked was, "Are there any courses offered at your college/university which could be classified as popular culture studies?" A response here would provide some indication of how well subjects understand the definition of popular culture as it is given in the instructions, and it would also indicate which schools have popular culture courses.

If subjects marked "yes" to the first question, a stronger indication of their understanding of Popular Culture would be revealed in the next and most important question, which asked them to list the courses on attached forms. (It would be the responsibility of the researchers to check these courses.) For convenience, space would be provided on these forms for additional information when it could be provided:

——a brief description of courses with ambiguous titles
——approximate number of students enrolled in each course
——the year that each course was first offered
——frequency of the course offering (i.e. how many times per year it is offered)

If this information could be given for most of the courses surveyed, then enough data would be available to answer many of the key questions.

Because one overall intention of the project was to measure the growth and development of Popular Culture as an educational movement, subjects were asked in a third question, "Do you have knowledge of courses relating to popular culture that are planned for the future?" If the answer was "yes," the professors were asked to list these courses by title, department and projected date of offering. A final question asked respondents if they thought the frequency of course offerings in Popular Culture would increase, decrease or remain the same. Subjects were encouraged to give a brief explanation. Because these responses would be opinions, this question is one means of gathering student, faculty and administration reactions to Popular Culture courses.

Pretesting and questionnaire problems

In September 1978 the first draft of the questionnaire was sent to twelve persons on the mailing list who have been long-time members of the Popular Culture Association. These persons were chosen because the primary purpose of the pretest was to test its sufficiency. Ten persons responded. Three completed the questionnaire and reported no difficulties in its format; six persons completed the questionnaire and offered helpful commentary for revisions; and one person was totally confused.

Most pretest subjects claimed the instructions were not clear enough, noting especially that the definitions of popular culture courses had to be better articulated. Two persons advised the use of less explanation and more examples. One person listed six courses that were not popular culture. Another reported fewer courses than she might have because, as she stated, "It isn't clear that you'll accept courses not offered through a Popular Culture program."

Several statements were made about the amount of work required to fill out the forms properly. One professor was offended at the idea of searching through every department at a school with 40,000 students. Others who expressed subtler versions of this feeling only reported courses from their own departments.

Thus before the questionnaire was mass mailed, it was revised according to the responses to the pretest. The number of pages was reduced from six to four and a half. The instruction page was re-written to give examples of Popular Culture courses and those commonly misunderstood as Popular Culture.

In deciding upon the most useful definition for the survey we had to keep in mind that Popular Culture is still a relatively new field and there is as yet no single statement agreed upon by all. Scholars are still debating, for example, the fundamental questions of what the term *popular* means in a conceptual sense, a descriptive sense and a critical sense.[10] Should a definition be based on aesthetics, consumption or economics? On what basis does a course offered in a History Department or a Journalism Department become a Popular Culture course? Since the purpose of the questionnaire was to outline the scope of the courses in popular culture rather than to dictate the nature of the subject itself, we decided it would be best to avoid these kinds of theoretical problems. Therefore Popular Culture was defined primarily in terms of the materials studied.[11] In any traditional field, if the beliefs, arts or artifacts studied are significant parts of the lives of large proportion of people in any given geographic area during any historical period, these are aspects of popular culture, whatever they might be. Courses which place a primary emphasis on an in-depth examination of these aspects are Popular Culture courses. This definition was demonstrated by examples.

Since every course would be checked before it was counted, subjects were encouraged to submit those they were not sure about. If a title obviously signified that the course was not the cultural study of popular phenomena, respondents were instructed not to add a description. Otherwise descriptions were requested. Stronger emphasis was given to the necessity of subjects looking outside their own departments.

As each questionnaire was returned, the forms were checked for errors. If a report from a sizeable school listed few or no popular culture courses, or if it appeared that the reporter had not looked beyond his or her own department, that questionnaire was later cross-checked with college bulletins.

As expected, some courses submitted in the survey did not follow the definition established and were therefore excluded. These were essentially those of traditional disciplines, even though some supplementary popular materials were used (e.g. a "History of American Art" course which studied popular art in the last week of the term). Another group of courses not accepted was professional or vocational training courses (i.e. "how to" courses) such as "Elements of Filmmaking," "Producing and Directing for Television," and "Principles of Advertising Writing." Even though these courses *use* popular culture materials, they are designed not to be analytical studies within any historical, social-scientific, or humanities context.[12] This is not to imply that only certain departments have Popular Culture courses. To the contrary, courses which studied popular materials from historical, social-scientific or humanities perspectives were found in almost every kind of department (e.g. "History and Philosophy of Sports" in a Physical Education department and "Technology and Society" in an Engineering Department).

The third type of courses which were excluded were those of folklore. Some scholars argue that folklore belongs within popular culture studies. They point to the overlap between the folk and mass arts in such areas as music and fiction and conclude it is improper to consider one apart from the other. Many scholars, however, insist that folklore is clearly a body of materials separate from popular culture. Folk culture, unlike the cultures of most ethnic subgroups, is usually studied outside the realm of the culture of the majority of the people living in a given geographic area. Folk culture is studied as an entity apart from the influences of mass society.

This argument over scholarly perspectives on folklore is unlikely to be resolved in the near future. It was therefore deemed best not to include the area in this survey. By not including such courses, the results may be interpreted as too conservative, but this seemed preferable to possible feelings that the survey is too broad.

Notes

[1]John Cawelti, "Popular Culture Programs," *Popular Culture and Curricula*, eds. Ray B. Browne and Ronald J. Ambrosetti (Bowling Green: Popular Press, 1972), p. 32.

[2]Noted by Bruce Lohof, "Popular Culture: The *Journal* and the State of the Study," *Journal of Popular Culture*, VI:3 (Winter 1972), p. 455.

[3]Lohof, p. 456.

[4]Completed by the writers using the April 1972 Popular Culture Association convention program.

[5]Ray B. Browne and Ronald J. Ambrosetti, eds. *Popular Culture and Curricula* (Bowling Green: Popular Press, 1972), from the introduction.

[6]Lohof, p. 455.

[7]Completed by the writers using the April 1979 PCA convention program.

[8]Established by Don A. Dillman in his book *Mail and Telephone Surveys* (New York: Wiley, 1978), chapters 1 and 2.

[9]Dillman, p. 2.

[10]The situation as it existed when the PCA began is discussed in considerable detail by Russel B. Nye, "Notes for an Introduction to a Discussion of Popular Culture," *Journal of Popular Culture,* IV:4 (Spring 1971), p. 1035.

The multiple possibilities for and disagreements for definition and methodology are shown in a special section of the *Journal of Popular Culture* IX:2 (Fall 1975). One example of ongoing debate stems from this issue of *JPC*. In an article, "Against Evaluation: The Role of the Critic of Popular Culture," Roger B. Rollin argues that popular culture materials should be studied apart from any aesthetic value judgments. A reaction to this position was published in the Summer 1978 issue of *JPC*, "A Critical Analysis of Roger B. Rollin's 'Against Evaluation' " by John Shelton Lawrence. And in the next article of this issue Rollin gives a reply to Lawrence's approach.

Every year at the National Popular Culture Association meeting a special session is devoted to theoretical problems with definition and methodology. It is not uncommon for articles which appear in the *Journal* to include some introductory comments about how the writer defines Popular culture for his or her purposes. The opening to an article by Leslie Fiedler, "Giving the Devil His Due" (*JPC*, Fall 1978) for example, Fiedler states "I am going to define for you what I mean by 'Popular Culture'...I consider my definition (which is not a historial one, not a sociological one, not an economic one, but a mythographic or a literary-anthropologic one) the best possible definition of Popular Culture" (p.197).

[11]Russell Nye, p.1031.

[12]In the previously cited article, Russell Nye explains the Popular Culture course as one in which the nvestigative techniques of the social sciences and the humanities converge. "Where such interests draw together—in examinations of social behavior, cultural patterns, communications media, social and cultural values—the study of popular culture provides a common ground where different disciplines may combine" (p.1036).

Chapter Two
Results

Subject Response

A total of 371 completed questionnaires were returned—138 from the initial mailing, and 233 from a follow-up mailing. Responses from 64 of these questionnaires were not used in tabulating the results.*

Questionnaires were sent to every state in the U.S. The number sent to each depended upon the maximum number that could be taken from the journal mailing lists. As Table 1 indicates, all states except Alaska, Nevada, Rhode Island, Wyoming, and Puerto Rico are represented in the data by at least one completed questionnaire. Forty-seven of these questionnaires reported no popular culture courses.

A regional breakdown of institutions with popular culture courses included in the survey, indicated in Table 2, shows that most of these institutions (54%) are from the East, Mid-America, and West. These are also the regions with the largest numbers of institutions in the mailing sample. The Northwest, which has the fewest number of institutions in the mailing sample, is represented by the fewest number of returns.

Of the 260 schools that reported popular culture courses, 157 are public (60%), and 103 are private (40%). As Table 3 indicates, the sizes of these schools vary from enrollment of under 1,000 to enrollments of over 30,000.

Course Returns

A total of 1,993 courses were gathered in the survey of 307 schools. A quick estimate based on simple division shows an average of 6.5 popular culture courses at each school surveyed. The average number of courses per school among only those 260 schools which have popular culture courses is 8. As will be seen later, this estimate is low. Of the total number of courses in the survey, 84% are undergraduate courses, and 16% are graduate.

As Table 4 indicates, most of the courses in the survey are from the East (482), Mid-America (392), and West (277) regions. The fewest number of courses is in the Northwest region (77). Most schools within every region—except the West—offer six to twenty courses each. Appendix A shows a breakdown of all courses in the survey according to the number within each state and the number at each institution.

In a breakdown of courses according to size of institution, indicated in

---

*Many of those not used were from students and teachers at two-year colleges and high schools. Others were from retired professors or those on sabbatical who were unable to get the information in time. Thirty returned questionnaires appeared inaccurate, and current bulletins were not available to check courses at these particular schools.

14

TABLE 1

Number of returned questionnaires
and
breakdown of regional and state representation of
institutions in survey

Region 1: NORTHEAST		Region 2: EAST		Region 3: SOUTHEAST	
Massachusetts	13	New York	23	Georgia	12
Vermont	6	Pennsylvania	20	South Carolina	7
Connecticut	5	New Jersey	8	North Carolina	5
Maine	2	Maryland	8	Florida	4
New Hampshire	1	Virginia	6	Virgin Islands	1
Rhode Island	0	West Virginia	4	Puerto Rico	0
		Dist.of Columbia	3		
		Delaware	1		
Total	27	Total	73	Total	29

Region 4: MIDDLE NORTH		Region 5: MID-AMERICA		Region 6: MIDDLE SOUTH	
Michigan	14	Kentucky	15	Tennessee	8
Wisconsin	10	Ohio	12	Alabama	5
Minnesota	6	Illinois	11	Louisiana	3
North Dakota	2	Iowa	6	Mississippi	3
South Dakota	2	Indiana	5	Arkansas	3
		Missouri	4		
		Kansas	2		
		Nebraska	2		
Total	34	Total	57	Total	22

Region 7: NORTHWEST		Region 8: WEST		Region 9: SOUTHWEST	
Washington	4	California	21	Texas	16
Oregon	3	Colorado	6	Oklahoma	4
Montana	2	Utah	4	Arizona	2
Idaho	1	Hawaii	1	New Mexico	1
Alaska	0	Wyoming	0		
		Nevada	0		
Total	10	Total	32	Total	23

TOTAL NUMBER OF RETURNS (N) = 307

TABLE 2

Breakdown by region of institutions
with popular culture courses included in survey

───
───

Total number of colleges represented in survey: 307
Total number of colleges with popular culture courses: 260

───

Region	No. of Colleges	%
NORTHEAST	19	7 %
EAST	67	26%
SOUTHEAST	22	8%
MIDDLE NORTH	28	11%
MID-AMERICA	44	17%
MIDDLE SOUTH	18	7%
NORTHWEST	10	4%
WEST	29	11%
SOUTHWEST	23	9%
	260	100%

───

N = 260

TABLE 3

Breakdown by enrollment size of institutions
with popular culture courses

Enrollment size	No. of colleges	%
under 1,000	24	9%
1,000 - 1,999	35	13%
2,000 - 2,999	29	11%
3,000 - 4,999	28	11%
5,000 - 9,999	64	25%
10,000 - 19,999	48	18%
20,000 - 29,999	26	10%
over 30,000	6	2%
	260	100%

N = 260

TABLE 4

Cross-tabulation of region of colleges with number of popular culture
courses offered

Total no. of courses	Region		No. of courses offered 1 - 5	6 - 10	11 - 15	16 - 20	21+
146	NORTHEAST	(19)	10	5	1	1	2
482	EAST	(67)	34	20	6	5	2
119	SOUTHEAST	(22)	16	4	1	0	1
227	MIDDLE NORTH	(28)	14	6	6	1	1
392	MID-AMERICA	(44)	23	7	9	2	3
91	MIDDLE SOUTH	(18)	13	2	1	1	1
77	NORTHWEST	(10)	6	1	1	2	0
277	WEST	(29)	13	7	2	3	4
182	SOUTHWEST	(23)	12	5	2	2	2
N= 1,993		(260)	141	57	29	17	16

This chart indicates the total number of courses offered within
each region (column at far left) as well as the number of schools in
each region that offers various numbers of courses (columns to the
right of region titles). The total number of schools in each region
is given to the right of the name (in parentheses). As can be seen
in the chart, the majority of schools in every region except the West
offer between one and five courses.

Table 5, an expected pattern is shown: the larger the school, the larger the number of courses offered. If the enrollment of a school is under 2,000, the average number of courses for that school is shown to be less than five. If a school has an enrollment between 2,000 and 10,000, the average number of courses is just over five. Schools 10,000 to 29,999 in size average between ten and fifteen courses. And schools 30,000 and over can be expected to have over twenty courses each.

Course and Department Taxonomy

Table 6 shows POPULAR LITERATURE is the category with the largest number of courses. Of the total 1,993 courses, 371 (or 18.5%) are literature courses. Of these, 112 are science fiction, 50 are detective fiction, and 57 are courses which cover a range of popular literature genres. Most schools in the survey offer at least one kind of popular literature course on a regular basis. As Table 8 indicates, 38% of the schools offer SCIENCE FICTION courses.[8] The results of POPULAR LITERATURE courses show that one or two more subcategories could have been previously established to handle the amount of data returned in this category—152 literature courses had to be placed under a category marked OTHER LITERATURE. Table 7 shows a breakdown of the miscellaneous literature courses which are included in this category.

Another category of courses which perhaps should have been further divided is FILM. Three hundred and twenty-seven courses out of the total 1,993 (or 16.4%) were about some aspect of movies and culture. Film courses are offered in every department shown in Table 6 as well as 110 offerings within non-designated departments (i.e. OTHER). More than one-third of the schools surveyed offer courses in film (see Table 8), and nearly half of all schools which have any popular culture courses have film courses.

Courses focusing on the MASS MEDIA are the third most common type of popular culture course collected by this survey. Two hundred and ninety-three of these were recorded, although some are cross-listings from FILM and TV/RADIO categories.* Table 8 shows that mass media courses are also offered at a large number of schools in the survey. Except for HISTORY, all the departments categorized in Table 9 offer courses in MASS MEDIA; over two-thirds of the MASS MEDIA courses are offered in SPEECH and JOURNALISM departments.

ETHNIC STUDIES is the fourth most common type with 165 courses reported. Because ethnic studies courses are relatively new and have gained quick acceptance into academic curricula, they have been reported from a wide span of college departments. As Table 6 indicates, 51 are offered in non-designated departments.

The fifth course type is TV/RADIO with 139 instances reported. It

---

*Film and TV/Radio are, of course, areas within mass media studies. But the purpose of this taxonomy is to break down as many types of courses as possible. Therefore MASS MEDIA courses as specified in the text here refer to survey or "umbrella"-type courses which lend fairly equal time to film, television, radio, press, and so on. If a course was described on the questionnaire as strictly a FILM or TV/RADIO study, it was placed under this category in Table 6 and is specified as such in the text. Some courses were described as studies of the electronic media (i.e. film, TV, and radio); each of these courses was listed under the FILM, RADIO/TV, and MASS MEDIA categories.

TABLE 5

Cross-tabulation of size of colleges with number of popular culture
courses offered

Total no. of courses	Ave.	Size		No. of courses offered				
				1 - 5	6 - 10	11 - 15	16 - 20	21+
75	3.1	under 1000	(24)	20	3	0	1	0
133	3.8	1000 - 1,999	(35)	27	6	1	1	0
176	6.1	2000 - 2,999	(29)	20	6	1	0	2
150	5.4	3000 - 4,999	(28)	16	8	3	1	0
394	6.2	5000 - 9,999	(64)	38	14	7	3	2
525	10.9	10,000 - 19,999	(48)	13	13	12	7	3
392	15.1	20,000 - 29,999	(26)	6	6	4	4	6
148	24.7	30,000 +	(6)	0	2	2	0	2
N= 1,993			(260)	140	58	30	17	15

This chart indicates the total number of courses offered at schools
according to size categories and the average number of course offerings
for each size (columns at far left). Also shown is the number of schools
within each size category that offers various numbers of courses. The total
number of schools in each category is given to the right of the enrollment
sizes as listed (in parentheses).

TABLE 6

Number and typology of courses--with breakdown by department

	ENGLISH	SOCIOLOGY	SPEECH/COMMUNICATION	HISTORY	AMERICAN STUDIES	BLACK STUDIES/ETHNIC STUDIES	JOURNALISM	ART	OTHER	Totals by Course Category
POPULAR LITERATURE:										371
SCIENCE FICTION	102	1	0	0	0	0	0	0	9	112
DETECTIVE FICTION	45	0	0	0	3	0	0	0	2	50
POPULAR LITERATURE GENRES	51	0	0	0	2	0	0	0	4	57
OTHER LITERATURE	135	1	0	0	3	0	0	0	13	152
TV/RADIO	7	1	75	0	8	3	8	7	30	139
FILM	84	3	68	24	8	1	4	25	110	327
MUSIC	1	1	4	1	4	1	0	4	98	114
SPORTS	3	11	0	9	6	2	0	0	32	63
ETHNIC STUDIES	16	23	3	21	15	32	0	4	51	165
HISTORY AND POPULAR CULTURE	0	1	0	91	3	0	2	1	17	115
MASS MEDIA	16	24	102	0	5	2	100	2	42	293
POPULAR ARTS	4	2	18	1	3	0	3	15	23	69
RELIGION	0	4	0	1	1	0	0	0	28	34
TECHNOLOGY AND SOCIETY	1	5	0	7	2	0	0	0	35	50
INTRODUCTION TO POPULAR CULTURE	18	16	2	18	19	0	0	0	17	90
RECREATION AND LEISURE	0	6	1	1	2	0	0	0	19	29
WOMEN'S STUDIES	14	8	1	16	2	0	0	1	29	71
OTHER	46	82	25	28	35	7	21	4	237	485

This chart indicates the number of popular culture courses offered according to a typology of course content. The "Totals by Course Category" are accurate figures. Totals by department here, however, would not be accurate because some courses (such as "Mass Media and the Afro-American Community") are listed more than once, under more than one category. The number of courses offered by each of the nine department categories is given in Table 9.

TABLE 7

Taxonomy of Literature Courses Placed under OTHER LITERATURE in Table 6

course title	no. of courses
Literature of Popular Culture (survey of various types and forms)	19
Topics in American Ethnic Literature	15
Images of Women in Literature	12
Western Fiction	10
Sports Literature	9
Fantasy	9
Popular American Humor	8
Literature of Occult/Supernatural	8
Topics in Childrens Literature	8
Topics in History of Popular Culture	8
Contemporary Popular Fiction	6
Film Literature	5
Literature and the Media	3
International Popular Literature (various topics)	3
Popular Song and Poetry	3
Popular Myths and Literature	2
Literature Read by Adolescents	2
American Heroes in Literature	2
Themes and Motifs in American Literature	2
Special Genres	2
Popular Non-fiction	2
Literature of Terror and Grotesque	1
Literature and Society	1
American Character	1
Love, Sex, and Marriage	1
Sex in Modern Fiction	1
Kentucky Literature	1
Mormon Literature	1
Policeman as Fictional Hero	1
Literature of Farm and Village	1
Small Town in American Literature	1
Literature of the Holocaust	1
Total OTHER LITERATURE	152

TABLE 8

Number of colleges offering courses in each course category

	No. of colleges offering courses	Percentage of 307 total colleges in survey	Percentage of 260 total colleges having P.C. courses
SCIENCE FICTION	116	38%	45%
DETECTIVE FICTION	50	16%	19%
POPULAR LIT. GENRES	52	17%	20%
OTHER LITERATURE	75	24%	29%
TV/RADIO	67	22%	26%
FILM	121	39%	47%
MUSIC	73	24%	28%
SPORTS	51	17%	20%
ETHNIC STUDIES	70	23%	27%
HISTORY AND POP. CULTURE	67	22%	26%
MASS MEDIA	121	39%	47%
POPULAR ARTS	42	14%	16%
RELIGION	22	7%	8%
TECHNOLOGY AND SOCIETY	40	13%	15%
INTRO. TO POPULAR CULTURE	80	26%	31%
RECREATION AND LEISURE	25	8%	10%
WOMEN'S STUDIES	48	16%	18%
OTHER	151	49%	58%

TABLE 9

Total number of courses by department

Department	No.	%
ENGLISH	439	22%
SOCIOLOGY	163	8%
SPEECH/COMMUNICATION	265	13%
HISTORY	143	7%
AMERICAN STUDIES	91	5%
BLACK STUDIES/ETHNIC STUDIES	41	2%
JOURNALISM	127	6%
ART	45	2%
OTHER	679	35%
Total number of courses	1,993	100%

N = 1,993

These figures represent the number of courses each department (in the survey) offers. Also given is the percentage of the total number of courses each department has.

should be noted that only 20 of the 139 course titles or descriptions given on the returned questionnaires specify a complete or even partial emphasis on radio. However, it is assumed that most courses in this category cover both radio and television (and film in some cases). Thirty-eight courses focus on television alone. Over half of the TV/RADIO courses are offered in SPEECH/COMMUNICATION departments, but some can be found in every other department listed except HISTORY.

The next five types of courses, in order of numbers reported, are: HISTORY AND POPULAR CULTURE (115); POPULAR MUSIC (114); INTRODUCTION TO POPULAR CULTURE (90); WOMEN'S STUDIES (71); and POPULAR ARTS (69). Courses listed as introductions to the study of popular culture were found at 80 of the schools in the survey (or 26%).

If the top five course types were arranged in another way, where FILM, TV/RADIO, and MUSIC were grouped as sub-categories of MASS MEDIA, MASS MEDIA overall would be the most common popular culture course in the survey. In fact, the total number of MASS MEDIA courses would be over 800, more than twice that of POPULAR LITERATURE courses. The top ten following would then be:

1 POPULAR LITERATURE (371)
2 ETHNIC STUDIES (165)
3 HISTORY AND POPULAR CULTURE (115)
4 INTRODUCTION TO POPULAR CULTURE (90)
5 WOMEN'S STUDIES (71)
6 POPULAR ARTS (69)
7 SPORTS (63)
8 TECHNOLOGY AND SOCIETY (50)
9 RELIGION (34)
10 RECREATION AND LEISURE (29)

The data returned in this survey and placed in Table 6 and Table 9 shows that popular culture studies have branched far beyond fourteen specific course types and eight departments. Most of these original categories, set up to assist in the processing of data, were chosen according to ones used in previous surveys.* Some new ones, which were thought to be common popular culture course types, were added. But 485 courses gathered in the survey—one-fourth of the total number of courses—focus on subjects other than those categorized. There is an unexpected 35 courses in international popular culture topics, for example.

Perhaps even more significant is the number of unexpected departments popular culture studies have entered. There are dozens of courses being offered in Music, Physical Education, Political Science, and other departments besides those given in Table 9. To get some idea of what the other courses and departments are, refer to Table 10 and 11.

So far the results of the most common course topics have been given only according to subject listings at 260 institutions. Another way to assess the most common topics is to consider the frequency at which these courses are offered. Of the frequency data reported and given in Table 12, FILM, SCIENCE FICTION, or MASS MEDIA courses seem to be offered more

---

*referring to the surveys by Cawelti and Lohof cited earlier.

TABLE 10

Breakdown of OTHER course category

International Popular Culture	35
Politics and Popular Culture	26
Collective Behavior/Social Movements	22
Popular Culture and Public Opinion/Propaganda	21
Topics in Myths, Heroes, Stereotypes, Icons, Rituals	18
Topics in Regional Popular Culture	18
Popular Theatre	15
Sex Roles	15
Architecture/Material Culture	12
Advertising	12
History of Costume/Clothing and Costume	10
Topics in Journalism	10
Futurism	10

These figures represent a further breakdown of the courses listed under "OTHER" in Table 6. Not all the "OTHERS" from Table 6 have been categorized here; only commalities are given. Included among the remaining "OTHERS" are numerous courses that overlap into existing categories; i.e. courses that fall under two or more categories in Table 6 (and are therefore counted at least twice), one of this is OTHER.

TABLE 11

Breakdown of OTHER department category

Music	81
General Studies/Interdisciplinary programs	48
Physical Education/Recreation	46
Film Studies	42
Drama/Theatre	39
Political Science	31
Foreign Languages	28
Religion	25
Biology/Chemistry/Physics	23
Anthropology	12
Social Sciences	12
Philosophy	9
Women's Studies	8
Psychology	7

These figures represent a further breakdown of the departments listed under "OTHER" in Table 9. Not all the "OTHER" departments from Table 9 have been categorized here; only commonalities are given. Included among the remaining "OTHERS" are numerous cases of joint-listed departments (e.g. English/Speech or History/Sociology) which were not used in this table.

TABLE 12

Frequency courses are offered by category

	1x/yr.	2x/yr.	3x/yr.	4x/yr.	Bi-annually	Other
LITERATURE						
SCIENCE FI.	47	20	4	4	12	15
DETECTIVE	18	8	1	4	9	4
POP. LIT. GENRES	11	9	6	6	11	7
OTHER	39	18	3	3	19	19
TV/FILM	36	13	1	3	5	4
FILM	103	33	9	5	27	21
MUSIC	26	16	3	1	6	5
SPORTS	14	5	2	1	6	6
ETHNIC/BLACK ST.	39	9	2	0	7	6
HISTORY AND P. C.	32	9	1	0	9	8
MASS MEDIA	76	41	12	3	12	12
POPULAR ARTS	21	5	4	1	5	4
RELIGION	6	2	0	0	6	4
TECHNOLOGY & SOC.	15	6	0	1	2	3
INTRO. TO POP. CULT.	43	14	2	2	6	5
RECREATION/LEISURE	5	1	0	0	3	1
WOMEN'S STUDIES	20	5	1	1	5	3
OTHER	145	27	18	5	33	34
	566	241	69	40	183	161

This chart indicates the frequency each course is offered each year, according to the course typology. Many respondents did not include this information; however, the table does indicate some general trends.

than any other type. Half of the 198 respondents who listed frequencies reported that film courses are offered at least once a year, while 33 marked twice per year, 9 marked three times per year, and 5 marked four times per year. SCIENCE FICTION seems to show a higher percentage rate of frequency, but less data is available. Forty-seven of 102 who responded claim SCIENCE FICTION courses are offered at least once a year, and 28 of the respondents (or 27.5%) marked more than once a year. POPULAR LITERATURE courses in the category marked OTHER shows a high frequency rate also; 39, out of 101 respondents marked once per year, and 24 marked more than once. But the highest percentage rate of frequency, which is based on the second largest amount of data, for a category, belongs to MASS MEDIA. Seventy-six of 156 respondents report umbrella-type media courses are offered at least once a year. More significant is the number who marked twice per year (41), and three times per year (12). Taken together, 35.6% of the response for MASS MEDIA courses was for more than once a year. Other high frequency rates are shown in POPULAR CULTURE, ETHNIC STUDIES, and INTRODUCTION TO POPULAR CULTURE (listed in order according to percentage of amount of data available).

Departments Where Most Courses Are Found
Of the eight departments given in Table 9, thought previously to be the usual departments offering popular culture courses, ENGLISH departments hold 439 courses, the highest number.* Not only do ENGLISH departments carry 333 literature courses, but a hundred courses in other categories are offered in English. The second ranking departmental category is SPEECH/COMMUNICATION with 265 total courses. A large number of the courses offered in SPEECH and/or COMMUNICATION departments are umbrella-type media courses (102). SOCIOLOGY is ranked third with 163 courses. The largest number of courses in the other category—82—fall under SOCIOLOGY.

A large amount of courses is offered within departments with titles other than those named above. Many of these are experimental or "new humanities" departments which are set up to study popular culture subjects. Forty-eight of the possible 796 department titles in the OTHER category of Table 11 are given as GENERAL STUDIES departments or INTER-DISCIPLINARY programs. Over 100 more are similar departments but are worded differently. Eight-one courses returned in the survey are offered in MUSIC departments; again, this high figure was not expected, so MUSIC does not appear as a department category in Table 9.

Enrollment
Survey respondents gave approximate yearly enrollment figures for 841 of the 1,993 total courses. The total number of yearly enrollment

---

*Department offerings from the eight categories used in the tables will be taken from Table 9 because it includes no cross-listings and gives the more accurate figures. The numbers of courses within the departments, however, will be taken from Table 6 to get an idea of what kinds of courses departments are involved with.

reported for the 841 courses is 48,468. Based on these results, the mean enrollment for a popular culture course is 57. As Table 13 indicates, the average yearly enrollment is highest for MUSIC courses; 39, respondents reported a total yearly enrollment of 3,010, bringing the mean to 77 students. It should be noted that MUSIC courses were shown to have a high rate of frequency in Table 12; thus one reason the yearly mean-per-course is high in MUSIC may be because many of ': ɔ courses are offered two or more times a year.

Following close behind according to mean-per-course are POPULAR LITERATURE at 76 students, HISTORY AND POPULAR CULTURE at 75 students, and RELIGION courses at 72. Each of these also have corresponding high rates of frequency (as shown in Table 12).

The largest gross number of total yearly enrollment (t.y.e.) for a given category is 14,960 students in POPULAR LITERATURE courses. This can be broken down into 5,397 t.y.e. reported for SCIENCE FICTION courses (ave. 62 per course); 4,475 t.y.e. for OTHER popular literature (ave. 48 per course); 3,143 t.y.e. for POPULAR LITERATURE GENRES; and 1,945 for DETECTIVE FICTION (ave. 49 per course). Thirty-one per cent of all yearly student enrollment reported in this survey lies within literature courses.

If TV/RADIO, FILM and MASS MEDIA were grouped together, the t.y.e. gross would be 17,561, which is higher than the POPULAR LITERATURE total and 36% of the t.y.e. for all courses. FILM itself has 9,712 the second largest number of enrollment for an individual course category.

HISTORY and RELIGION courses have high average yearly enrollments per course at 75 and 72. The HISTORY figure is based on more data, however, and is therefore a more dependable signifier. The total yearly enrollment for HISTORY reported from 47 courses is 3,545 students. T.y.e. for RELIGION is 649 from 9 enrollment reports. There may be a strong student draw in popular religion courses, but only 34 total RELIGION courses were reported in this survey.

Most persons who reported INTRODUCTION TO POPULAR CULTURE courses also gave enrollments, and the figures turn out to be high. The t.y.e. is 3,703 from 66 courses, which brings the average-per-course enrollment to 56. High enrollments might be expected here since this course type has already shown a corresponding high rate of frequency. It may be interesting to note that only three of the 90 INTRODUCTION TO POPULAR CULTURE courses are offered by a formal popular culture department.* The implication may be that these courses draw high enrollments for a number of traditional departments.

Years of First Course Offerings
According to the results of this survey, the year most popular culture courses were first introduced into academic curricula was 1974. As Table 14 indicates, during that year 156 courses were reported to have begun.**

---

*That being the one at Bowling Green State University.
**Not all respondents reported year first offered.

TABLE 13

Enrollment Patterns

	No. of Course Enrollment Reports	Total Enrollment	Mean Enrollment
LITERATURE	258	14,960	58
SCIENCE FICTION	86	5,397	62
DETECTIVE FICTION	39	1,945	49
POPULAR LIT. GENRES	41	3,143	76
OTHER LITERATURE	92	4,475	48
TV/RADIO	41	1,678	40
FILM	152	9,712	63
MUSIC	39	3,010	77
SPORTS	27	1,293	47
ETHNIC STUDIES	35	1,139	32
HISTORY	47	3,545	75
MASS MEDIA	97	6,171	63
ARTS	39	1,897	59
RELIGION	9	649	72
TECHNOLOGY & SOCIETY	8	565	31
INTRO. TO POPULAR CULTURE	66	3,703	56
RECREATION AND LEISURE	5	135	27
WOMEN'S STUDIES	18	582	32
OTHER	190	9,452	49
Total	841	48,468	57

N = 841

These figures indicate enrollment patterns of the popular culture courses in the survey. The enrollments reported and listed here are average-per-year enrollments. The "Total Enrollment" figures are only partially accurate, since many course enrollments were not reported. The "Mean Enrollment" figures, however, can be assumed to be generally accurate for the entire survey.

TABLE 14

Breakdown by year first offered

	1968	'69	'70	'71	'72	'73	'74	'75	'76	'77	'78	'79
LITERATURE	7	3	14	10	18	25	35	31	32	30	31	7
SCIENCE FICTION	3	1	5	1	7	10	14	11	14	6	13	7
DETECTIVE FICTION	1	0	0	1	4	2	4	3	7	6	6	6
POP. LIT. GENRES	2	0	4	3	2	7	3	4	4	6	3	7
OTHER	1	2	5	5	5	6	14	13	7	12	9	12
TV/RADIO	0	0	3	2	1	2	7	6	3	5	8	9
FILM	1	2	8	2	8	11	29	18	16	16	14	19
MUSIC	0	0	3	0	1	5	4	5	5	1	3	7
SPORTS	0	0	1	0	0	3	5	1	2	5	8	3
ETHNIC/BLACK STUDIES	0	1	1	1	1	4	7	4	5	2	3	3
HISTORY AND POP. CULT.	0	1	3	2	1	4	3	9	8	7	6	6
MASS MEDIA	2	0	9	0	6	3	11	9	7	12	6	11
ARTS	1	1	3	1	2	3	3	3	2	2	3	2
RELIGION	1	0	1	0	0	1	0	0	3	1	0	2
TECHNOLOGY & SOCIETY	1	0	1	0	1	2	1	5	0	1	4	1
INTRO. TO POP. CULT.	2	1	3	2	6	6	7	9	7	12	7	5
RECREATION/LEISURE	0	0	0	0	1	0	1	1	0	0	1	1
WOMEN'S STUDIES	0	0	2	0	1	1	5	5	0	3	2	0
OTHER	5	2	10	4	8	17	28	19	31	18	25	33
Total	20	11	62	24	55	87	156	125	121	115	121	134

This chart indicates the number of courses first offered each year (from 1968 to 1979), according to course typology. NOTE: Information was not available for all courses.

There were 15 reports of years before 1968

Thirty-five of these are POPULAR LITERATURE—14 SCIENCE FICTION, 4 DETECTIVE FICTION, 3 POPULAR LITERATURE GENRES, and 14 OTHERS. Twenty-nine are FILM, 11 MASS MEDIA, and 7 TV/RADIO. Seven ETHNIC STUDIES courses began in 1974 as did 7 INTRODUCTION TO POPULAR CULTURE. There are 22 offerings in the remaining course categories and 28 in the OTHER category.

New course offerings dropped after 1974 to 125 in 1975, then 121 in 1976, and 115 in 1977. The figure rose back to 121 new offerings in 1978 and then up to 134 in 1979.

Strangely, 1974 is the peak year in a range of popular culture courses which has developed somewhat sporadically since the 1960s. In only one previous year was there a number of first offerings even half the size of that in 1974; the year before, in 1973, 87 courses were first offered. A total of 15 courses reported were first offered in years before 1968. In 1968, 20 courses first appeared. The number dropped to 11 in 1969, but rose sharply to 62 in 1970. There was another drop in 1971 to 24 offerings, but this number more than doubled to 55 in 1972. Course frequencies on the basis of first offerings have thus grown in two noticeable intervals, shown in the graph of Table 15. The first began in the early 1960s and ended in 1970. The second and greatest began in 1971 and culminated in the 156 courses of 1974. Since 1974 first offerings have balanced out to about 121 per year, except for 1979 when the number rose to 134.

Future Prospects

As a final part of the questionnaire, respondents were asked if they thought the number of popular culture courses at their college or university would increase, decrease or remain the same. As Table 16 indicates, 229 persons responded to this question. Most believed the number would remain the same, and many predicted an increase in the future. Only 5 persons believed the number will decrease.

The most common reason given for the claim that courses will increase, shown in Table 17, is STUDENT DEMAND. Students were said to favor popular culture courses and to often choose them as electives. Many others believed increases would occur because of favorable FACULTY ATTITUDES or ADMINISTRATIVE ATTITUDES toward the field of popular culture. Respondents felt the number of courses will remain the same for a variety of reasons; negative FACULTY and ADMINISTRATIVE ATTITUDES towards popular culture were the most common. Four out of five persons who projected decreases in course offerings reported this was because of negative ADMINISTRATIVE ATTITUDES.

An attempt was made to isolate some possible variable behind the reasons given for future prospects. Cross-tabulations were made to determine whether the size, region, or source of funding (i.e. public or private) of institutions shows a relationship to the reason given for future prospects. For the most part, the cross-tabulations revealed little of significance—the major problem being that the low number of institutions reporting any one particular answer limited the possibilities of noting any trends.

TABLE 15

Breakdown of total number of popular culture courses given with years first offered with a graph showing rises and falls of years first offered

Year	Total no. of courses first offered
1968	20
1969	11
1970	62
1971	24
1972	55
1973	87
1974	156
1975	125
1976	121
1977	115
1978	121
1979	134

No. of courses first offered

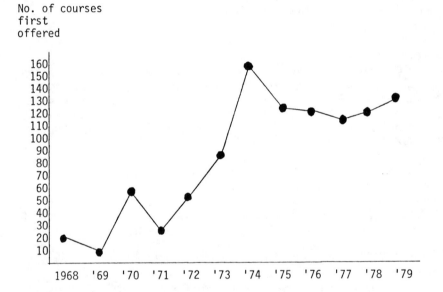

The dots are located on the graph according to the total number of popular culture courses offered each year.

TABLE 16

Future Prospects

		%
Increase	105	40%
Remain the same	119	46%
Decrease	5	2%
No Response	31	12%

TABLE 17

Reasons for future prospects

	Student Demand	Reputation of Subject	Enrollment Patterns	Admin. Attitudes	Faculty Attitudes	Other
Increase	34.6%	2.9%	1.9%	12.5%	13.5%	15.4%
Remain the Same	4.2%	2.4%	6.4%	16.8%	16.0%	33.6%

These figures indicate the most common reasons (by percentage) given by the colleges that responded "Increase" and "Remain the Same" to the question of Table 14. There were not enough "Decrease" answers to provide meaningful statistics except to note that 4 of the 5 colleges indicated "Administrative Attitudes."

Three points, however, can be made with some degree of validity:

1 As a reason for determining that a school was expected to have an increase in popular culture courses, STUDENT DEMAND seemed stronger than average in West, Southwest, and Middle South states, and weaker than average in East and Middle North states.

2 In public schools, ADMINISTRATIVE ATTITUDES were reported unusually high numbers as a reason for popular culture course prospects remaining the same, while FACULTY ATTITUDES were in high numbers as a reason for expecting an increase in courses.

3 The exact opposite is true of private schools, where FACULTY ATTITUDES were cited as a strong cause for prospects to remain the same, and ADMINISTRATIVE ATTITUDES were cited as a strong cause for an increase.

Bulletin Checks

Forty-five of the 307 returned questionnaires in the survey appeared inaccurate and were placed in a designated file. These suspicious returns were later cross-checked with current bulletins from the colleges and universities in question. The results show a general incompleteness in terms of how well popular culture . courses were reported by some respondents. Because of the time required to complete the questionnaire, it was expected that a few courses would be missed by most respondents. In several cases the respondents missed only a few courses, but in most cases the reports were severly inaccurate. If a school with no courses reported was found to have some, it was included in the 260 schools (given earlier) which offer popular culture courses.

Only one of 18 schools checked was accurate in reporting no popular culture courses. The other 27 had an average of 4 courses per school, as shown in Table 18. Seven schools had more than 4 courses; one had 12.

As Table 19 indicates, not one of the remaining 27 suspicious reports checked was accurate. The closest was a person reporting seven courses at a school where only one other course was found. The worst slighting was a report from a large school in the Mid-America region—57 additional courses were discovered. A person from a university in the East reported five courses when 44 others could be found. A representative from a small private college in the Northeast region only listed one course, but ten others were found. Even a report of 18 popular culture courses from a university in the West, which was accidently placed in the suspicious returns file, was short by 17 courses.

The differences between the numbers of courses reported in the bulletin checks and the questionnaires were serious enough to call into question an earlier average of 8 courses per school. The average-per-school from the 45 bulletins checked and listed in Tables 18 and 19 is 14.4 A reasonable and compromising average based on the new evidence, then, is 11 courses per school. To test this figure, ten more college bulletins were checked. These were chosen at random from available resources, and with the exception of two from California, the schools used are of differing sizes and are located in different states. The results of this random bulletin check are that all of the schools have popular culture courses. The fewest number is one at a

TABLE 18

Results of bulletin checks: Colleges which reported no courses

	Report	Courses Discovered
1)	NO	0
2)	NO	1
3)	NO	1
4)	NO	2
5)	NO	2
6)	NO	2
7)	NO	3
8)	NO	4
9)	NO	4
10)	NO	4
11)	NO	4
12)	NO	5
13)	NO	5
14)	NO	6
15)	NO	6
16)	NO	9
17)	NO	9
18)	NO	12

This table indicates the results of bulletin checks for those questionnaires which reported no popular culture courses. The figures in the right column are the numbers of courses found.

TABLE 19

Results of bulletin checks: Colleges which reported courses

	Courses Reported	Additonal Courses Discovered
1)	1	10
2)	2	16
3)	2	16
4)	3	8
5)	3	10
6)	3	16
7)	4	14
8)	4	15
9)	4	19
10)	5	2
11)	5	13
12)	5	44
13)	5	57
14)	6	2
15)	6	7
16)	6	9
17)	7	1
18)	7	4
19)	7	16
20)	8	3
21)	8	11
22)	9	2
23)	9	43
24)	10	28
25)	12	4
26)	18	17
27)	21	6

   This table indicates the results of bulletin checks for those
questionnaires from medium-sized to large colleges which reported
a suspicious few courses. The column on the left is the number
reported. The right column is the number found in the bulletin.

relatively small university in the Northwest region. The largest number is 24 at a fairly large school in Mid-America. The average for the ten schools is 11.9 (See Table 20).

TABLE 20

Result of random bulletin check

	Undergraduate Courses	Graduate Courses	Undergraduate /Graduate
1)	6	0	0
2)	11	0	7
3)	0	0	4
4)	10	1	0
5)	1	0	0
6)	7	5	12
7)	13	0	0
8)	1	1	9
9)	17	1	0
10)	11	6	5

Average number of courses per institution: 11.9

This table indicates the results of a random national sampling of university bulletins. The sampling represents all geographical areas and various sizes.

Chapter Three
Discussion

How Many Popular Culture Courses Are There?

The results of this survey confirm 1,993 popular culture courses of all kinds offered among 260 four-year colleges and universities in the United States. The average number of courses per school is eight. Because a check of college bulletins and course descriptions revealed a much higher number of courses per school, an average of eight is undoubtedly too conservative. If every school represented in this survey was cross-checked with bulletins, it would be no surprise to find an average of over 12. The average-per-school reached after the two bulletin checks discussed in the preceeding chapter is 11.

The question of a bias factor undermining this entire survey must be addressed here. Namely, in using a specialized sample of subjects, does the research represent mostly schools which are likely to have many popular culture courses and mostly professors who are likely to report them?

It is likely that many college contacts who are associated with the Popular Culture Association are going to be teaching one or more popular courses. The specialized sampling allowed more courses to be reported, which was a primary intention of the research. One would think it might also slant any overall conclusions made. But there are other variables to consider. The obvious bias is largely offset by the fact that most academic institutions in the U.S. have only one, if any, professors who belongs to the PCA. And there is seldom any major influences one or two persons can bring to an overall college curriculum. Moreover, the results of bulletin checks, where courses are described objectively, show even PCA members miss many courses offered in departments of which they are not a member.

Naturally, there is some degree of human error in this study on the part of those who were asked to report courses at schools (especially the larger ones) and those of us who compiled the results. But there is also enough data gathered to make a reasonable estimation of the total number of popular culture courses offered among all four-year colleges. The United States has 1,780 such schools.[1] The 307 covered in this survey constitute about 1/6 of that total. If there are 1,993 courses recorded here, and this figure is multiplied by six, the number of courses currently offered at four-year colleges is nearly 12,000. If the number of courses nationwide is consistent with the course average indicated in the sample bulletins checked, the total number of popular courses in American high education is doubled, almost 20,000.

What are Common Types of Popular Culture Courses?

The survey shows the most common popular culture courses are still popular literature and mass media courses. As the field in general has flowed into many tributary areas, these two "pioneer" areas have progressed at a strong enough pace to maintain the lead. On the other hand, each has also become diversified within itself. Of the total 371 literature courses, 152 are something other than science fiction, detective fiction and other popular literature genres (See Table 7). There are courses in everything from "19th Century Children's Books" to "Mormon Literature" and "The Policeman as Fictional Hero."

A majority of specialized media studies courses, as in the 1960s, still focus on film, but one third of media courses now treat TV or radio as separate media. Mass media courses in general have spilled into every department categorized in the survey, including political science, foreign languages, anthropology and philosophy.

Both the total number of literature courses and the number of media courses recorded in this survey far exceed the number of colleges which had popular culture courses. Only one of the 45 bulletins checked did not have one of the two types of courses. It should be safe to say that about 90% of all the four-year colleges in the U.S. offer either courses in popular literature or mass media or both.

In 1972 John Cawelti figured from his survey that literature courses were the leading type of popular culture course. Courses in ethnic studies and cultural subgroups placed a close second. Mass media and film courses were found to be the third most common, popular music fourth, and popular arts and architecture fifth. A survey of PCA convention topics in 1972 revealed a stronger concentration of popular literature topics and much less activity in ethnic studies. The current shape of things is considerably different. The tremendous growth of media studies within liberal arts and social science disciplines and the consequential segmentation into specific areas of film and television are obvious developments according to the results of this survey. The number of mass media courses reported (i.e. survey courses, film, and television) is nearly twice that of the collective number of popular literature courses.

Ethnic courses is currently a common type of popular culture course, whether Cawelti predicted this or not. In this survey, 165 courses focus on cultural subgroups, the fourth highest number of courses in any category. Most of these, as expected, are Afro-American studies; but there is a considerable number of other ethnic subgroups, like Chicanos and Japanese-Americans, being studied. Except for Journalism, ethnic studies courses pervade every department categorized in the survey, with high concentrations in history, sociology and "Other" departments, such as music and theatre.

Other common popular culture courses currently existing are historical popular culture, popular music, courses on the popular arts, and topics in international popular culture. Perhaps the most surprising discovery of the survey is 90 instances of courses entitled "Introduction to Popular Culture," making it the ninth highest number. These courses are offered at 80 institutions, nearly 30% of those reporting. This particular reportage is probably the result of the specialized survey mailing and an advantage of it. While "Introduction to Popular Culture" may not be a common course at this time, it is becoming more common each year. The chart listing years when courses are first offered, given in Chapter III, shows a relatively high average of eight new "Introduction to Popular Culture" courses every year since 1974. The total number of "Introduction to Popular Culture" courses collected in this study indicates a general growth in the entire field of Popular Culture. If a school is going to introduce students to an area of study, and the course is successful, it will probably follow up with more courses.

What Range of Subjects are Studied from a Popular Culture Perspective?

The answer to this question is *all* kinds of subjects. Possibly the most important finding in this survey is the number of courses and departments which had to be categorized as OTHER. With all this diversity in subjects covered by a variety of new and traditional departments, it seems that popular culture courses are reaching that degree of eclecticism and broadness the subject itself demands. In light of this diversity, it is surprising that so few organized programs exist. According to the bulletin findings, though, it seems most academics are not even aware of half the number of popular culture courses on their own campuses.

Some of the most common instances of popular culture being crossed with the teaching of traditional subjects are in sociological approaches to behavior patterns, population movements, cultural subgroups and social programs. Courses offered in history departments, such as "Popular Culture in 20th Century America," and "19th Century England and Popular Culture" reveal that many historical periods are taught with an emphasis on the popular culture of those periods. Foreign language departments have recently turned to teaching the cultural context from which a language is naturally spoken; many culture courses offered in these departments are taught from a popular culture perspective. Political scientists are obviously seeing the need to examine the mass media and popular arts; there are 26 reports of courses like "Politics in the Media," "Public Opinion and Mass Society," and "Politics in Film."

Popular culture materials are reportedly used most often in three general areas: (1) the teaching of humanities courses—literature, languages, history, art, etc.; (2) Speech and Communication departments; and (3) among the social sciences. This is where the field was centered eight years ago. Today, however, popular culture courses are also a part of nearly every academic discipline. The result in this survey is hundreds of course titles like "Technology and Society," "Advertising and Audience Behavior," "Physics and Living," "Survey of Sport in America," "Clothing and Culture," "The American House," "Sex Roles and Cultural Stereotypes," and "Elvis."

What Departments Offer Large Numbers of Popular Culture Courses?

It was assumed in the early 1970s that 90% of all popular culture courses in existence were offered through four departments—English, History,

Communications and Journalism. The present survey shows the top four departments to be (in order) English, Speech/Communication, Sociology and History (Journalism is a close fifth). Taken together, however, only about 50% of the total courses surveyed are offered in these departments. About a third of all courses are offered through departments other than the eight thought to have the most. Of these others, the traditional fields of music, health and physical education (because of a growing trend in courses on sports and recreation), theatre/drama and political science appear most frequently.

Even though there are twice as many media-related courses recorded in the survey than literature courses, English departments offer almost twice as many total popular culture courses than Speech/Communication departments. English began to offer courses in mass media and various forms of popular writing in the 1960s.

Speech/Communication departments are usually oriented toward vocational curricula, but the academic study of mass media within these departments is common. Media studies are growing annually. The indication is that soon a survey of mass media in society will be as mandatory to Speech/Communications as Shakespeare is to English. It might be noted that whereas few non-media-related popular culture courses are offered through Speech/Communication departments, there are recent instances of popular arts courses here (e.g. comics, music, advertising art).

In terms of flexibility and openness, sociology is becoming to the social sciences what English is to the humanities. A precious assortment of popular culture topics—everything from counter-culture heroes to the American worker—is offered by sociology departments. (More "Other" courses were recorded from sociology than from any other department; in fact, about twice as many.) There are strong shows of media courses, ethnic studies, and introductions to popular culture. This outcome should be no surprise since so much of the study of society today is the (at least indirect) study of popular culture. What the survey shows is an increasing willingness among sociologists to examine nearly all types of popular phenomena.

Another department which has offered an abundance of popular culture courses in recent years is history. Studying popular culture historically has led to interesting insights and possibilities, as historian Russel Nye, in *The Unembarrassed Muse,* demonstrated. It has also led to some fascinating new courses like "The Great Escape: Radio, the Movies and Depression in America."

One department which unexpectedly does not offer many popular culture courses, despite its interdisciplinary basis, is American Studies. It reported the largest number of introductions to popular culture, but little else.

Ethnic Studies was included as one of the eight major department categories because it was thought to be a common interdisciplinary department. Only six courses were recorded under this category, but a wealth of new course types were submitted as parts of special interdisciplinary programs such as College Humanities and General Studies. Because Popular Culture was originally intended to be interdisciplinary in approach, this trend should be viewed as positive.

Courses are usually treated as "experimental" studies when they are located in these places, though, which reflects an attitude of newness and relative uncertainty toward the courses on the part of curriculum planners. Often the courses are only offered as electives or as partial-credit courses—another sign that after twelve years popular culture study still lacks recognition.

How Often Are Courses Offered?

Respondents listed course frequencies for 1,260 of the total 1,993 courses reported. Of these 1,260 courses, 566 are offered once per year; 241 are offered twice a year; 69 are offered three times a year; 40 are offered 4 times a year; and 183 are offered every other year. One hundred and sixty-one courses are offered at a different frequency than these. An estimate based on these reports is that nearly half of all popular culture courses are offered at least one time per year, while about one of every four is offered more than once a year.

Highest frequency rates were found in film, popular literature and mass media courses. These are the oldest and evidently most firmly established of all such courses. They have gained greater acceptancy as the years have passed and seem consistently to attract the interest of more students. Other courses which were reported to be offered frequently, with the likelihood of more than once per year, are courses in TV/radio, history and popular culture, ethnic studies, and introduction to popular culture.

Many persons who reported other kinds of courses stated these were "being tried"or offered on a "one shot" basis. If enrollments were strong enough, the course would be offered again. In general the indication is that popular culture courses offered by traditional departments do attract students. The difficulty is getting a course pushed through administrations, as the data returned for future prospects show. Once a course becomes a part of a department, it usually remains.

What is Student Enrollment Like in Popular Culture Courses?

In 1977 a faction of the National Education Association helped to stress a nationwide "Back to Basics" movement. Commenting on this drive, NEA president John Ryor said he favored it in some ways. "But I am afraid that this new trend may treat symptoms and not get at causes."[2] Certain college administrators in the 1970s have been especially concerned about both quality in education and quantity—not only what students want and what students need, but also what they will take. During the past decade student attitudes have shifted away from liberal arts courses, and the general tendency seems to be toward "professional" or "practical" courses which lead to degrees which in turn lead to jobs. This has presented no crisis for business schools, but it has come down hard on the heads of humanities colleges. The addition of popular culture courses is, according to this survey, a possible solution.

Even the decision-makers have had to be practical on this issue, and enrollment patterns often influence them to adopt new courses. If this is the case, then a valuable piece of information for popular culturists is the number of students currently enrolled in popular culture courses.

Enrollment reports from 841 courses in this survey show an average of 57 students per course per year. Earlier an average of 6.5 courses per institution was made, then shown to be conservative. A more reasonable and still conservative average would be 10 courses per institution. Based on this average, if there are 1,780 four-year institutions and thus 17,800 popular culture courses in the U.S., and if each course draws a yearly enrollment of 57, then the total number of students taking popular culture courses in 1979 was 1,014,600. Considering the 11,000,000 students enrolled in colleges across the country,[3] it may be that one out of eleven students took a popular culture course this year. The bulletin checks described in Chapter 2 indicate that the actual numbers are in fact probably greater (See Tables 19 and 20).

These persons probably took a course in history, popular music, mass media, or popular literature, since these tend to draw the most students. If it was literature, it was probably a course on popular literature genres. If it was mass media, it was probably film.

With the exception of ethnic studies and women's studies courses, all of the top twelve popular culture course types show an average-per-year enrollment of at least 40. It becomes odd, then, to encounter a respondent who reports a low enrollment remark, "students go for more common, acceptable courses." So the question is, in the face of this kind of view, will student enrollment overall be sustained or even increase in the coming years? The answer to this crucial question is yes, once the "Catch-22" is discovered: students who do not take popular culture courses are under the impression that they are not common, acceptable courses; popular culture courses are not common and acceptable because students are advised not to take them. The figures clearly show that all the assumptions of this logical merry-go-round are false.

What Trends in Subject Matter Have Risen Since 1972 and What Trends Have Fallen?

Certain basic trends in Popular Culture which began in the late 1960s have become stronger and more expansive in the past decade, and it is difficult to detect dying trends. One of the first scholarly movements of popular culture study was a new methodological approach to popular arts. Popular arts were seen to have separate structural forms than the elite arts, but forms just as complex.[4] There were thematic studies of popular literature and mass media arts which defined them and investigate their relationship to an audience. This trend has been maintained in the literature genres of science fiction, detective fiction and westerns, primarily, and it has spread to other forms of literature and popular art. English departments applied these approaches to film and continue to do so. In fact, English departments offer the largest number of courses in film.

Of the media arts, film is presently getting the most attention; focal studies of film genres, styles and historical periods are on the rise more now than ever before. In the last four years more film courses have been added to curricula than any other type. Forty-one film courses were reported from departments distinctly entitled Film Studies. Television as popular art is included in many of these courses.

The study of television from a content-analysis approach and as it relates to its audience has really broken off into a trend of its own. Aside from literature, film and media survey courses, the television course is the most common type of popular culture course reported, although it is often offered in conjunction with other topics.

It seems the interest in film, literature and television has monopolized popular arts study, however. When Cawelti took his survey in 1972, arts and entertainments courses were varied. This survey turned up a relatively small number of arts courses, and popular entertainment courses seem to be especially difficult to find (e.g. popular theatre).

The shift in the concept of "culture" set by early popular culture scholars[5] allowed the range of cultural phenomena which could be given serious study to be broadened. Everyday architecture became icon; celebrities on TV became cultural heroes; and rock concerts became theatrical rituals. The gambit was to seek out new materials and bring them under humanistic analysis for the first time in academic history. Today this trend continues, and it has finally been taken up by non-humanities departments. One common new area of study, for example, is sports and recreation, in which physical education and sociology departments have shown a special interest.

Another trend which continues from the early seventies is the study of popular culture of ethnic subgroups, most of these courses taught in Afro-American studies. These courses were the second most common type in Cawelti's survey. They have moved to fourth in this one, although the number of courses on black culture, chicano culture, American Indian culture has risen considerably since 1972. There has always been a lack of international popular culture courses and courses on foreign subgroups in America, but this situation may be changing. "Modern Japanese Society," "Contemporary German Life" and other topics in foreign culture made up the largest number of "other" course types in the survey.

Where Are Popular Culture Studies Likely to Go in the Future?

Every indication from the data reported is that popular culture courses will increase in the future. One hundred and five of the respondents predicted an increase at their respective schools. The number who thought course offerings would stay the same in the foreseeable future is 119. Only five persons believe the number of courses will decrease.

The two most common reasons given for increases in popular culture course offerings are student demand and faculty attitudes. The most common reason given by faculty for projected decreases in course offerings is negative administrative attitudes toward Popular Culture. The survey shows, then, that positive student response to popular culture courses is the strongest force behind the growth of the field. If student response is maintained or if it increases, this factor will probably sway the attitudes of those administrators who have thus far been opposed to such courses in their curricula. As administrative attitudes change, or if they change, the number of faculty interested in Popular Culture has already been shown to be high enough to provide new popular culture courses.

One factor which must be considered, however, as a possible deterrent to popular culture course offerings is the general decline in college student enrollment in the U.S. during the last year or so, a situation likely to worsen in coming years. Many persons surveyed from institutions already experiencing sustained or falling enrollments stated that this situation has caused administrators to keep curricula conservative. Traditional, "practical" courses are given precedence over new types. Only a few persons made comments which suggested that the addition of new types of courses (e.g. popular culture) to the curricula might be a means to stimulate student enrollment. Again, the reason why this alternative is seldom considered is probably because such a strategy is assumed not to be worth the effort. Perhaps evidence such as that shown throughout this survey can be used to counter this assumption.

Conclusion

Popular Culture courses in American higher education are still suffering somewhat through a period of public and academic condescension and criticism similar to that experienced by courses in English literature near the turn of the century, by American literature when it was introduced forty years ago, and by programs in American studies during the 1930s and '40s. All four academic areas were new at the time of being attacked and all three were presenting what was considered subject matter of questionable merit. As late as the summer of 1979 the public revelation that Sonoma State University in California was offering a course on the frisbee was condemned in newspaper editorials from coast to coast and was the topic of a tritely ironic feature on the *CBS Evening News*. Peter Diamandopoalos, President of Sonoma State, in a nationally distributed newspaper column responding to the condemnation of the course, nicely summed up negative attitudes toward not only the course at his university but toward the entire spectrum of popular culture study:

> Higher education, by its very nature, must be evolving its own standards and adjusting its strategies and shifting its targets to an ever-changing world. Whatever contributes to the vigor of the academy and is consistent with the seriousness of the enterprise should be encouraged to excel....
>
> The real issue then is not Frisbee but rather what too often confronts American higher education—the world's practical and not always flexible attitudes toward new talent, ideas and initiatives.

The results of this survey confirm Professor Dianandopoulos' remarks. During the 1970s, while the introduction of popular culture courses into American higher education was under attack by academic traditionalists, the courses themselves became a part of nearly every American college and university curriculum. Higher education has indeed been evolving and popular culture has been an ever-present element of that evolution. Popular culture courses quite obviously should be subject to the same evaluative standards as any other courses. At the same time, educators must face the fact that some million students per year are enrolled in courses that may be labeled Popular Culture in virtually every type of academic department within the arts and sciences. The argument over whether or not Popular Culture belongs on the campus is no longer relevant. In the future meaningful debate about the proper place for popular culture in the classroom should not center on the degree of acceptability of its subject matter but rather on how a specific college or university might best be served by the popular culture courses it already has and the additional courses it is likely to add in the near future.

The surprisingly large variety of courses in popular culture that have been developed during the past decade indicate the breadth of materials and complexity of approaches potentially available to teachers and students. Although comments on the survey suggest that only a few formal programs in popular culture studies are likely to be implemented during the next few years, specific courses in popular culture are quite obviously "adjusting the strategies" and "shifting the targets" of long established disciplines such as English, history and sociology and comparatively new disciplines such as ethnic and women's studies. Ray B. Browne, co-founder of the Popular Culture Association, is fond of referring to popular culture studies as "the New Humanities." He could just as easily say the new mass communications, the new social sciences and even the new physical education and the new home economics.

This survey clearly suggests that schools, programs and departments sensitive to student demands and flexible about their future are already finding popular culture courses a valuable part of their offerings. Popular culture's struggles for life during its academic infancy are over. Teachers of popular culture may now look forward with confidence to the maturity of their subject matter as an important contributor to American higher education.

Notes

[1] The source for this figure is the National Center for Educational Statistics—a branch of the U.S. Department of Health, Education and Welfare—1978 findings.

[2] Quote taken from a speech reprinted in part by the editors of the *Reader's Digest 1978 Almanac and Yearbook* and placed in a special section on American education, p. 202.

[3] Statistics from the National Center for Educational Statistics.

[4] One of the important popular culture studies which came out of this trend is John G. Cawelti, *Adventure, Mystery, and Romance* (Chicago: University of Chicago Press, 1976).

[5] Discussed by Russel Nye in "Notes for an Introduction to a Discussion of Popular Culture," *Journal of Popular Culture*, IV: 4 (Spring 1971), pp. 1031-1038.

Part II
University Programs and Course Syllabi

Introduction

The following descriptions of programs and courses in popular culture are meant to be detailed illustrations of the data presented in Part I. All of these descriptions were written by those who participate in the programs or teach the courses. They were selected from materials submitted from a call for syllabi published in the Spring 1979 issue of *Popular Culture Methods*. Those wanting their programs or courses published submitted rough descriptions and then revised their descriptions according to general guidelines intended to make them as accessible as possible to general readers. The outlines selected to be included here were chosen because they show the broad range of popular culture courses currently being offered nationally and because they illustrate how popular culture materials relate to traditional courses and disciplines.

The first section of Part II includes descriptions of three programs in popular culture currently being offered. They are arranged according to the formal complexity of their structures. The first essay presents the new minor in popular culture offered by the History Department of Metropolitan State College in Denver. Next comes a detailing of Michigan State University where it is possible to specialize in popular culture within the course requirements of the English Department. Finally there is a description of Bowling Green State University in Ohio which has a Department of Popular Culture and where students may earn both B.A. and M.A. degrees in popular culture.

The course syllabi are divided into some of the major categories discussed in Part I. General or introductory popular culture courses are included, for example, because they are probably the "purest" type of popular culture courses and because more then eighty of them appeared on the survey. Popular literature is a rather limited subject area but it appears in this section as a separate category because it was the largest single subject area in the survey. The courses within traditional disciplines begin to show how popular culture can be used to revitalize a curriculum and how popular culture materials can be used within a traditional course framework. The last category, General Topics, is especially important because it illustrates the broad range of subject matters and teaching strategies that are used in popular culture courses.

Anyone intending to read a number of the syllabi will find wide diversity and several instances of intentional duplication. Within the media section, for instance, there are two courses on American popular music which are both primarily interested in recorded pop music, especially after 1950. Materials that analyse the 1930s appear in more than half a dozen syllabi. There is a course on the Depression. In addition, a film course restricts itself to the 1930s and 1940s. Some other materials on the 30s appear in courses on The Family, Freud in America, the popular music courses and in Professor Plesur's survey of American popular culture. The purpose of this overlap is to demonstrate the different directions popular culture instructors are going with similar subject matter. In the first chapter the difficulties of defining popular culture were discussed. Along with the problem of definition is a corresponding problem of a lack of an accepted methodology. Putting it simply, popular culture is studied in as many different ways as there are disciplines offering courses in popular culture subject matter. On one hand, this has caused problems in gaining academic recognition for popular culture. On the other hand, as these course syllabi demonstrate, the lack of a singular method of study provides the popular culture instructor with rich opportunities for innovative teaching approaches and the advantage of seeing everyday subject matters from a near-infinity of interesting perspectives.

University Programs

"Selling" Popular Culture
at an Urban Institution

Most likely the History Department at Metropolitan State College in Denver, Colorado, became involved with popular culture for the wrong reason: we were looking for ways to increase and/or stabilize our enrollments and courses on movies, sports and rock music seemed able to attract students who normally flooded introductory psychology and sociology courses. In past years we had taken advantage of momentary trends to boost our student credit hour production. In Spring 1978 we offered "The Fabulous Fifties," a course intellectually undemanding designed to cash in on the Happy Days/1950s nostalgia craze. Posters advertised it all over campus and a popular AM radio disc jockey heard about it and mentioned on the air that he might attend class. It filled the largest classroom in the college and we felt we had a good idea.

We began to change our attitude about popular culture by Fall 1978. The spring course had been a teaching disaster. I ran it as a zoo to keep students happy and in the end it upset me, and made our involvement with popular culture suspect. We reoffered Fab 50s that fall and attracted nearly as many students as the first time. This time, however, I assigned books and organized and ran the course as any other valuable course. As a result, this second offering of the course received much higher student approval in our regular semester evaluations. Perhaps it was the success of this course (only our immensely popular Colorado History survey did better), or perhaps the popular culturists inside us were fighting to get out, but one afternoon we bandied ideas and forth. Dolph Grundman, an excellent constitutional historian, with his avocational love of sports trivia and his general knowledge, expressed interest in a course on sports and society. Dick Aquila, who had published on American Indians, talked about rock music, lyrics and social impact. I had always used movies as examples of popular trends, beliefs and attitudes in regular history courses. Charles Angeletti had a longtime interest in popular culture and futurology; he offered us his file of materials and his advice. It seemed like one of those 1930s Mickey Rooney/Judy Garland musicals. "Hey gang! You can sing, I can dance, they can play music. Let's put on a musical to save the orphanage!" We had personal interest, some source material, and an institution that looked kindly upon—if not encouraged—innovations. Somehow Dick and I decided to work up something. Charles gave us his information, and we began planning.

Why were we attracted to Popular Culture and why were we qualified to teach it? First Dick and I had to convince ourselves before we convinced anyone else. Neither of us is an elitist historian by nature. Talking over our approaches to various history courses, we recognized that we included a great deal of popular culture (and social history) without labelling it. Certainly it ought to attract students. More important, MSC is an urban institution drawing students from a variety of ethnic, age, geographic and vocational backgrounds. Could traditional history courses completely meet our mission to assist this kind of nontraditional student body? Was popular culture automatically less rigorous and responsible simply because it was non-elitist?

Reading through Charles' file—much of it from the Popular Culture people at Bowling Green State University—we found convincing reasons why popular culture deserved academic respectability. In terms of our attitudes about teaching, we realized that using certain mass phenomena as movies, rock music, sports or popular literature, we could make clear why many people believed as they did, behaved as they did, acted as they did. We could discuss whether mass values come from above—either authority or the source of the mass phenomena—or spring up from below. We were—and are—devoted to the historical process and believed that looking into popular culture might well help explain the past better than such traditional areas of historians' concern as politics, diplomacy and elite culture. We also convinced ourselves that, given the difficulty of creating an independent (and new) department of Popular Culture within the college, history was the department best suited to handle courses. History—and the academic freedom within our department—was ideal. It was more than popular culture being helpful to us; we also decided that, as a minor option, it had great benefits for students. In business, marketing majors would gain insight into mass culture and phenomena. We have a large communications area—industrial, business, public relations, etc.—and students there had to gain from courses in popular culture. Clearly, journalism, literature, psychology, sociology and anthropology majors all would benefit. Anyone interested in some aspects of modern, urban culture would benefit. We were sure that we had an idea whose time at Metro had come.

Following the administrative ladder, we began approaching the powers-that-be to learn if it were worth our effort to design a minor option in popular culture. Our department chairman, Stephen Leonard, instantly saw the potential to attract students, recognized its academic credibility and noted his approval. Given his knowledge of the ways of bureaucracy, he cautioned us to expect some hassles and he was proved correct. Some people might question this idea; and some would worry about their department's enrollments and think our minor option might draw students normally registering for their courses (and choosing their minors); some simply would nitpick. The Dean of Liberal Arts, Philip Boxer, enthusiastically encouraged us. He approved our general plan to obtain a minor option program in history, work toward an interdisciplinary major (possibly requiring a grant to underwrite costs), and establish a resource center for the Denver area. At a reception for faculty involved in our Elderhostel program, Dick had a few minutes with our new college president, Donald J. MacIntyre, who indicated his strong support for popular culture and a minor option in history. We felt the final process, once we drew up our proposal, would be smooth sailing.

Dick and I began discussing what courses should constitute the popular culture minor option. We wanted to call it "The Popular Culture Minor Option in History" and require 21 hours of study (a typical minor at Metro). We needed new courses, a rationale for the program, arguments to demonstrate that we were not repackaging history courses (the Curriculum Committee might disapprove a shuffling of existing courses), and proof that we did not require additional faculty resources. Within our department we had discussions about courses. Some of our colleagues felt we should include traditional upper division U.S. chronological history courses; obviously we questioned the value of those courses in a popular culture program. We did not wish to water down our proposal or compromise the integrity of popular culture; either it was valid or it was not. A few people warned us the Curriculum Committee might be scared off by the title "Popular Culture," and convinced us we should title it "American Culture"—a title which proved to be a mistake. Others wondered if we were sacrificing our credibility as a department to teach seemingly questionable courses; if there were a back-to-basics movement, we might find ourselves stuck in popular culture.

From these discussions but largely on our own we created the proposal. We used the general justification for Popular Culture programs sent us by the people at the Popular Culture Program at Bowling Green State University. We organized it along the lines of such successful submissions to the Curriculum Committee as our American West option. We decided since we were using history to examine popular culture (looking at it over time), we would require our HIS 122, "American History Since 1865" course. Students should have some sense of the past before concentrating on popular culture. We reconstructed our HIS 150, "Popular Culture" course. It had dealt with changing topics (e.g. Rock Music & Social History, Sports in America, The Fabulous Fifties) and was therefore repeatable with credit; we wanted to pattern it after the PC 160 course at BGSU—an introductory lecture course in popular culture [see syllabi]. We created HIS 384, "Topics in Popular Culture," where we would offer courses previously listed under the HIS 150 number—Movies & History, Rock Music & Social History, Sports in America, Popular Literature and Culture—or anything else we felt we had a particular competence and interest to teach. We made HIS 485, "Seminar in Popular Culture," a required course. It would serve as a sort of quality control for the minor option and help us build our resource center for popular culture in the Denver area. We also devised HIS 385, "American Social History." We believed that a folklore course was desirable but we did not have the teaching strengths to suggest it nor was the Curriculum Committee likely to approve a great many new courses in one submission. By having students take at least two of our HIS 384 offerings, we had a core of 18 hours (HIS 122, 150, 384, 385, 484). We compromised and agreed that, with permission of the department, we would count other courses. Our HIS 110, "American West," for example, fit within our broad theme. The course deals with the contrast between reality and popular myths, in perception, in the changing ways different generations of Americans have viewed the West (often having little to do with reality). Movies, music, literature, and tales are used. Other courses as our HIS 396, "Heroes in U.S. History," also seemed to fit our overall goals. While the package was not perfect—we had a compromise title and some questionable courses—it was the best we could do given our resources. And we could amend it in time.

The Curriculum Committee meeting came as a sober shock to our enthusiastic optimism. Mickey and Judy always successfully staged a smash-hit show; the academic environment is different from those MGM backlots. We thought we had covered all bases. We had all the necessary administrative approvals. The student newspaper, *The Metropolitan,* which reaches nearly 30,000 students, faculty and staff on the Auraria campus, thought the proposal worthy and gave it a big writeup. We had explained our ideas to the student government president and student members of the Curriculum Committee. They approved and since they voted as a bloc we felt assured of a relatively easy time. We had sent each member of the curriculum committee our packet of information. But when we went to the meeting we were in for a surprise. Representatives from Business, Engineering Technology and Science and Mathematics gave their assent. The trouble came from representatives from areas that we had expected to support expanded interest in popular culture.

Representatives from the Center for Interdisciplinary and Urban Studies questioned a program on "American Culture" that did not automatically include courses from their areas. They may well have been motivated by fear of inadequate enrollments; it may have been a failure of communications on our part by misnaming the proposed minor option. In any case dissent was strong and vocal. The Liberal Arts representative believed our 400-level seminar course duplicated ENG 102, a basic course required of students at the college, and felt it unnecessary. This may have been our fault since our syllabus had overly stressed the importance of writing and research in this course. I wanted to force a vote regardless of possible ill feelings; I wanted the minor option and thought the objections tangential to our proposal, reflecting faculty politics more than useful comments on popular culture. Our chairman, far wiser, suggested postponing a decision by the committee and modifying the proposal to meet some of the objections.

We renamed the minor option "American Popular Culture Minor Option in History" and that correctly identified our proposal. It concentrated on this country—our area of limited expertise, it was about popular culture (not watered-down American Studies), and it would be offered through the History Department. We explained in an expanded course syllabus that, in examining the relationship between mass phenomena and mass culture, we would deal with minorities and women. We clarified provisions in the minor which would allow for inclusion of popular culture courses from other departments. We defended HIS 484 arguing that a basic course in research and paper writing techniques taught by the English Department was not comparable to an advanced course in the methodology of popular culture and history.

The next meeting of the Curriculum Committee was anticlimactic. Either because we had done our homework well or because our most vocal critics did not attend, the proposal passed without a dissenting vote.

As of this writing—December 1979—the situation looks promising. In Fall of 1979 we offered Rock Music & Social History and Sports in America and attracted large numbers of students. Preliminary (mail-in) registration figures for Spring 1980 indicate good support for our three popular culture offerings: Rock Music & Social History, Sports in America, and Movies & History. While schoolwide enrollments remained stable, the History Department enrollment increased 15% and popular culture helped lead the way. Students signing up for popular culture remain second only to our Colorado History surveys. It seems students are interested; we must wonder about the reasons that attracted them to our popular culture courses. Our experiences in previous HIS 150 offerings would suggest that many students believed the courses would offer easy times, little work and good grades. While it was relatively easy to convince our colleagues that popular culture was a valid field of study, we found students expecting something less rigorous and much less demanding than typical college classes. We are currently discussing ways to convince students that the interesting appeal of popular culture courses does not mean they lack academic vitality. Many students signed up for Rock Music & Social History expecting the class to consist of one recent (post 1976) record after another and our role as instructors reduced to introducing the next album cut. Tom Altherr, who replaced Dick Aquila when he moved on to Ball State University, showed students that class could be much more than they imagined. Starting with rock music's antecedents, he used rock music—especially lyrics—to discuss recent culture and social history. He used the music as a vehicle to arrive at truths about modern youth culture and the sources of mass phenomena. Dolph Grundman easily moved beyond the kind of internal, sports trivia class that many students expected and used sports—spectator and participatory—to discuss values of modern, urban America and the relationship of sports to popular culture.

The true test will come soon. We will succeed when students begin choosing our classes or entering our minor program because they recognize the importance (and enjoyment) of popular culture. It is an educating process; we will begin advertising after the beginning of the Spring 1980 semester to raise student consciousness about popular culture studies. When they are convinced it is an important part of their education, then we will have the broad-based support to further our commitment to popular culture. As students show increasing interest, it will be easier to attract faculty attention and gain further academic acceptance.

It is an ongoing and continuing process. Hopefully we are on the proper path and a reasonable goal awaits us over the next semester or two. We certainly are interested in sharing our experiences and learning from the experiences of others, particularly other History Departments. We welcome advice, comments, suggestions. The more we exchange ideas—learn what has worked elsewhere, avoid what has not worked so well—the easier all our paths will be. As we all seek to demonstrate the need and academic validity of popular culture studies, it is nice to know that there are like-minded people facing similar experiences.

Charles M. Dobbs
Department of History
Metropolitan State College, Denver

Emphasis on Popular Culture
At Michigan State University

Legend has it that descriptions of popular culture courses began to appear magically in the Michigan State University catalogue with the publication of Distinguished Professor Russel B. Nye's *The Unembarrassed Muse* in 1970, but actually the study of the popular arts from a cultural perspective had always been a part of Nye's interests and it was in his graduate seminars that legends began. His seminar in *American Literature* (ENG 983) in 1969-70, for example, focused on "the popular genres of art, music and literature" and resulted in the collection of student essays published as *New Dimensions of Popular Culture* (Bowling Green University Popular Press, 1972). In 1971-72 Nye taught a two-term seminar in *American Literature and Culture* (ENG 986) which examined "the theoretical principles of the study of American popular culture," and in 1973-74 he conducted a seminar on *Studies in Popular Culture* (ENG 986) concerned with the history, theory and methodology of popular culture. It was the demand for Nye's seminars and the practical realization among members of the Department of English that courses in popular culture should be available to a broader base of students that led to the establishment of a series of courses on the undergraduate level and the expansion of graduate options to include emphases in popular culture on both the Masters and Doctoral levels.

The Master of Arts Program in American Studies (Program IV) allows for fifteen credits in popular culture. On the Ph.D. level students may take courses and independent study leading to an examination in popular culture as one of three areas of expertise. Courses which periodically examine popular culture include *Proseminar for Master's Degree Candidates* (ENG 880), the 983 and 986 seminars noted above, and *Graduate Reading Course* (ENG 970) in supervised study. The flexibility of the graduate programs provide for considerable background and opportunities for intensive investigation of popular culture.

The Department of English also offers a thematic emphasis in popular culture as a part of the undergraduate program in English. Courses may be taken as electives in a traditional emphasis on preparation for graduate study in literature, or as a sequence of courses in preparation for careers other than English. The popular culture sequence includes four basic courses, including *Introduction to Popular Culture* (ENG 241), which also satisfies one-third of the university's general education requirement in the humanities. *Introduction to Popular Culture* examines the basic concepts of popular culture through the exploration of present and past imagery. The course examines narrative and visual conventions, and generic innovations in graphic art, fiction, film, radio and television, material culture, celebrity processes, sport and related matters, with emphasis on the development of a coherent critical perspective on contemporary popular culture. *Popular Literary Genres* (ENG 242) provides the opportunity for the extensive examination of the origins and development of popular genres through fiction and other media. The course has focused on Hollywood, spy, detective, science, horror and gothic fiction, and has treated radio drama and non-fiction genres. *Studies in Popular Culture* (ENG 340) examines aspects of the popular culture of the United States and England in some depth. Included among the topics that have received attention are the hero in America, popular rites of passage, the Western myth, the changing image of the Orient in the United States and England, popular film genres, documentary impressions of contemporary culture, sport, and images of women in popular culture.

Several other English courses occasionally concentrate on popular culture topics. *Literature and Film* (ENG 347) emphasizes the relationship between film and literature through the study of themes, style and structure in selected film masterpieces from different periods and cultures. The course has featured both popular films and those received by relatively narrow audiences. Other courses have from time to time emphasized matters of interest to students of popular culture. *Perspectives on Literature and English Language* (ENG 399), for example, has provided a rich variety of perspectives on such areas as science fiction, musical theatre, the Sixties, popular film, the detective novel, supernatural fiction, the literature of the perverse, contemporary images of women and other popular forms.

While the major emphasis of popular culture has come from courses within the Department of English where a generalist perspective has been allowed to flourish, other disciplines have been active as well. Lyman Briggs College, a residential college within the university, has developed *Popular Culture and Technical Change* (LBC 378) which is now cross-listed with the American Studies program (AMS 378). The course explores the influence of technical change on the form and quality of American life through examinations of a series of case studies from the early 1800s to the present. Case studies include the development of Coney Island and the origins and popular form of Las Vegas among others.

The Department of History offers two courses which include or focus on popular culture. *American Society and Culture since 1945* (HST 405) provides a broad cultural perspective that is not limited to popular culture, but includes discussion of it as a significant aspect of the course. Constructed in two parts which emphasize movements and beliefs, the course treats expressions of youthful rebellion through the discussion of delinquents, heroes, rock music and early protests, best sellers, movies, television and music before 1960; the second part covers campus protests, the counterculture, environmental and consumer movements, and popular culture to the present. A second course, *History of Sport in America* (HST 403), traces sport from colonial through modern times, focusing on its social and cultural ramifications. The course examines the nature of colonial sport, the rise of organized sport, the social significance of sport in recent times, and related matters.

The Department of Telecommunications offers an array of courses in audience research, technical communications systems, and the production of radio, television and film programming. Courses available to non-majors include *Telecommunication in the United States* (TC 120), which examines the history, economics, public control, programming and social effects of broadcasting and cable systems. *Television Program Development* (TC 437) introduces seniors in other fields to a working knowledge of production planning and practices, with *Cable Communication* (TC 415) providing students of junior standing with the history, public policy, practices, and social effects of broadband cable systems. A course in *Audience Survey Analysis* (TC 335) examines research design techniques. *International Telecommunication* (TC 498) is a course in comparative systems which discusses selected national and international development, as well as the distribution of information and propaganda. Courses offered jointly with the departments of Advertising and Art and the College of Education focus on Media Research and the use of media in education. *History of the Motion Picture* (TC 280) and *The Documentary Film* (TC 396), which provide technical and theoretical background for film study, also provide practical preparation for *Cinema I* (TC 390) and *Cinema II* (TC 490), the courses in filmmaking offered by the department.

The Department of Human Environment and Design offers one course particularly oriented to popular culture and several others that provide important background for its study. *Culture, Society and Dress* (HED 434) provides a systematic examination of dress and adornment as self-expression, artifact, symbol of culture and social organization, and as an indicator of socio-cultural change. The course draws extensively from interdisciplinary perspectives. Other courses include *Survey of World Dress* (HED 256), which examines the relationship of clothing to aesthetic and social interests through cross-cultural examples, while courses in the history of interior design, *Ancient to Medieval* (HED 230), *Medieval to Rococo* (HED 330), *Rococo to Victorian* (HED 430) and *Modern* (HED 431), consider the development of furniture, textiles and accessories as they relate to interiors.

In addition to courses which have their focus on the design and management of recreation areas, the Department of Park and Recreation Resources offers courses related to the study of popular culture. *Environmental Attitudes and Concepts* (PRR 302) explores beliefs and attitudes toward land, with consideration of industrialism and issues of environmental quality. *Leisure and Recreation Resources* (PRR 344) considers the history, philosophy and significance of leisure in modern society, as well as its impact on urban and natural resource development. On a more advanced level, *Dimensions of Recreation and Leisure* (PRR 801) examines concepts, definitions, values, historical roots and educational aspects of recreation and leisure in the United States, and their implications for professional development.

Other departments within this major university designed to accomodate over 43,000 students offer courses with popular culture components on both undergraduate and graduate levels. Undergraduates who wish to develop a strong emphasis in popular culture may do so by committing themselves to any of several majors which allow flexibility in the selection of electives. The department of English, for example, offers in addition to the emphasis of twelve hours of popular culture a choice of cognates that allows twenty-seven hours of cognate courses outside of English in three or more departments, and electives beyond general education requirements and departmental requirements to the total of the 180 required for graduation. In other words, students may earn the equivalent of an undergraduate major in popular culture while earning a major in English. Graduate students may enter the M.A. or Ph.D. programs in English or American Studies and pursue a program that is individually designed to include a strong emphasis in popular culture while earning degrees in traditional fields.

Larry N. Landrum
Department of English
Michigan State University

The Curriculum of
The Department of Popular Culture
At Bowling Green State University

Courses in Popular Culture at Bowling Green State University were first offered in the late 1960s by the Department of English, principally through the energies of Ray B. Browne. At about this time Browne had also initiated at Bowling Green the Center for the Study of Popular Culture, mainly a collection of primary resources, and had also begun to publish the *Journal of Popular Culture*. Faculty ambition and student interest in Popular Culture on both the undergraduate and graduate levels during the next several years gradually increased beyond the resources of the Department of English. In 1973, after the usual rounds of committee debates, the University approved Popular Culture for departmental status within the College of Arts and Sciences. It was the first (and, as of 1980, only) Department of Popular Culture in American colleges and universities. During this period BGSU also approved the granting of both the Master's (first) and the Bachelor's degrees in Popular Culture. Initial teaching faculty for the new department was two regular faculty, one single year appointee and five graduate teaching assistants. By the end of the 1970s this number has grown to six full time faculty and a dozen teaching assistants.

The Undergraduate Curriculum
The first courses offered by the new Department of Popular Culture were inherited, in name at least, from the Department of English. These included an "introduction" to the subject, two upper level courses in folklore, including "Literature and Folklore," and one upper level course in popular literature. All new courses would have to be proposed by the Department and approved through regular university channels. In order to provide a rationale for new courses, a department curriculum committee was formed in 1974, composed of faculty and graduate students, to form a blueprint for future curricular additions.

The curriculum committee was instructed by the chair to provide both specific course suggestions and an overall perspective on an ideal departmental curriculum for popular culture studies. General discussions led to agreement on three overall objectives:
1. The curriculum should be media oriented but not exclusively so. Four national meetings of the Popular Culture Association had shown that most popular culture studies were being done on specific mass media. It was therefore appropriate that our curriculum reflect that direction within the profession. On the other hand, so much of popular culture is multi-media or non-mass media that the door must be left open for the study of these areas as well.
2. The curriculum should be flexible. The subject matter of popular culture is immense. New research in popular culture constantly suggests broad new areas of interest. Therefore, several courses should remain open ended to allow for the inclusion of new materials.
3. The curriculum should be patterned. Too many departments, the committee agreed, had allowed their courses to build up in a rag-tag fashion,

often through the whims or personal expertise of individual faculty members. With the advantage of being able to begin a series of courses from scratch, the committee insisted the popular culture courses should relate to one another. Lower level courses should be broad overviews while upper level courses should examine similar areas but more specifically and in greater depth. Lower level courses should be offered quarterly while senior level courses should be offered every other year.

Using these objectives as guidelines, the Department has added courses as faculty and resources have become available. By 1980 twenty courses were being offered regularly:

POPC 160. INTRODUCTION TO POPULAR CULTURE. Basic theories of, approaches to, and topics within popular culture; several selected topics and use of various theories and approaches.

POPC 161. POPULAR CULTURE AND MEDIA. Various types of culture and media which affect our lives—artistic and aesthetic accomplishments and failures; obvious and subtle forces and infuences.

POPC 220. INTRODUCTION TO FOLKLORE AND FOLKLIFE. Study and collecting of folklore; ballads, myths, tall tales, heroes, folk medicines, superstitions, proverbs, arts and crafts.

POPC 230. PERSPECTIVES ON POPULAR CULTURE. Study of theme, era, or problem of popular culture. Topics in the past have included "Popular Religions in America," "Images of Women in Popular Culture," etc.

POPC 240. HISTORY OF POPULAR CULTURE. From classical world to present; relationship between society and its popular culture; constant needs of man such as play, sex, ritual, etc.; changing needs of man in changing society.

POPC 150 INTRODUCTION TO POPULAR FILM. Popular film as mass entertainment medium; Hollywood studios, popular film formulae, genres, relationships between popular films and movie-going public.

POPC 270. INTRODUCTION TO CONTEMPORARY POPULAR LITERATURE. Popular literary formulae, publishing industry, relationship between popular literature and reading public, functions of popular literature in society.

POPC 280. INTRODUCTION TO POPULAR MUSIC. Relationship between music world and listening-viewing audience; musical styles, trends in popular music, popular performers and entertainers and what they reveal about popular culture; appropriate music listening.

POPC 290. TELEVISION AS POPULAR CULTURE. Relationship between popular television programming and American society; viewing of appropriate television.

POPC 350. ADVANCED STUDIES IN POPULAR FILM. In-depth study of particular aspects of popular film: single genre, particular director, specific studio, etc. May be repeated once if topics are different; viewing of appropriate films.

POPC 355. STUDIES IN HISTORY OF AMERICAN POPULAR FILM.
Study of specific period in American popular film: silent era, films of
Depression, films of post World War II, etc. May be repeated once if topics
are different; viewing of appropriate films.
(Note: all three film courses also serve as components of an
interdisciplinary "Film Studies" program at BGSU.)
POPC 370. POPULAR LITERATURE. A survey of detective, science
fiction, western, mystery, best sellers, poetry, magazine fiction, etc.
Prerequisite: any 200-level literature course or permission of instructor.
POPC 380. CONTEXTS OF POPULAR MUSIC. In-depth investigation
into single aspect of popular music: specific popular music genres, specific
musical themes in popular music, popular music industry, etc. May be
repeated to eight hours if topics are different.
POPC 390. ELECTRIC MEDIA. Cultural media theory as related to aural
and visual electric media, especially radio and television. Impact of these
media on contemporary culture. Prerequisite: one course in mass media or
permission of instructor.

POPC 400. SENIOR SEMINAR IN POPULAR CULTURE.
Interdepartmental seminar for seniors in POPC program. Selected topics
approached from several points of view. Prerequisites: senior standing and
major in POPC or in discipline represented in POPC program.
POPC 426. TOPICS IN FOLKLORE. In-depth study of a single topic. May
be repeated once if topics are clearly different. Prerequisite: POPC 220 or
permission of the instructor.
POPC 426. POPULAR ENTERTAINMENTS. Cultural significance of
popular entertainments, past and present: circuses, carnivals, parades,
vaudeville, professional and amateur sports, camping, etc. Prerequisite:
POPC 160 or POPC 161.
POPC 460. POPULAR CULTURE: ADVANCED STUDIES. In-depth
study of particular problem: development of hero in popular arts; minorities
in popular culture, etc. May be repeated once if subject matter is different.
POPC 470. POPULAR LITERARY GENRES. Study of particular genre:
science fiction, western, detective novel, etc. May be repeated once if genres
are different. Prerequisite: POPC 370 or permission of instructor.
POPC 490. PROBLEMS IN POPULAR CULTURE. For advanced
students, independent study. Prerequisite: consent of director of POPC
program to proposal approved by staff member three weeks prior to end of
quarter. May be repeated to eight hours.

About one half of the courses deal directly with mass media. Flexibility
is achieved on all levels above 100. POPC 230 allows instructors freedom of
subject choice at the introductory level and 460 gives this same freedom in a
course meant for juniors and seniors. These courses also allow faculty from
other departments to teach courses on popular culture materials. Upper
level courses in film, music, folklore and literature each allow the specific
subject matter to change with each offering. The overall curricular pattern,
generally, is as follows:

100s—General introductions
200s—Introductions to specific areas of popular culture
300s and 400s—Intensive studies of specific subject matter

Few popular culture majors or minors are served by these courses—10-15 majors in a given year and about 25 minors. Students select courses from several departments besides Popular Culture and work closely with an advisor to construct a personal, interdisciplinary program. Most students, however, elect to enroll in courses in the Popular Culture Department because they fulfill general requirements or simply because they find the material interesting. For this reason, most courses below the 400 (senior) level do not have prerequisites.

Enrollments in upper division courses, mainly because of the low number of majors, is moderate except when "cult" courses such as "Science Fiction" or "The Hard-Boiled Detective in Film and Fiction" are offered. Lower division courses, on the other hand, cannot begin to accommodate the number of students who request them. Currently we are register some 2000 students each year. Overall, enrollment in the Department of Popular Culture undergraduate courses is about 90% of capacity, one of the highest in the College of Arts and Sciences.

The Master of Arts Program

The M.A. Program in Popular Culture at BGSU in some ways is quite similar to graduate, interdisciplinary degree programs elsewhere. Courses from several departments outside of Popular Culture are required. Candidates take general comprehensive examinations based on a core reading list and then select either to write a thesis or to take additional course work and a set of individual exams. Three courses are required: POPC 501, Introduction to Graduate Study in Popular Culture; POPC 597, Theories and Methods of Popular Culture; and one course in folklore. Graduate assistants in addition must take POPC 590, Teaching Popular Culture.

In 1977 this quite conventional plan of studies underwent some important modifications. Although basic requirements remained the same, three separate "tracks" were begun in order to accommodate the needs of modern graduate students who quite probably did not plan on a future career in college teaching. The threefold "track" system allows for individual student interests and needs but at the same time creates patterns of coursework through which students may begin to prepare for their vocational futures.

The "Professional" Track

The aim of the professional track is to prepare students for work in a particular vocational area of popular culture—e.g., record sales, media work, student union programming, advertising, etc. It is intended for terminal Master's students with specific vocational aims.

When the student and the Graduate Advisor have worked out a tentative degree plan they work with a faculty consultant(s) in the department(s) in which supportive course work is necessary to plan out the area of specialization. For example, a candidate wanting to work in student union programming might work with someone in the College of Business to plan a specialization that would include work in Management, Accounting, and Business Law in addition to formal course work in Popular Culture Studies.

Special requirements:

a) An area of specialization. A minimum of 20 hours of courses directly related to the vocational interests of the candidate.

b) Internship. 12 credits. The culmination of the internship is to be a written evaluation of the experience or an investigation of some problem central to the experience. (For example, someone working in record sales might want to center on the problem of determining why certain records sell well in certain markets.) This written evaluation, or investigation, serves in the place of a thesis for students in the professional track. Students have elected to do internships at such places as student activities offices on other campuses, cable TV companies, popular magazine publishers, and museums.

The "Research" Track

The research track is intended for those candidates whose goal is to pursue their formal education beyond the Master's level. It may also serve the needs of those students who intend to pursue a career in research.

Special Requirements:

1) A student following the research track is required to take at least *one* course in the following areas:

a) media analysis (can include "informal" media—e.g., speech as well as the electric media);

b) social science, a course which stresses quantitative methods.

2) Thesis research/writing (4-9 hours).

The "Teaching" Track

The teaching track is intended for those candidates who intend to pursue a teaching vocation on the secondary or junior/community college level.

Required Courses:

1. POPC 590, Teaching Popular Culture;

2. POPC 571, Course and Curriculum Planning in Popular Culture (this course is team-taught by a faculty member from Popular Culture and a faculty member from the College of Education);

3. A graduate course in Adolescent Studies;

4. A graduate course in media analysis or media use.

Other Requirements:

If thesis option is pursued, the thesis must deal with an educational issue.

The number of Masters' candidates per year since 1977 has averaged between 15 and 20. The appropriateness of the revision of the program toward the track system was borne out in a survey of Popular Culture M.A. recipients done in 1979. The survey revealed that about one-fifth were in high school or junior college teaching positions; slightly more than one-quarter went on to further graduate study; and about one-half sought out jobs in private businesses. From the beginning the Popular Culture program has prospered sometimes with the cooperation of some departments (such as Sociology, Music and the Ethnic Studies Program) and the active support of the administration of the College of Arts and Sciences, the Dean (and several departments, notably Marketing) of Business Administration, as well as the higher administration. Support from various other departments on campus is growing steadily.

Syllabi

Popular Culture Courses
in General Popular Culture

Popular Culture 160
Introduction to Popular Culture
(4 credits—10 week quarter)

Introduction.

"Introduction to Popular Culture" was the first course developed by the Department of Popular Culture when Popular Culture Studies was given departmental status in 1973. The course was initially designed to serve as an elective for freshman and sophomore level students who wished to satisfy course requirements in the humanities. This has proven consistently to be the case. About three-fourths of the students who enroll in PC 160 do so to satisfy a college general humanities requirement and slightly more than 60% of the students who enroll come from outside the College of Arts and Sciences. Since the Department has few undergraduate majors, they have never been an important factor in the planning of the course.

During 1974, its first full year, "Introduction to Popular Culture" was offered to about 60 students per quarter. Since that time demand has increased each year, until by the end of the '70s it had become one of the most demanded non-science electives at the university. Currently, about 1000 students per year enroll in PC 160. Computer printouts show student requests for the course are double the seats available. Because of the heavy demand, some large sections of 200 students are offered annually. Most students, however, are handled in sections of 30 students where informal discussions can easily take place. The give-and-take atmosphere of these small sections seems appropriately attuned to the overall objectives of PC 160.

Unlike many "introduction" courses which are aimed mainly at presenting an overview of a discipline and are intended to be followed by additional courses within the discipline, PC 160 is a course which is meant to stand on its own and which emphasizes practical application rather than broad disciplinary perspectives. During the first class sessions, the course is described as a "survival manual" and it is explained as presenting a series of "tools" that will help students understand the popular culture environment within which they spend a great majority of their lives.

The course is structured to meet this central objective. Basically, class lectures, discussions and assignments proceed along a triple path, always arriving at the goal of applying concepts to the direct interpretation of the meaning of elements of the popular culture environment, both past and present. Each new area of the course begins with abstract definition and theory, proceeds to multiple examples of and directions on how to analyze the area and, finally, ends with tests and writing assignments that demand that students apply the general concepts to central materials that have not been dealt with in class (see outline and special features). The overall structure also reflects practical objectives by proceeding from general concepts of culture and a discussion of what is popular culture to the "tools" of the discipline and, finally, to discussions at the end of the course of the meaning of current popular artifacts.

Outline of Course.

Part I. Overview of the Subject and an Introduction to the Foundations of
    All Culture: Beliefs and Myths (3 weeks.)
    A. Topics discussed in general overview:
        1. What is culture?
        2. What is popular culture?
        3. Differences between elite, folk and popular culture.
    B. Topics presented in discusssion of beliefs and myths:
        1. Limited consciousness, world view and popular culture's
           place within these concepts.
        2. Beliefs as the abstract basis upon which people conduct
           their lives.
        3. Myths as basic beliefs structuring fundamental questions
           about life.
        4. How cultural beliefs are exploited in ads and politics.
    C. Some modern beliefs discussed: It is good to be young;
       it is good to be thin.
    D. Some modern myths discussed: Myth of material success.
       Myth of rural goodness. Myth of technology as
       savior. Myth of sacred individualism. Myth of
       endless abundance.
    E. Sources for examples: Magazine advertisements, political
       quotes, myths as seen on prime time television.
The first unit concludes with a 55 minute examination.
One short paper is assigned during the unit asking students to identify a
popular myth on a prime time TV show.

Part II. The "tools" for the Study of Popular Culture. (5 weeks.)
    The students are told several times during this section of the course that
they are learning a set of categories of popular culture artifacts that will act
as "tools" enabling them to recognize popular myths and beliefs. In
addition, they are given lists of questions to ask about an artifact which are
meant to aid them in interpreting the abstract cultural significance that is
at the core of the popularity of that artifact. When examples are discussed,
the emphasis is upon the beliefs suggested by the artifact.

A. Popular Icons.
   1. Def. An object that has meaning for people beyond its use.
   2. Class examples: cars, jeans, sunglasses, guns, pinball
      machines, McDonalds, etc.
B. Popular Stereotypes.
   1. Def. An oversimplification in which individual people
      are seen as identical members of a classification.
      The classification is publicly agreed upon.
   2. Class Examples: Various ethnic minority groups.
      American regional stereotypes. Sexual stereotypes.
      Popular fictional stereotypes.
   3. Unit Emphasis: It is stressed that stereotypes in themselves
      are neither good nor bad. Some uses of stereotypes
      in fiction serve a useful purpose, for example, while
      most negative ethnic stereotypes have a destructive purpose.
C. Popular Heroes.
   1. Def. People who represent the ideals of a culture.
   2. Types: a) Traditional Heroes; b) Rebel Heroes; c) Celebrities.
   3. Class Examples: Babe Ruth, Jack Johnson, The Lone Ranger,
      the cover stories in recent *People* magazines,
      Butch Cassidy and the Sundance Kid, etc.
D. Popular Rituals.
   1. Def. Elaborately repeated acts participated in or watched
      by large groups of people.
   2. Types: a) Rites of Passage; b) Rites of Season; c) Rites of Unity;
      d) Rites of Reversal.
   3. Class Examples: Spectator sports, national holidays, weddings,
      funerals, campus homecoming, initiation ceremonies, etc.
E. Popular Formulas.
   1. Popular story forms in which the audience expects certain
      conventional elements including locale, characters,
      plotline and iconic props.
   2. Class Examples: Westerns, true confession stories,
      horror movies, soap operas, etc.
During this second unit, audio visual examples are used almost daily.
The unit concludes with a 55 minute examination.
Four short papers are completed during the unit (on four of the five
   "tools") and a long paper is assigned.

Part III. Concluding Overview (2 weeks.)
   This section includes a series of class activities which integrate the
course "tools" in examinations of specific cultural artifacts. For example,
we watch and discuss a half hour TV sitcom looking for stereotypes, icons,
etc. and conclude with a discussion of the beliefs the program seems to
confirm for its audience. Another class is devoted to an analysis of the past
decade based on selected popular music. It is explained to the students that
this is meant to prepare them for the final exam and for completion of their
large paper.
   The unit concludes with a 2 hour final examination.

The large paper is collected half way through the unit. (See special features.)

Special Features.

PAPER ASSIGNMENTS. Paper assignments are the most crucial element of the course because they force students to apply ideas within the course to materials with which they are unfamiliar. Five short papers (about 2 pages each) are assigned in which the students must use individual elements of the course. One longer paper is also required. This long paper asks for an examination of a popular artifact from an unfamiliar time period and demands use of all the "tools" taught in the class.

Short Assignment Example:

Select a popular non-religious ritual that you personally have within a month either attended or participated in. For example: homecoming, a wedding, fraternity or sorority ceremonies, Halloween parties, etc. Then write the paper in which you do two main things: 1) Describe the specific ritual you were involved in. 2) Analyze the ritual you were involved in and explain one myth or belief the ritual suggests that the participatants have confirmed for them by the ritual itself.

Long Paper Example:

Go to the library and select one issue of one magazine that was produced in America before 1960. Magazines you may select from are *Life, Look, The Saturday Evening Post, Ebony, Colliers, Liberty, Ladies Home Journal, The American Magazine.* After an intensive study of the magazine in which you use all of the tools of PC 160, write the paper on the following topic:

Discuss in detail three important myths/or beliefs that the people of the time the magazine was published believed based on what is suggested by the contents of the magazine itself.

Try to do two things in the paper:

1) Get beneath the surface of the magazine. Think creatively and in depth about what you are examining.

2) Be detailed in proving your ideas. Cite abundant evidence for all your generalizations.

TESTS. In keeping with the course objectives, all tests are essay type with the questions aimed at new integrations of course materials. The two hour final exam, for example, demands that students, as in the long paper, use course tools for analysis of the beliefs hidden in a television show or a magazine ad that is shown to them for the first time during the test itself.

Test Example:

Match one item from list A with one from list B and from list C. Then write a detailed paragraph in which you explain your reasons for the match. Be specific. Then do the matching twice more so that when you are finished with the question you have three different matches and three carefully developed paragraphs. Do not use any item more than once.

List A

John Wayne
Babe Ruth
Jack Johnson
The Lone Ranger
Farrah
"Sambo"

List B

Pinball
The Super Bowl
Demolition Derbies
Automobiles
Disco
Marlboros

List C

Myth of Material Success
Myth of Endless Abundance
"Epic Moment" in American History
Myth of Rural Simplicity
Myth of Sacred Individualism
Myth of Technology as Savior

(All of the above items would have received individual classroom attention but they would not have been previously discussed together.)

Bibliography
Texts

Nachbar, Jack, Deborah Weiser and John L. Wright, eds. *The Popular Culture Reader.*
    Bowling Green, Ohio: Bowling Green Popular Press, 1978. An anthology of critical
    articles divided according to the divisions used in the course itself.
    Each section includes a descriptive introduction. Used in all sections
    of the course.

Other Texts: Each instructor chooses his/her own primary source readings. A few of those that
have been used successfully include current issues of *People, The National Observer* and
confession magazines; any available novel by Horatio Alger, Jr.; Irving Wallace's novel *The Fan
Club,* anthologies of *Doonesbury* cartoons and *National Lampoon's 1964 High School Yearbook.*

Selected Background Reading:

Arens, W. and Susan P. Montague, eds. *The American Dimension.* Port Washington, N.Y.: Alfred,
    1976. Anthology of essays on popular rituals written by anthropologists.
Boorstin, Daniel J. *The Image: A Guide to Pseudo-Events in America.* New York: Harper and
    Row, 1964. Primer on celebrityhood and other problems in mass-mediated America.
Browne, Ray B. and Marshall Fishwick, ed. *Icons of America.* Bowling Green, Ohio: Bowling
    Green Popular Press, 1978. An anthology of essays on American icons both past
    and present.

Cawelti, John G. *Adventure, Mystery and Romance.* Chicago: University of Chicago Press, 1976. An important study of the concept of popular formula.

Eliade, Mircea. Any of professor Eliade's books will provide valuable insights into the cultural functions of myths and ritual.

Nye, Russel B. *The Unembarrassed Muse: The Popular Arts in America.* New York: Dial Press, 1970. The best historical overview of the subject.

Real, Michael. *Mass-Mediated Culture.* Englewood Cliffs, N.J.: Prentice—Hall, 1977. Marxist oriented essays on Disneyland, The Super Bowl, etc., as cultural metaphors.

Jack Nachbar
Department of Popular Culture
Bowling Green State University

American Studies 403
American Popular Culture
(4 credits—10 week quarter)

Introduction

"American Popular Culture" has been considered an essential part of American Studies since the inception of the department in 1959. Considered as an elective within both the American Studies academic and teaching credential program, it is offered three times a year and has an average enrollment of 25 students. Faculty is selected from several disciplines (sociology, English, American Studies, speech communication), and each professor designs the course according to his/her own scholarly orientation and interest.

For this particular course I stress discovery rather than instruction. This is made clear in the syllabus which opens with the Marcel Proust line, "The real voyage of discovery consists not in seeking new landscapes, but in having new eyes." Toward this goal, students are required to actively investigate, accurately describe and analyze artifacts, activities and ideas labeled as "Popular Culture." They then learn to create hypotheses about the role and significance of these elements in American life.

The final grade for A.S. 403 is determined by graded fulfillment of the following: "Radioanalysis," 5 points; "Iconorama," 15 points; Research project—oral presentation, 20 points, written presentation, 20 points; in-class final exam, 40 points.

I have taught two variations of this course. "Course Outline" describes those activities utilized in both variations while "Special Features" describes those activities utilized in only one or the other of the variants.

Course Outline

A. *TV Analysis* (Used on the first class meeting before syllabi are distributed.)

"What can you learn about American culture by watching and analyzing a TV game show?" (This question is written on the blackboard for students to see as they enter class.)

After watching 15 minutes of a game show, be prepared to discuss the following questions. What themes are presented? What are the hidden messages? Who is the audience? What elements give you the clues for analysis? Does this show influence its audience or does it reflect current values? What values are revealed?

B. *Radioanalysis*

Divide into groups of two or four. Each group should select an AM radio station with which the students are familiar. (This should be done one week before the analysis date, with radios brought to class to check station transmission capabilities to campus area.) On the "Radioanalysis" date, do not come to class. Instead, each group should have a quiet meeting place on campus, bring a battery operated radio and keep an accurate log of the assigned station noting everything that is heard from 10:00 to 10:30. (Divide duties within the group, e.g. one person note time and item, another note content, etc.)

The Log: Write down the exact time and details of everything heard. 1) Music: list title, artist kind (soul? rock? pop?). What is the message? Are titles and artists announced? If not, what does this mean? 2) Talk: list topics, deejay's tone and point of view; 3) commercials: kinds and prices of products, style of sell; 4) News: summarize items and tone of presentation; 5) Public service announcements; kinds? 6) Weather; 7) Traffic; 8) Other.

After compiling the log, tablulate the number of commercials, songs, talk, news, etc., and try to figure out the ratio of each for the half hour. Examine the messages of songs, news and talk, Analyze your findings.

From the information compiled, what assumptions can you make about the audience? Who are they? Where do they live? What is their educational background? financial status? consumer habits? age? values? fears? concerns?

What about the Deejay? Analyze his/her style, vocabulary, attitude toward the audience. What did you learn about him/her? What about the station? Do they exploit their audience or do they provide useful service information? Do they enforce continuity or are they movers and shakers, encouraging social action?

On the class meeting following the "radioanalysis" date, be prepared for each group's discussion of findings which will be turned in with logs, tabulations and summaries.

What did you learn from this experience?

C. *Iconorama*

Select an icon or icons for a five to seven minute creative presentation and display. Be prepared to give reasons for your selection of this particular object or objects as icon. You are to convince the class that this item qualifies as an icon and you must create an ad to sell it, including the ad in your presentation. Some questions to consider: Which audience uses this icon? What societal values are revealed by its use? How does your icon relate to icon characteristics described in the readings?

D. *Phonographics*

Bring at least three different kinds of record jackets for an exhibit. (Leave the records home if it's a hot day.) All covers will be taped to the wall for examination, enjoyment and focus of discussion. Questions to consider: Are record jackets a form of art?—a new form of art? What is the relationship of visual presentation to style of music, to time period?

Music Trade Publications
What can you learn about popular music by studying "the trades"? (Bring current and back issues of *Billboard, Cashbox* and *Record Rack* into class.)

Divide into dyads and examine these publications creating hypotheses about the nature of the music industry. Questions to consider for an in-class discussion: What is the procedure for analyzing a magazine? What do you look for? Where are the clues? Relate your questions and discoveries to the "Phonographics" and "Radioanalysis" exercises.

Special Features

A. Popular Music Research Project
What does popular music reveal about those who compose it, listen to it, sing it? dance to it? buy copies of it?

Select a songwriter (lyricist) popular in America at any time and prepare both a written and oral presentation including biographical data, career information, and an analysis of ideas, rhyme, and vocabulary from a minimum of five of the writer's songs. When analyzing the lyrics, listen to them in the context of the music. Do not limit yourself to just the printed word.

You are to interpret the writer's success (or lack of it), and the influence on his/her audience, making a final statement as to the significance of the writer's work and what it reveals about the society in which he/she lived or lives. Be sure to consider the social and historical events influencing the writer, his/her popularity, themes, messages.

The written presentation requires the inclusion of lyric samples with analysis and a discography. The oral presentation should include the playing of examples with a summary statement about the meaning of the artist's work in American culture.

B. 30 Day Self-Improvement Plan
Select a current book (last 5 years) presenting a self-improvement or self-help scheme (beauty, health, success, personality, etc.). Follow the instructions of the book, map out a plan, and track your progress daily in a notebook. Record problems and successes, and note whether instructions were followed as prescribed or adjusted. Keep track of supportive and non-supportive responses from friends and family. At the end of 30 days you will evaluate the process in both written and oral form. You will be required to analyze the value and effectiveness of your particular self-improvement program, discussing its significance related to the concepts of progress and success.

(To assist the students, a counselor from a Student Health Center came in to lead a group session on problems, benefits, limitations, rewards and feasibility of short-term goals. This opened up important issues on self-improvement and its role in the American lifestyle.)

C. Festival of Home Movies

Bring your own home movies and slides for a grab bag film festival. Why do we photograph what we photograph? With whom do we share our "frozen memories"? Which family member decides what to memorialize?

D. Create an Ad—Discover the Difference Between Radio and TV.

What is the difference between an audio and an audio-visual presentation? Divide into groups of four. As a group select one object and create both a TV ad and a radio ad for the same product. You will have the entire class time to make your decision and plans (1 hour 40 minutes). On the next class meeting there will be a video set-up (camera, deck, and monitor) and a tape recorder set-up available in the classroom. Each group will take turns performing and producing its own presentation.

After the playback session, apply what you have learned as a participant and a viewer to a discussion of differences between the two media.

E. The Manipulation of Popular Culture—Guest Lecture

A freelance writer, Joe Posner, was invited to describe his process of selecting a marketable fad, pyramid power, and exploiting it through the creation of his screenplay, "The Cheops Effect." To demonstrate the process, he led the class through the steps of selecting other fads manipulating them into the creation of an outline for a potentially salable film product directed toward a target audience.

bliography*
Texts:
Browne, Ray B. and Marshall Fishwick. *Icons of America.* Bowling Green, Ohio: Popular Press, 1978. Basic readings for the course.
McFadden, Cyra. *The Serial.* New York: Signet, 1978. Hilarious and important to any study of contemporary life.
McLuhan, Herbert Marshall and Quentin Fiore. *The Medium is the Massage.* New York: Random House, 1967.
————————. *Understanding Media.* New York: McGraw Hill, 1964. A useful get-acquainted-with-media classic.
Palmer, Tony. *All You Need Is Love.* New York: Penguin, 1977. Overview of pop music with good visuals.
Whetmore, Edward Jay. *Mediamerica: Form, Content and Consequence of Mass Communication.* Belmont, CA: Wadsworth Publishing Co., 1979. Very good overview and format with useful discussion questions.

Selected Background Reading:
Akeret, Robert U. *Photoanalysis: How to Interpret the Hidden Psychological Meaning of Personal Photographs.* New York: Simon and Schuster, 1973. Useful for "Festival of Home Movies" offering another interpretation of photos.
Benedict, Brad and Linda Barton. *Phonographics: Contemporary Album Cover Art and Design.* New York: McMillan Pub. Co., 1977. Colorful coverage of covers.
Hipgnosis and Rogert Dean, ed. *Album Cover Art.* New York: Dragon's World Ltd., 1977. Useful historical data on record album art with excellent graphics.
Lasch, Christopher. *Culture of Narcissism.* New York: W.W. Norton, 1978. Critical to any study of Self-Improvement.

74   Popular Culture Studies in America

McLuhan, Marshall and Kathryn Hutchon and Eric McLuhan. *City As Classroom*. Agincourt,
Ontario: Book Society of Canada, Ltd. 1977. While designed for younger students, exercises
and questions about media are adaptable and useful to college classes.

Norine Dresser
Department of American Studies
California State University, Los Angeles

Honors 50 GH
The Development and Function of Popular Culture in Twentieth-Century America
(3 credits—16 week semester)

Introduction:

I developed this course for both personal and educational reasons. I am
from Tupelo, Mississippi, the birthplace of Elvis Presley, and movies and
rock and roll have been extremely important experiences in my life.
Although my academic training is in Russian literature, I have for some
time felt frustrated while teaching high culture because it intimidates
Missouri students, and therefore makes communication difficult.

More generally, though, I find the increasing specialization and
emphasis on practicality in higher education in the seventies a disturbing
trend. For one thing, it is very unlikely that within five years of graduation
students will be directly applying what they studied in college, but it is very
likely that they will be going to movies and watching television. No matter
what one's occupation, it is virtually impossible to live in American society
without experiencing popular culture. Popular culture gives us our
expectation, our sex roles, and our conceptions of the world; therefore, to
study popular culture is to study one's self. American universities offer
many subjects, but few of them enhance the students' personal growth and
self-awareness as the study of popular culture does.

I offered this course in our Honors College, which provides possibilities
for new and innovative courses which might not, for whatever reason, meet
with the approval of the Curriculum Committee. Only students with a 3.3
average (out of 4) may enroll in Honors College course, and this inevitably
limits enrollment (I had 15 students in the course). Since I cannot offer the
course in my home department (Germanic and Slavic Studies), I have
discussed the possibility of offering it in Speech and Dramatic Art with the
chairman of that department, but since I have no appointment there,
obvious difficulties arise. At this writing, I plan to teach the course in the
Honors College one more time, but after that my plans are uncertain.
(Incidentally, although the course is given in the Honors College, it does
count toward the humanities courses in the general education requirements
for a B.A.)

My general purpose in the course is to attack what someone has called
"the bubble gum fallacy," a fallacy perfectly expressed in the Rolling
Stones' song "It's Only Rock and Roll (But I Like It)." Whether consciously
or unconsciously (mostly unconsciously), people think of popular culture as
a form of bubble gum—you chew it for a while, and then, when it won't
bubble any more, you spit it out—and that's that. I consider this a fallacy
both because popular culture expresses the same enduring themes and

concerns of America as high culture (democracy versus elitism, for example) and because popular culture gives us our expectations about life, and concepts of the world, and does so all the more insidiously because people rarely analyze it. Moreover, both academics and students often resist analyzing popular culture because our Puritan heritage, in its contemporary form, says that it's all right to have a good time as long as you don't think about it.

Outline of Courses:

Since I am a passionate McLuhanite, I have generally limited the course material to American popular culture in the 20th century, since this enables me to deal with development of popular culture as a function of changes in communications media. I begin the course by asking the students to fill out a "Popular Culture Survey," in which I ask them whether they have seen some well-known movies of the past few years, what television programs they watch, and I ask them to identify people like Norman Lear and Peter Asher. I do this in order to find out what common experiences the class has had, and what references I can make. I then devote a class period to discussing McLuhan's *Understanding Media,* and its implications for interpreting popular culture.

I grew up reading murder mysteries. I therefore begin the course proper with a history of the murder mysteries. We read Poe's "The Murders in the Rue Morgue," Doyle's *A Study in Scarlet* and *the Sign of Four,* Agatha Christie's *The Big Four,* Raymond Chandler's *The Big Sleep,* Spillane's *I, the Jury* and MacDonald's *One Fearful Yellow Eye.* In discussing the great detectives, I emphasize the way in which the features of the great detectives such as Dupin, Holmes, Poirot and so forth constitute a response to the growing anonymity and uniformity of city life. To take the most obvious case, Holmes finds meaning all around him in cigar ashes and so forth, where most people find none.

After murder mysteries comes a unit in which the students really start to open up and to which they usually respond strongly—"The Mythology of High School." I use Ralph Keyes' *Is There Life After High School?* to make the points that high school is the one nearly universal experience in American life, and that it forms (and/or de-forms) people for the rest of their lives. Since I key the course to the university film series, I was able to show *Rebel Without a Cause* in class, and then assign the students to see *American Graffiti* (which was shown in the film series) immediately afterward. Each film deals with the ubiquitous conflict in American life of the "innies" and the "outies," but does so in a way which is characteristic of the fifties and the seventies.

What could follow high school but cars and sports? I discuss the history of football and baseball as social phenomena, and the meaning of the car in popular culture.

After mid-term, the second half of the course consists primarily of popular culture as media history. I do a series of classes on radio, television and rock and roll. I begin with pre-television radio, playing records of such comedy stars as Amos 'n' Andy, Jack Benny and Fred Allen, and analyzing the way they used verbal humor, as opposed to the visual humor of television. Then comes television itself; I show an excerpt from a CBS special on television in the fifties, and discuss in some detail the development of television programming. I'm especially interested in the progressive externalization of the situations of major shows. In the fifties, we find many shows taking place in the home, and using a family as its principal characters (*Mama; My Three Sons; Ozzie and Harriet*); in the sixties with *Bonanza* and *The Dick Van Dyke Show* we find a merger of the family situation and the work situation. *Bonanza* combined these completely, since the Cartwrights work on their own ranch; *Dick Van Dyke* alternated between the two—sometimes the show took place at home, and sometimes at the office. In the seventies, we find more and more shows which take place primarily in the work situation (*Taxi, Alice, WKRP in Cincinnati),* but treat the group of workers as a family, with close, warm ties among the people, who give each other mutual support in times of difficulty. Even *Charlie's Angels,* with all it owes to James Bond movies, fits into this pattern.

I allowed a week (next time it will be two weeks) for a cultural history of rock and roll. I call this segment of the course a "cultural" history because I can emphasize, not the individual stars so much as the context of rock and roll—the social groups from which the individual stars came, and the way in which the music filled social needs; and the changes in musical styles as manifestations of changes in recording techniques.

The segment of the course on media concludes with a guest speaker, in this case the program director of a local rock station, who discussed the nitty-gritty of running a rock station, how he plans programming, what records he decides to play and not to play.

Because I use the university film series, I scheduled a segment on Westerns at the very end of the course, since *High Noon* and *The Man Who Shot Liberty Valance* were being shown within a week of each other. I began the segment with Owen Wister's *The Virginian,* the source of many of the standard conventions of Westerns, such as "Smile when you say that, pardner," and one of the most important and significant examples of popular writing in American culture.

Special Features:

The first two writing assignments in the course involve autobiography, but require understanding of the self in a social context. For "A Media Biography," I ask the students to describe the changes in their media experiences, and relate those changes to their lives. We all know that our students started out watching cartoons on television, but what happened after that? I want answers to questions like: When (if ever) did you get tired of cartoons? What was the first significant movie which you remember seeing? When (if ever) did rock and roll become important to you? (I say "if ever" here because a significant percentage of the students in my class knew very little about rock and roll—either they were interested in jazz, or weren't interested in music at all.) Then comes the assignment which produced the most moving and eloquent batch of student papers it has ever been my privilege to read: "What I Liked/Hated Most About High School." Virtually everyone has strong feelings about high school, and these students were no exception. I have never in my life read such bitterness and resentment toward an institution. A student poignantly asked, "Was there no better way we could have spent our adolescent years?" Some were able to find humor in the pain, though; one girl called her paper, "I Never Saw a Fat

Cheerleader (and Other Realities of Adolescent Life)."

The other two writing assignments had less to do with autobiography. At the beginning of the semester I asked the students to make a commitment to watch a weekly television show, to make notes on the plots, characters and relationships in the show, and write this up. And finally, I asked them to do a fairly detailed analysis of a rock and roll album paying particular attention to matters like influences, production techniques, use of instruments and the like. (Students are not accustomed to verbalizing their reactions to rock and roll, and I later found out that they generally considered this the most difficult assignment.)

Since we talked about high school so much during the first half of the course, I included the following question on the mid-term:

Just before the chicken race in *Rebel Without a Cause,* Jim asks Buzz, "Why do we do this?" and Buzz replies, "You gotta do something." Explain the nature of the social and technological forces in American society which this scene expresses. In what sense can you say that *American Graffiti* both resolves these forces and acknowledges their continued effects?

I gave a take-home final which had a very general question: "Discuss the relationships among individual, place, and community as they appear in American popular culture." I phrased the question in this way because I wanted to find out how they would organize and integrate these recurring themes in the course.

Bibliography

McLuhan, Marshall. *Understanding Media* (New York: McGraw-Hill, 1964). Essential for understanding the relationships among art, technology and social process.

Keyes, Ralph. *Is There Life After High School?* (Boston: Little, Brown, 1976). A stimulating, well-researched analysis of the meaning of high school in American life.

Newcombe, Horace, ed. *Television: A Critical View* (New York: Oxford Press, 1978). Collection of articles.

Nachbar, Jack, ed. *Focus on the Western* (Englewood Cliffs: Prentice-Hall, 1974). Collection of articles on the Western.

Suggested Background Reading

Fiedler, Leslie. *Love and Death in the American Novel* (New York: Stein and Day, 1966). Seminal analysis of some of the most enduring myths in American life.

Marcus, Griel. *Mystery Train* (New York: Dutton, 1975). The best book ever written on rock and roll.

Wright, Will. *Sixguns and Society* (Berkeley: Univ. of California Press, 1975). Structural study of the Western.

James M. Curtis
Germanic & Slavic Studies
University of Missouri—Columbia

Popular Culture Courses
in Popular Literature

English 210
Detective and Espionage Fiction
(3 credits—15 week semester)

Introduction

Detective and Espionage Fiction, purposely offered to attract students who reject traditional English courses, was first given in the spring of 1978 and repeated in 1979. In 1980 in response to requests from local educators, it will appear as English 301 and emphasize the use of course materials in the secondary school classroom. Although English 210 has encountered no overt hostility from other department members and received warm support from some, I consider its position roughly comparable to that of an illegitimate child—tolerated but not fully accepted. The course has met at eight in the morning both times it has been offered to undergraduates, and the spring schedule of classes stipulates that it "cannot be applied to English major requirements." It does, however, meet general humanities requirements, and English majors may take it as an elective. I plan to offer the course in its original form during the 1980-81 academic year.

A literary, historical and sociological analysis of selected short stories and novels featuring detection, mystery and espionage, English 210 provides disciplined and serious study of two popular fictional sub-genres whose relatively short life spans allow students to witness the development of literary forms from their beginnings to the present and to understand the relationship between socio-historical and literary change. Since I do not believe that most detective and espionage fiction deserves or repays the kind of sustained *literary* analysis one would give to a Donne elegy or a Shakespeare play, for example, and since my own critical orientation is socio-historical, the course is designed to emphasize establishment of formulas peculiar to each genre, specific changes which have modified existing formulas, and long-term trends which reflect the relationship between each form and the society in which it originated and developed. Therefore, such subjects as the rise of the middle class and the spread of literacy in the eighteenth century, the impact of technology upon popular art, conditions in the publishing industry, and the characteristics of a mass audience are as integral a part of the course as traditional literary considerations. Literary influences are, of course, crucial and the impact of Poe upon detective fiction, incalculable, but one must also consider the importance of the democratic and essentially law-abiding societies in which

78

the detective story was born. No one questions the contributions of Buchan, Ambler, or Le Carre to espionage fiction, but it is not possible to understand these authors or their popularity without also understanding England before 1914, fascism in the 1930s and the Cold War.

The primary aims of English 210 are to provide students with a sound grasp of the development of detective and espionage fiction, to acquaint them with major writers in each genre, to develop their skills in literary interpretation, and to enable them to see that popular literature, like all art, is rooted in the political, social and historical milieu in which it is produced.

Outline of Course
Part I. Detective Fiction (10 weeks).
A. What is detective fiction? Who reads it and why? Does it answer certain psychological needs or appeal to specific personality types?

B. Literary and historical background of development of the form: growth of the middle class, establishment of police forces, improvements in printing and presses and growth of a cheap popular press. Popularity of crime literature, both factual and fictional in eighteenth and early nineteenth centuries; literary precursors in Gothic novels, Newgate calendars, melodrama. Specific attention to Godwin's *Caleb Williams* and the *Memoirs* of Vidocq.

C. Edgar Allan Poe: detailed discussion of the elements of detective fiction found with Poe in order to establish a pattern from which to view future developments.

D. Victorian Sensation Fiction: discussion of penny dreadfuls and shilling shockers, the work of Emile Gaboriau; definition of sensation fiction, its appeal and function in the novels of Dickens, emphasis upon Collins' *The Moonstone*, especially the character of Sgt. Cuff, narrative technique and the author's use of the unconscious.

E. Conan Doyle and Holmes in perspective: looking back at Dupin and Cuff and forward to Poirot and other detectives of Golden Age fiction. Guest lecture on "The Logic of Sherlock Holmes."
At this point in the course each student presents an oral report based upon his reading of two short stories by early twentieth-century authors such as Chesterton, Morrison, Futrelle, Freeman, Leblanc, Hornung and Barr. In order to enlarge their knowledge of both period and form, students analyze their stories according to these criteria: character of detective, plot structure and social milieu.

F. Golden Age Detective Fiction: general characteristics of interwar English detective stories with emphasis upon E.C. Bentley's *Trent's Last Case* and the work of Christie, Sayers, Allingham and Marsh. Pointed contrast between the worlds of the novels and actual conditions in Great Britain; attention to authors' attitudes toward social class.

G. Formula Fiction: Definition and Function. At this time students are introduced to important critical commentaries on the genre and read such essays as Auden's "The Guilty Vicarage," Barzun's "The Delights of Detection," and Wilson's "Who Cares Who Killed Roger Ackroyd?"

H. American Detective Fiction with emphasis upon the hard-boiled tradition of Hammett, Chandler and MacDonald. All students read Chandler's "The Simple Art of Murder," and we discuss the specific differences between these authors and their English contemporaries and attempt to analyze the differences through attention to historical circumstances, national character and linguistic patterns. Our discussion of formula fiction is continued and expanded.

I. Ross Macdonald: the fusing of two traditions. Macdonald combines the American private eye with the elaborate plotting of English tradition and provides us with opportunities to discuss the impact of Freudian psychology on modern literature and the use of detective stories as vehicles for social criticism. The concept of California as a lost paradise in both Chandler and Macdonald revealed the importance of archetypes and myths in popular fiction.

J. The Police Procedural: a new variant. Continued discussion of social criticism with added emphasis upon the relationship between authors' political opinions and the form and content of their works.

K. Guest Lecturer: Jorge Luis Borges and the expansion of the genre.

Part II. Espionage Fiction (5 weeks)

A. General introduction and background: traditional attitudes toward spies; importance of Dreyfus case, Anglo-German military rivalry, and World War I upon the development of the form; patriotism. Early examples of genre: Kipling's *Kim* as precursor; Oppenheim, Childers, LeQueux.

B. John Buchan: establishment of thriller pattern in *The Thirty-Nine Steps;* relationship between Kipling's *Kim* and Buchan's political, religious and social attitudes, especially their joint emphases upon the ennobling nature of espionage work and their shared imperialist political stances.

C. Changing Attitudes: Maugham's *Ashenden,* Greene, Ambler. Cynicism, shades of grey, and liberal political views. The impact of fascism. The novels of the thirties demonstrate, with remarkable clarity, the relationship between historical events and literary change.

D. From World War II to the Sixties: fiction of and about the war; Alistair MacLean; Ian Fleming; communism, the new adversary; the cold war; increased use of technology in the genre. The last point is of considerable importance and reflects change not only in fiction but also in modern warfare and in espionage itself.

E. John Le Carre: the shift to realism. Impact on English authors of Great Britain's reduced political power in the years following World War II and Suez; influence of the career of Kim Philby; the professional agent.

F. Len Deighton: the end of the old boy network. Deighton illustrates two major shifts in espionage fiction: the rise to prominence of lower-middle or working-class agents with consequent satire of established personnel and attitudes; and a skillful exploitation of the marvels of modern science.

G. Summary: where have we been? where will we go? Attention to distinction between the two genres in plotting, characterization, milieu, social attitudes, responsiveness to social and historical change.

Special Features

Paper Assignments: the first short paper, a comparison of English and American detective fiction, was designed to allow the student to use and integrate his knowledge of course materials. Each student read two hard-boiled detective short stories and analyzed, according to the following criteria, their differences from "genteel" English fiction: plot, characterization, language and social milieu. This paper also reinforced the main approach of the course since it forced students to deal with distinctions arising from national and historical traditions.

The final, long paper allowed students to develop their own interests and approaches; subjects chosen included the influence of Freud on Ross Macdonald, a survey of the elements of formula in Ian Fleming's Bond novels, and an analysis of symbolic presentations of masculinity in several detective story writers. All student papers were read aloud to the class so that we could share the insights and knowledge of the authors.

Bibliography
Assigned Readings in Chronological Order for the Course:

Poe, E.A. "The Murders in the Rue Morgue," "The Mystery of Marie Roget," "The Purloined Letter," "The Gold Bug," "Thou Art the Man."
Collins, Wilkie. *The Moonstone.*
Doyle, Arthur Conan. *The Adventures of Sherlock Holmes.*
Christie, Agatha. *The Murder of Roger Ackroyd.*
Wilson, Edmund. "Who Cares Who Killed Roger Ackroyd?"
Chandler, Raymond. *Farewell, My Lovely* and "the Simple Art of Murder."
Macdonald, Ross. *The Blue Hammer.*
Sjowall, Maj, and Per Wahloo. *The Laughing Policeman.*
Borges, Jorge Luis. "Death and the Compass."
Buchan, John. *The Thirty-Nine Steps.*
Ambler, Eric. *Cause for Alarm.*
Deighton, Len. *Catch a Falling Spy.*

Selected Secondary Sources:

Altick, Richard. *Victorian Studies in Scarlet.* Victorian attitudes toward crime: stage, page and life.
Cawelti, John. *Adventure, Mystery, and Romance: Formula Stories as Art and Popular Culture.* Superb analysis of literary formulas.
Harper, Ralph. *The World of the Thriller.* An existentialist approach to thriller analysis; it is simply the best thing ever done on the subject.
Hartman, Mary S. *Victorian Murderesses.* Excellent account which provides insight into the social and sexual mores of the period.
Landrum, Larry, Pat Browne and Ray B. Browne, eds. *Dimensions of Detective Fiction.* Very useful anthology of critical essays.
Ruhn, Herbert, ed. *The Hard-Boiled Detective: Stories from Black Mask Magazine.* Excellent introduction which traces the development of hard-boiled detective fiction and defines its nature.

Jeanne F. Bedell
Humanities Department
University of Missouri—Rolla

Popular Culture 230
Magazines as Popular Culture
(4 credits—10 week quarter)

Introduction
"Magazines as Popular Culture" was originated in the Spring of 1979

as an opportunity for students to take an in-depth look at an aspect of popular culture so widespread that we tend to ignore or take for granted its relevance and importance: popular magazines. It was hoped that only those students with a genuine interest in the subject would enroll, but, as is unfortunately the case with many Popular Culture courses students queued up to register for it like rock fans at a Who concert. As a result, there was a large number of soon-to-be-graduated seniors who needed only one more course, and thus many underclasspersons who attempted to enroll were rejected by the computer. Another significant percentage of the class consisted of Journalism majors, who it turned out, contributed a great deal to the course. The course was considered innovative and successful enough to be offered again in 1979-80.

The class met twice a week for two hours, a format to which almost any course is adaptable, but one especially suitable to this course, as there were five main components to each class, and 20 to 25 minutes is quite a long stretch of time for anybody's attention span. The movement of each class period was from the specific (history of magazines) to the general (genre work) and back to the specific (one particular magazine within a genre). The remainder of each class was taken up by individual student reports on other specific magazines within the genre of the day, and class discussion following that. Thus a typical class would begin with a twenty-minute lecture covering one specific period of magazine history (e.g. 1800-1825), but would then turn to a general discussion of the genre assigned for that day, for instance, gossip (or "personality journalism") magazines. This discussion would then lead into a close examination of one magazine, a magazine assigned previously, belonging to that genre—*People*, for example. There would then be time for two oral presentations by students on other magazines of the genre, in this case *Us* and *Rona Barrett's Hollywood*. This would be followed by a general discussion of the differences between magazines of that particular genre.

Of course this is a highly flexible and rarely followed schedule, and could only be followed after several classes had been devoted to establishing, defining and developing a method of approaching individual magazines for the purpose of analysis. This method was focused on the determination of *style, appeal* and *impact*.

Approach

A. Style

Here we examined not only writing styles and formulae but also the more nebulous *overall* styles of individual magazines: the *Esquire* style, the *Newsweek* style, the *Hustler* style, etc.

Some Questions:

1) What makes up the individual styles of the various magazines? (rhetorical analysis; typesize and style; photographic techniques— emphasis on closeups, for instance.)

2) How does the writing differ from one magazine to another, not only from genre to genre (e.g. from *People* to *Sports Illustrated*) but within particular genres (e.g. from *People* to *Us*)?

3) How are articles (particularly in the Time/Life group) structured so that even the dullest information can be conveyed in an entertaining

manner? (Why do we get excited over an article on Bolivian forest mammals of the sea?)

4) Does the size of a magazine make a difference? (Do we impress ourselves more by reading a 900-page issue of *Better Homes and Gardens* or a 25-page issue of the *New Republic*?)

B. Appeal

Here we examined some of the bases for our appreciation of the magazines.

1) What are the internal ratios between "serious" and "humorous" articles? (In *Esquire,* say, or *Playboy,* how many humorous articles does it take before we no longer take the magazine seriously?)

2) How do prose and photography work to balance each other out?

3) How do titles (or headlines) function?

4) Which magazines advertise in other magazines—in which ones? What assumptions, then, are made about the audience?

5) To whom do the advertisements appeal? How do advertisements for the same product vary from magazine to magazine? What does this tell us?

6) How do themes and motifs function to draw us into certain magazines? (See 1. in Special Features.)

C. Impact

Here we examined the effect of popular magazines on American culture.

1) How are we affected by the magazines, both individually and as a group?

2) How do we read them? Do most of us simply skim, or do we read the whole thing?

3) How much do we read them? Answering this question involves some demographic work by the students—surveying other students at the university, etc.

4) To what extent do we believe or *obey* magazines? Is there really such a thing as the *Cosmopolitan* Girl? How does she let the magazine shape her personality and appearance? What sort of man reads *Playboy*? How are his beliefs and appearance shaped by the magazine?

Using this approach, the ultimate goal of the course, apart from an analysis of style, appeal and impact, is to come to a clear understanding of the relationship between information and entertainment, and how magazines exploit that relationship.

Outline of Course

As outlined in the Introduction, each class is generally divided into five sections, that is, once methods of approach have been established and explained. As the quarter progresses, less time can be spent on the lecture and more on reports and discussion.

1) Introduction to course. Requirements, review of syllabus, etc.

2) Discussion of methods of approach (style, appeal, impact, etc.).

3) More discussion of methods. Lecture: The Origins of Magazines, 45 B.C.—1800. Assign: *People.*

4) Discussion of Personality Journalism (including historical background).

5) Practical application of methods to *People* and *Us.*

6) Lecture: Magazines 1800-1825; Joseph Dennie's *Port Folio*; the

Weeklies.

7) Discussion of General Magazines: *Life* in the '50s. Assign: *Life.*

8) General Magazines Today: *Life* (current issue); *Saturday Evening Post.* Assign: *Reader's Digest.*

9) Lecture: The Golden Age of Magazines: 1825-1850; Magazines and Politics. Discussion: *Reader's Digest.* Assign: *Time.*

10) Lecture: The Magazinists. Discussion: News Magazines: *Time.* Student reports: *Newsweek, U.S. News & World Report, New Republic.* Assign: *Good Housekeeping.*

11) Lecture: The Civil War, and After: The Big Guys. Discussion: Homemaking Magazines: *Good Housekeepling.* Reports: *Better Homes and Gardens, Ladies Home Journal, Family Circle.*

12) Midterm Examination. Assign: *Cosmopolitan.*

13) Lecture: The Second Golden Age: The New Editors. Discussion: Women's Magazines: *Cosmopolitan.* Reports: *Glamour, Mademoiselle, McCall's, Playgirl.* Assign: *Playboy.*

14) Lecture: Religious Magazines. Discussion: Men's Magazines: *Playboy.* Reports: *Penthouse, Hustler.* Assign: *Sports Illustrated.*

15) Lecture: Into the Twentieth Century: The 10-cent Magazines. Discussion: Sports and Hobby Magazines: *Sports Illustrated.* Reports: *Sport, The Sporting News, Field & Stream, Popular Mechanics.* Assign: *Ohio.*

16) Lecture: Curtis, Bok and Larimer: Big Business. Discussion: Regional Magazines: *Ohio.* Reports: *New York Magazine, Cleveland, Columbus.* Assign: *National Lampoon, Teen.*

17) Lecture: Postwar Magazines, Little Magazines for Elitists. Discussion: Humor and Teen Magazines: *National Lampoon, Teen.* Reports: *Mad, Co-Ed, Tiger Beat, Seventeen.* Assign: *National Geographic.*

18) Lecture: The Twenties and Thirties. Discussion: Cultural and Special Interest Magazines: *National Geographic.* Reports: *Psychology Today, Omni, Rolling Stone, Money.* Assign: *60 Minutes.*

19) Lecture: Magazines Today. Discussion: Magazines on TV: *60 Minutes.* Reports: *20/20.*

20) Summary.

21) Final Examination.

Special Features

1) Thematic Analysis of Magazines;

Any magazine, we discovered, can be analyzed not only for its style and appeal but also for its fondness for a recurrent theme. Most articles in *People,* for example, no matter what they are ostensibly concerned with, actually revolve around the theme of motherhood and the family. Articles about Patty Hearst are really about her relationship with her mother and the breakup of her family; Margaret Trudeau is important because she represents a threat to the traditional family; a condemned murderer is significant and newsworthy not because of his crime but because of the broken home he grew up in. *Life* magazine, similarly, is concerned with *power; Time* articles center around *thrust* and the lack of it.

2) Student Reports:

These generally last about fifteen minutes and deal with the following:

a) A brief history of the magazine.
b) Circulation figures.
c) Advertising rates.
d) Percentage of space devoted to advertising.
e) Ratio of photography to text.
f) Writing style.
g) Themes, motifs.
h) Tone, and consistency thereof.
i) Appeal: who reads it and why.
j) Comparison to other magazines in the genre.
3) Papers (2):

a) Changes in one magazine over a ten-year period. The papers utilize the methods outlined above and also discuss changes in the magazine in terms of changes in the country. 10 pages.

b) Although this is by no means a creative writing class, if the students can learn to effectively imitate the various writing styles, they will come to a clear understanding of exactly what constitutes those styles. To this end, students are expected to write one five-page article imitating the style of the magazine of their choice.

Bibliography

1) Textbooks: None. Just the magazines themselves.
2) Background readings: Most of the materials for the lectures on the history of American magazines came from John Tebbel's *The American Magazine: A Compact History* (New York: Hawthorn, 1969). The book is invaluable. Other useful books for background material: Association of National Advertisers. *Magazine Circulation and Rate Trends: 1940-1967.* New York: Association of National Advertisers, 1969. A compilation of circulation data for 62 magazines.
Audits & Surveys Co., Inc. *The Audiences of Five Magazines.* New York: Newsweek, 1962. *Newsweek, Time, U.S. News & World Report, Saturday Evening Post.*
Kimbrough, Marvin. *Black Magazines: An Exploratory Study.* Austin: Center for Communication Research, 1973. Useful for bibliography.
Katz, William and Berry Richards. *Magazines for Libraries.* New York: R.R. Bowker, 1978.
Mott, Frank Luther. *A History of American Magazines 1741-1930.* Cambridge: Harvard Belknap, 1957. The classic study.
Opinion Research Corporation. *Holiday Audience.* Princeton, N.J. 1959.
Peterson, Theodore. *Magazines in the Twentieth Century.* Urbana: Univ. of Illinois Press, 1964.
Politz Research Inc., *A Study of the Accumulative Audience of "Life."* New York: Time, Inc. 1950.
Wolseley, Ronald E. *The Changing Magazine.* New York; Hastings House, 1973.
———————*The Magazine World.* New York: Prentice Hall, 1951.
———————*Understanding Magazines.* Ames: Iowa State Univ. Press, 1969.
Wood, James P. *Magazines in the United States.* New York: Ronald, 1956.

Adam Hammer
American Culture Program
Bowling Green State University

English 242
Popular Literary Forms (Science Fiction)
(10 weeks)

Introduction
    Popular Literary Forms is one of three courses in popular culture introduced by the Department of English at Michigan State University in 1973. The course is flexible enough to appeal to both majors and non-majors and, as the catalog description indicates, it is intended to allow for the widest possible exploration of genre:

Study of a particular genre of popular literature (e.g., science fiction, western, gothic) through reading, discussion and writing, with attention to the genre's development in media other than print.

    The course is open to freshmen and sophomores each term and students may enroll up to two times for a total of six quarter hours. General practice is to combine lecture, discussion and the presentation of media, with class sizes ranging from twenty to fifty or more students. Several members of the department have cooperated in the teaching of detective fiction, spy fiction, Hollywood fiction, supernatural horror fiction, radio drama, science fiction and gothic fiction during the past seven years. A ten-week session in science fiction has been one of the more successful of these offerings.
    Science fiction has been attractive in a number of disciplines as a way of extrapolating an image of the future from present conditions. The emergence of anthologies of readings in science fiction for courses in sociology, anthropology, political issues, philosophy, the various sciences and literature indicates something of the evocative power of the genre. Literary approaches have focused on the literary history of the genre, its major authors, and the issues it raises. A popular culture approach should attempt to be something of all of these through exploration of the genre's meaning in its deepest and most significant senses. Science fiction is particularly rich in generic variations and archetypal imagery, and is intimately concerned with basic structures of the imagination—space, time, our ability to distinguish between reality and illusion, the bestiary of the unconscious. As a genre it reflects the tensions of its culture through a sensibility bounded by a set of narrative assumptions, and through its transformation of the iconology and beliefs of contemporary everyday life.
    The implications for teaching science fiction that such a perspective of genre can bring are numerous and challenging. It is useful to establish the boundaries of science fiction by discussing early its relationships to those genres that it shades into on every side, such as fantasy, utopias, the lost race tradition, action-adventure fiction, and experimental fiction. Simply tracing the social and political paradigm of H.G. Wells and the technological paradigm of Jules Verne is too narrow an approach, but it should be shown that science fiction's popularity has kept pace with society's sensitivity to the issues of social and technological complexity. The comparative use of media is probably the most effective way to discuss this sensitivity. As a general rule the media through which the genre is presented is of less importance than the genre itself, but the genre can be fully understood only when it is considered in the forms of all the media in

which it appears.

While novels remain the fullest expression of science fiction, it has been a part of film since its beginnings, surfaced in early comic strips, played a significant part in radio's golden age, was adapted early to television, and provided the inspiration for the first commercial comics. The imagery of science fiction appears in cartoons, posters, a multitude of ephemera, and has at times pervaded such parasitic genres as advertising and campaign oratory—times when the authors become celebrities and consultants to business and government. Since today we are immersed in the techniques of rational speculation, computer projections, cultural scenarios, theories of technological change and the literature of prophecy as well as the imagery of science fiction, it is valuable to gain critical distance when discussing motifs. It is suprisingly easy to overlook the extent to which speculation, future-orientation and anthropomorphism of technology have become a part of contemporary ideology.

Outline of Course

A Distancing Mini-unit

All audio-visual collections contain short non-fiction films developed for training people in the proper orientation to some aspect of technology. *Motor Mania, Freeway Phobia* (Parts I and II) and *Magic Highway, USA* were produced by Disney Studios for early driver education programs. The first two animations portray Goofy as Common Man fumbling with technology (a dominant source of humor in contemporary advertising) and the latter shows his problems solved by the technology of the future. Rather than having to learn proper freeway tactics he is whisked away in his car directly to his office door through perfect machine-machine symbiosis. A story that may be read along with the viewing of these films is Robert Heinlein's *The Roads Must Roll* (1940) where, as a result of an energy crisis, moving highway strips are developed to rapidly move great masses of people over long distances. The strips are patrolled and administered by trained cadets and are maintained by underground workers. An administrator without cadet training who has psychological problems urges the maintenance men to strike, but the cadets crush the strike and the roads roll once again. Both the story and the films reveal a naive booster ideology, but the story also reveals the aspect of maintenance that *Magic Highway* ignores in mythic fashion. Many further comparisons and contrasts can be evoked from this and other distancing units.

Practice

Students are required to keep journals in which they collect and respond to science fiction imagery in the print media, and keep notes on listening and viewing experiences. They are encouraged to note the ways innovative technologies affect everyday life, and are alerted to related items found in such sources as *Science News, Scientific American* and other available periodicals. A slide lecture on reading visual imagery greatly enhances the quality of journal entries and papers dealing with visual media. An illustated lecture on the iconology of the future helps students identify and comment on material culture. Weekly papers of about two pages are required through the first half of the course, and two longer papers and a final examination are required in the second half. The first part of the course focuses on short fiction, background information, media and mini-units, while the second half focuses primarily on the novels and the contemporary feature film.

Special Materials

A volume of short stories such as Volume I of *The Science Fiction Hall of Fame* series (Avon, 1971) and from three to five novels are essential. The number of novels used depends on the media budget and the amount of time set aside for assignments in Special Collections (graphic materials), Assigned Reading (non-fiction articles and excerpts and critical materials) and the Audio Library (music, interviews with authors, radio programs) and other matters. A thematic checklist of fiction is appended. Robert Scholes and Eric S. Rabkin's *Science Fiction: History, Science and Vision* (Oxford, 1977) contains a literary history of the genre, a brief discussion of media, consideration of themes, reviews of ten representative novels, and an annotated bibliography. Other secondary materials are too abundant to list here.

Several films may be used, preferably with some distance among production dates. *Metropolis* (1926), *Forbidden Planet* (1956) and *2001: A Space Odyssey* (1968) or *A Clockwork Orange* (1971) are representative. Students are generally reluctant to be drawn into a film like *Metropolis*, and it is useful to provide a gloss on the film's visual aspects and its expressionistic tendencies. This approach will reap great benefits when working with more accessible films such as *A Clockwork Orange*, which has marked expressionistic qualities. When budgets shrink, short films can be used. *THX-1138* first appeared as a short, and many experimental films have science fiction themes. A weekly survey of television movies will turn up surprises.

Lists of science fiction materials on television and radio, comic strips, comic books and recordings can be compiled from standard sources where specialized materials are not available. John Dunning's *Tune in Yesterday* (1976) contains synopses of radio programs, and I have made use of *Science Fiction on Radio* (1973), a mimeographed publication by Meade and Penny Frierson of 3705 Woodvale Road, Birmingham, AL 35223, which summarizes chapters of adult science fiction radio shows. Tapes of programs are widely available through commercial dealers and traders.

Students will often be able to supply examples of comics if a popular culture collection is not available, though an extensive collection is essential for the purposes of many projects. The DC weird comics, Buck Rogers strips and many other comic materials, including Gahan Wilson cartoons have appeared in collected editions. Randall Scott of the MSU library has compiled an index to the superhero comics and heads a lively organization whose members publish a newsletter and numerous motif indexes. I have collected cartoons, advertisements and ephemera through the good graces of my students and associates, but once the sense of the course begins to emerge students will note and collect an ample number of these for reproduction and circulation. Brief discussions of the iconology and assumptions found in television advertisements will provide the basis for development of this area by students.

Television programs can be obtained from commercial distributors, but many can be seen as reruns and current broadcasts. Information about them can be obtained from Vincent Terrace's *Television Programming 1947-1976* (1976), Tim Brooks and Earle Marsh's *The Complete Directory to Prime Time Network TV Shows, 1946-Present* (1979), and Nina David's *TV Season*, an annual that began coverage with the 1974-75 season (1976). There are also the extensive writings on *Star Trek*, together with scripts, adaptations and fanzines.

Bibliography
(Thematic Checklist Compiled with R. Glenn Wright)

Anthologies and Collections
Ballard, James G. *Chronopolis and Other Stories* (1971)
The Best of Fredrick Brown, ed. Robert Block (1976)
Borges, Jorges Louis. *Ficciones* (1962)
Bova, Ben. *The Science Fiction Hall of Fame*, vols. IIa and IIb (1973)
Bradbury, Ray. *The Illustrated Man* (1951)
_____. *The Martian Chronicles* (1950)
Clarke, Arthur C. *The Nine Billion Names of God* (1974)
Delany, Samuel R. *Driftglass* (1971)
Disch, Thomas. *Getting Into Death and Other Stories* (1976)
Ellison, Harlan, ed. *Dangerous Visions* (1967); *Again Dangerous Visions* (1972)
Haldeman, Joe. *Infinite Dreams* (1978)
Knight, Damon. *Orbit* (numbered series) (1968)
LeGuin, Ursula K. *The Wind's Twelve Quarters* (1975)
Merril, Judith. *England Swings SF* (1965) and *The Best of Sci Fi* (series)
Silverberg, Robert, ed. *Science Fiction Hall of Fame*, vol. I (1970)
Spinrad, Norman, ed. *Modern Science Fiction* (1974)
Wilson, Robin Scott. *Those Who Can: A Science Fiction Reader* (1973)
Wollheim, Donald, ed. *Men On the Moon* (1969)
_____ and Terry Carr, eds. *World's Best Science Fiction* (1965-)

Adventure/Space Opera
Anderson, Pohl. (Most of his work.)
Burroughs, Edgar Rice. (Martian and Venusian novels.)
Haldeman, Joe. *The Forever War* (1974)
Harrison, Harry. (Space Rats of the CCC series.)
_____ *Bill, the Gallactic Hero* (1965)
Heinlein, Robert. *Glory Road*
Nowlan, Philip. *Armageddon 2419 A.D.* (1928)
Panshin, Alexei. *Rite of Passage* (1969)
Smith, Cordwainer. *The Game of Rat and Dragon*
Smith, E.E. (Doc). (All of his work.)

Cautionary Epics
Asimov, Isaac. *Foundation* (1950), *Foundation and Empire* (1951) and *Second Foundation* (1952)
Herbert, Frank. *Dune* (1965), *Dune Messiah* (1969) and *Children of Dune* (1976)
LeGuin, Ursula K. The Earth-Sea Trilogy (*The Furthest Shore, The Tombs of Atuan*, and *A Wizard of Earthsea*: 1968, 1971, 1972)
Lewis, C.S. *Out of the Silent Planet* (1938), *Perelandra* (1943) and *That Hideous Strength* (1945)
Smith, E.E. (Doc). Lensman series (*First Lensman, Second Stage Lensman*, and *Children of the Lens*: 1934-47 in serial)
Stapledon, Olaf. *Last and First Men* (1931)

Alternate History
DeCamp, L. Sprague. *Lest Darkness Fall*

Dick, Philip K. *Man in the High Castle* (1962)
Harrison, Harry. *Tunnel through the Deeps* (1972)
Moorcock, Michael. *Behold the Man* (1966)

Robotics
Asimov, Isaac. *The Bicentennial Man* (1976)
____*I, Robot* (1950)
____*The Rest of the Robots* (1964)
Bate, Harry. "Farewell to the Master" (1940)
Capek, Karel. *R.U.R.* (1920)
Dick, Philip K. *Do Androids Dream of Electric Sheep?* (1968)
Kuttner, Henry. *Happy Ending*
Williamson, Jack. *The Humanoids* (1948)

Time Problems and Paradoxes
Anderson, Poul. "Delenda Est"
Blish, James. *Common Time* (1953)
Dick, Philip K. *A Little Something For Us Tempunauts*
Heinlein, Robert. *All You Zombies* (1960)
____*Door Into Summer*
Leiber, Fritz. "Catch That Zeppelin!"
Moore, Ward. "Bring the Jubilee"
Niven, Larry. "All the Myriad Ways"
Wells, H.G. "The Time Machine" (1895)

Projected Physics
Asimov, Isaac, "Old Fashioned"
Delany, Samuel R. *Einstein Intersection* (1967)
____. *Nova*

Space Flight
Blish, James. *Cities In Flight* (1970): collects *They Shall Have Stars* (1957), *A Life for the Stars* (1962), *Earthman Come Home* (1955) and *The Triumph of Time* (1958).
Burdrys, A.J. *Rogue Moon* (1960)
Clarke, Arthur C. *Rendezvous with Rama* (1973)
____, "The Sentinel" (1951)

Biological Change
LeGuin, Ursula K. *The Left Hand of Darkness* (1963)
Stapledon, Olaf. *Last and First Men* (1931)
Sturgeon, Theodore. *More Than Human* (1952)
Wells, H.G. *The Island of Dr. Moreau* (1896)

Paranormal Humans
Heinlein, Robert. *Stranger in a Strange Land* (1962)
Herbert, Frank. *The Santaroga Barrier* (1968)
Russ, Joanna. *And Chaos Died* (1935)
Stapledon, Olaf. *Odd John* (1935)
Sturgeon, Theodore. *More Than Human (1952)*
Van Vogt, A.E. *Slan* (1941).

Social Change/Criticism
Wilhelm, Kate. "Baby, You Were Great!" (1969)
____. "The Red Canary"
Leiber, Fritz. "Coming Attractions"
And most other science fiction after WWII

Future City
Brunner, John. *Stand On Zanzibar* (1968)
Campbell, John. "Twilight" (1934)
Clarke, Arthur C. *The City and the Stars* (1956)
Knight, Damon, ed. *Cities of Wonder* (1967)

The Machine World/Computers
Brunner, John. *Shockwave Rider)*
Ellison, Harlan. "Catman" (1974)
_____. "Repent Harlequin, Said the Ticktock Man" (1965)
Forster, E.M. "The Machine Stops" (1928)
Heinlein, Robert. *The Moon is a Harsh Mistress* (1967)
Malzberg, Barry N. "The Wonderful, All-Purpose Transmogrifier"
Vonnegut, Kurt. *Piano Player* (1952)

Alien Encounter
Berryman, John. "Berom"
Knight, Damon. "Straight Station" (1956)
Lem, Stanislaw. *Solaris* (1971)
Lester, Murray. "First Contact"
Nourse, Alan. *The Counterfeit* (1952)
Pohl, Frederik. "We Purchase People"
Wells, H.G. *War of the Worlds* (1998)
Wyndham, John. *The Day of the Triffids* (1950).

Last Survivors
Dick, Philip K. *Dr. Bloodmoney, or How We Got Along After the Bomb*
Heinlein, Robert. *Farnham's Freehold* (1964)
Miller, Walter M. Jr. *A Canticle for Leibowitc* (1959)
Orwell, George. *1984* (1949)
Pangborn, Edgar. *Davy* (1964)
Roshwal, Mordecai. *Level 7* (1959)
Schoonever, Lawrence. *Central Passage* (1962)
Shelley, Mary. *The Last Man* (1826)
Shute, Nevil. *On the Beach* (1954)
Stewart, George. *Earth Abides* (1951)
Tiptree, James, Jr. "Her Smoke Rose Up Forever"

Authoritarian Society
Burgess, Anthony. *A Clockwork Orange* (1962)
_____. *The Wanting Seed* (1962)
Disch, Thomas M. *Camp Concentration* (1968)
Hersey, John. *The Child Buyer* (1960)
Huxley, Aldous. *Brave New World* (1930)
Karp, David. *One* (1953)
Orwell, George. *1984 (*1949)
Rand, Ayn. *Anthem* (1946)
Zamiatin, Eugene. *We* (1924)

Advertising and Future Image-Making
Hartley, L.P. *Facial Justice*
Mead, Shepherd. *The Big Ball of Wax* (1954)
Pohl, Frederick and Cyril Kornbluth. *The Space Merchants* (1953)
Spinrad, Norman. *Bug Jack Barron* (1969)

Philosophical/Theological
Ballard, J.G. "Terminal Beach" (1964)
Blish, James. *A Case of Conscience* (1958)
Clarke, Arthur C. "Against the Fall of Night"
LeGuin, Ursula. *The Lathe of Heaven* (1971)
Lewis, C.S. *Out of the Silent Planet* (1938)
_____. *Perelandra* (1943)
_____. *That Hideous Strength* (1945)
Miller, Walter. *A Canticle for Leibowitz* (1959)
Vonnegut, Kurt. *The Sirens of Titan* (1959)
Zelazny, Roger. (His work is oriented to Eastern Thought.)

Altered States of Consciousness
Aldiss, Brian. *Barefoot in the Head* (1969)
_____. "Diagram for Three Enigmatic Stories"
Dick, Philip K. *Eye in the Sky* (1957)
_____. *Ubik* (1969)
Lem, Stanislaw. *The Futurological Congess* (1971)

Experimental Language
Aldis, Brian. *Barefoot in the Head* (1969)
Burgess, Anthony. *A Clockwork Orange* (1963)
Delany, Samuel R. *Dahlgren* (1975)
Lem, Stanislaw. *The Futurological Congress* (1971)

Sword and Sorcery
Howard Robert E. *Conan* (A touchstone series to which other writers have contributed.)

Fantasy
Beagle, Peter. *The Last Unicorn* (1968)
Cabell, James Branch. *Jurgen* (1919)
Carroll, Lewis. *Alice in Wonderland (1865)*
D'Engle, Madeleine. *A Wrinkle in Time*
Hudson,W.H. *Green Mansions*
Rabkin, Eric S. *Fantastic Worlds: Myths, Tales, and Stories* (1979)
Swift, Jonathan. *Gulliver's Travels*
Tolkien, J.R.R. Fellowship of the Ring (trilogy, 1954-55).

Larry N. Landrum
Department of English
Michigan State University

Popular Culture Courses in Specific Mass Media

American Studies 298
Popular Music in American Society
(3 credits—16 week semester)

Introduction

"Popular Music in American Society" was developed in 1975 and first offered at the University of Maryland in the spring of 1976. It represents an outgrowth of a doctoral dissertation in psychology which explored the links between popular music and elements of youth culture. The course, in all its variations, has now been taught 14 times. Initially there were two versions, one a history of popular music and another using popular music to illustrate a number of key psychological and sociological concepts (e.g. adolescent adjustment; attitudes toward war, women, death and religion; the "generation gap"). The present version of the course combines both approaches and is described as follows:

The course will examine America and its music since 1940, using excerpts from songs and corollary documentary material. Classes will focus on people, styles, issues, events, fads, media, products and mores, trace them through four decades. This approach, emphasizing a lyrical content analysis, will seek to document popular music as an integral part of American culture, reflecting and affecting important aspects of society.

From its beginnings as a General Honors seminar (enrollment 12), AMST 298 has grown so that it now averages 250 students per class. It is always taught as a three hour course (i.e. one day or one night per week). Because of the personalized format and resources necessary for that format, it has only been taught by one instructor. During Spring 1980, however, a former TA (for two terms) will teach the course using tapes made for previous semesters.

AMST 298 is a lower-level elective that fulfills a three-credit General Education Requirement in Arts & Humanities. It is recommended, though not required, in the American Studies program. Student evaluations indicate that it is drawing students from all classes and all majors, with Radio, Television and Film (RTVF) contributing the largest number.

The course has been well received by both students and administrators. In addition to having been taught on the College Park campus, AMST 298 has also been offered (by request) in the University's overseas division. Students in Germany, Japan and Okinawa have had opportunites to take the course. Numerous units of the course have been aired on radio, from half-hour public service to six-hour specials.

The objectives for AMST 298 are several. The most important is to teach students about contemporary history and culture through the medium of music. For example, most undergraduate students are too young to have been affected by the Vietnam war. Still, almost all are familiar with the devisiveness that conflict generated in our society. Music, through examples such as "Ballad of the Green Berets" and "Stop the War, Now," makes it easy to explore the different sides taken during the war years. The course also teaches the extent to which music and other manifestations of popular culture permeate our lives. Though claims that rock music has been responsible for everything from drug use to an increase in teenage pregnancies are impossible to prove (and therefore disprove), the course explores the effect that music may have on shaping values in such areas as romance and courtship. By highlighting fads, teenage concerns, social issues and every other imaginable topic, popular music fills in much of the background that traditional historians ignore. AMST 298 underscores how popular songs can serve as a catalyst to understanding the evolution of American society during the past 40 years. Two years ago a foreign student summarized the course by saying that during the previous 15 weeks she had learned more about the "real" America than in her six years of American history in school.

Outline of Course

The course is organized so that while historical material is presented in its correct chronology there is also an opportunity to introduce contemporary music in the classes covering the '40s and '50s. This is accomplished by including cultural "themes" which can be traced from the '40s to the present. The fifteen units are set up as follows:

1. Introduction to Popular Culture and the definition of Popular Music. Timeless music (ASCAP's selection of America's most popular songs) vs. Topical music (dealing with people, events, issues, fads, etc.). Music and radio in the early '40s with an emphasis on the Big Bands. Popular Music before, during and after World War II.
2. The American hero in the '40s (cowboys and baseball players). Overview of Country and Western music including late '50s TV westerns. Broadway's contribution to popular music (from *Oklahoma* to *The Wiz*).
3. The Cold War era including the Korean War and McCarthyism. Popular music and the romantic love (old sentimentality) theme. Popular music's treatment of the religious theme.
4. The early '50s and the impact of television (excerpts from *Texaco Star Theater* to the *Mickey Mouse Club*). *Your Hit Parade* and early '50s pop (Como, Fisher, Clooney, Page, etc.). Rhythm & Blues and "cover records."
5. Role models for '50s youths (Brando, Dean) and the beginning of Rock & Roll. The pioneers of Rock & Roll (Fats Domino, Chuck Berry, Little Richard, etc.).

Elvis Presley from "That's All Right Mama" to his death in 1977.
Rock & Roll comes of age (Buddy Holly, Everly Brothers, Coasters, etc.).
6. Rock Exploitation (films) and backlash (calypso).
American Bandstand and the rise of youth culture.
   The adolescent experience, featuring clothing, grooming, fads, high school, summer vacations and teenage idols.
7. "Camelot" and the early '60s.
   Goodtime music, including dancing, surfing and racing cars.
MIDTERM EXAMINATION
8. The Beatles and the British invasion (Rolling Stones, Kinks, Who). Television in the mid-'60s (doctors, sitcoms, private eyes, etc.).
   1960s films, including "beach" movies, James Bond and musicals.
9. Martin Luther King, Jr. and the Civil Rights Movement (1956-1968).
   Black music of the '50s (Nat King Cole, Johnny Mathis), the '60s (Motown, Memphis Soul, James Brown) and the '70s (Philly Soul, Disco).
10. Alienation based on age, social class and lifestyle.
    Social and political alienation; the revival of folk music (Pete Seeger, Bob Dylan, Chad Mitchell Trio, etc.).
    Popular music and the Vietnam war.
    The San Francisco counter-culture; acid rock (Jefferson Airplane, Joplin, Hendrix).
11. The late 1960s featuring the "incredible year" (1968), including political conventions and the assassination of Martin Luther King, Jr. and Robert Kennedy.
    The musical impact of Woodstock.
    The alleged connection between drug songs and drug use.
12. Popular music and the changing image of women (from "Rosie the Riveter" to Meg Christian).
    Social issues of the early '70s; ecology, population growth, the American Indian.
    Sex-role identification in popular songs.
13. Events and non-events in the mid-'70s (Watergate, the Bicentennial, etc.).
    Music and other media in the '70s (films, television, books, *Rolling Stone,* etc.).
    Popular music and the "new sentimentality."
    1970's musical styles (e.g. "glittter," MOR, mellow, pop/country).
14. The sexual liberation of pop lyrics ("pornographic pop" or orgasm rock").
    The music and culture of disco.
    Popular music and the anti-nuclear power movement.
    New Wave/Punk's musical message for the '80s.
    *Billboard'*s all-time top records.
    All class projects are due.
15. FINAL EXAMINATION

Special Features
All the musical and documentary materials heard in class are presented on tape. Each tape is approximately one hour in length and includes from 65 to 150 musical and non-musical excerpts. Duplicate copies of each tape, plus complete discographies (see example below), are placed in the undergraduate library following each class.

Examples on Ecology tape:
1. Mercy Mercy Me (The Ecology)-Marvin Gaye
2. Rachel Carson sounds her "Silent Spring" warning (63)
3. Whose Garden Was This-John Denver
4. Big Yellow Taxi-Joni Mitchell
5. President Nixon campaigns on the ecology issue (70)

In addition to the taped material, the course makes extensive use of cultural artifacts. A bulletin board with appropriate newspapers, magazines, comics, movie posters, record jackets, bubblegum cards, photographs and other memorabilia is prepared prior to each class. Students are also urged to leaf through a large selection of paperback books (e.g. *The Silent Spring, Helter Skelter, 'Twixt Twelve and Twenty*) before and after each class. Examinations contain questions based on these materials.

Course requirements include a mid-term and final examination for all students. The size of the class dictates that a large portion of the tests be "objective." Types of questions used include sound identifications (students identify and place in context some of the documentary material they have heard), matchings, fill-ins and two-point short answers (e.g. define Payola). Each examination, however, also includes three or four five-point essay questions. Examples from past tests include, "Describe the qualities that transform a rock star into a pop culture superstar," "Trace how Motown reflected the Civil Rights Movement of the 1960s," and "What does Disco tell us about American society in the late '70s?"

Students wishing to earn an "A" in the course are required to do an original paper or project. Directions for form and content are provided in a handout. Books that are not available in the campus library can be borrowed from the instructor. Similarly, students who need hard-to-find musical material for tapes they are doing can request up to a dozen songs. Recent projects have included a taped interview with an Elvis imitator, a musical simulation of the Beatles' reunion, and an analysis of Billy Joel's lyrics as a window to the '70s. Other students may do projects to raise a grade, but they are not encouraged to do so. All projects must have prior approval from the instructor or TA before they are accepted.

Bibliography
Texts:

Manchester, William, *The Glory and the Dream*. New York: Bantam, 1975. An anecdotal history of America from the Depression to Watergate. All the required readings are from this book.
The course has used a number of books on music in its four year history. None has proved

adequate for the time span (1940 to the present), and the range of subject matter. The most useful titles for selected portions of the course are included below.

Berry, Peter E., *"____And the Hits Just Keep on Comin'."* Syracuse: Syracuse University Press, 1977. Statistics on twenty years of popular songs (1955-76). Lists top songs, artists, million sellers, etc.

Denisoff, R. Serge and Richard A. Peterson. *The Sounds of Social Change.* Chicago: Rand McNally, 1972. Anthology of writings relating popular music and culture.

Eisen, Jonathan (ed). *The Age of Rock (Vol. 1 & 2).* New York: Vintage Books, 1969, 1970. Collections of some of the best writings on rock culture and the rock business.

Jahn, Mike. *Rock—from Elvis Presley to the Rolling Stones.* New York: Quadrangle, 1973. A year-to-year coverage of Rock 'n' Roll. Currently out of print.

Miller, Jim (ed.). *The Rolling Stone Illustrated History of Rock & Roll.* New York: Rolling Stone Press, 1976. A profusely illustrated critical history of the artists and the styles. Includes useful discographies.

Shaw, Arnold. *The Rockin' '50s.* New York: Hawthorn, 1974. A good reference for the pre-rock era. Information and background on individual artists, specific musical styles (e.g. Rhythm & Blues), the music industry and other aspects of Pop/Rock music can be scattered among the more than 750 books which have been published in the past twenty years.

Hugo A. Keesing
American Studies Program
University of Maryland, College Park

Humanities 46
American Popular Music
(4 credits—15 week trimester)

Introduction

While 1980 will be the first time the course American Popular Music will be offered at Franklin University, the roots of the course go back much farther. The course, to be offered as a 15 week semester course, had its initial trial as a 10 week course at Bowling Green State University in 1976. The course was received very enthusiastically there, and we anticipate a similar reception at Franklin University.

The reason for our confidence is the success we have had with our Introduction to Popular Culture course; that course currently enrolls a full load even during our slowest trimester, Summer. Furthermore, the American Popular Music course is perfect for the type of student Franklin attracts. We are a small college with degree programs in Business, Public Administration and Science and Technology; therefore, most of our Humanities offerings are self-contained and are designed to reach students on the broadest possible levels. For that reason a survey such as this course will be immediately appealing. Another factor contributing to the success of such courses here is that we face a wide range of cultural, age and social levels (we enroll many from the inner city and the average age of our evening students is approximately 28 years old). This also helps make survey courses and courses dealing with specific, relevant topics interesting and marketable. We hope, moreover, to avail ourselves of a fine continuing education program to encourage wide community participation. In order to achieve this goal the course will be offered both as a credit course and as a continuing education course, with different tuitions charged for each category.

American Popular Music is a 4 credit hour course that will be offered once or twice a year. It will be offered on Sunday afternoons initially as part of an experiment Franklin is conducting to encourage new students to enroll. The course will be taught by a faculty member who has had two years of music training on the college level in Theory and Sightsinging, and advanced composition. The course, however, could be taught by anyone with a strong background in history, the social sciences, or the humanities as long as that person also has some musical knowledge, either formal or acquired through professional experience.

Because the course is a broad survey of a popular art there are four basic objectives we hope to achieve:

1) To introduce the student to trends in culture, popular thought, and history via concentration on one art form.

2) To explore the relationship between (a) the audience and the artist in the creation of music and song and (b) the artist, the medium, and the audience, to better demonstrate exactly what role that audience plays in the creation of popular culture; this will also provide dramatic proof of the dynamic nature of culture in general.

3) To expose students to popular music in America and illuminate the various types and functions of popular music; to make them more sensitive to not only mainstream popular music but also to the music of the various subcultures which feed into the main arteries of the culture.

4) To provide students with some theoretical concepts to help them evaluate popular music and what role it plays in their lives and the lives of the people around them.

To fulfill the objectives of the survey, the primary teaching methods will be lecture-discussion supplemented by slides and musical selections illustrating the various people, productions, periods and trends in American music. Each unit will be presented by beginning with a survey of the time period (1910-1920 or 1940-1950, for example) and what major events musical, media and otherwise occurred; then we will explore the origins of various musical movements (i.e. where did Kern get his ideas and inspiration for the type of musical theatre he produced in *Show Boat*?) and the role various individuals played in the creation of a particular type of music.

Outline of Course

WEEK 1—Introduction to Popular Music and Society. General discussion of the impact of music on culture and of the culture on music. Discussion of the importation of popular song to the U.S. in the 19th century and of native American forms of song; Stephen Foster and the Sentimental tradition are featured with minor emphasis given to Gottshalk and MacDowell.

WEEK 2—The Birth of 20th century popular music. The role of Charles K. Harris as musical entrepreneur is analyzed, and different trends in music as well as the evolution of Tin Pan Alley, 1898-1910, are discussed; a unit is begun on ragtime, concentrating on Scott Joplin and Irving Berlin, the then King of Ragtime. Other music of the period as well as sheet music sales are treated here and also the dance craze and invention of the phonograph.

WEEK 3—Birth of 20th century music continued. The unit on ragtime is completed with an analysis of some of Joplin's rags. Next, the Musical Theatre 1910-1920 is discussed; particular emphasis is placed on George M. Cohan and Jerome Kern; selections from their music and slides of various productions are presented.

WEEK 4—The Jazz Age. The great watershed years of the 1020s with the invention of radio, the birth of talking pictures, and the introduction of jazz into the music mainstream are covered. Special emphasis is placed on such people as George Gershwin, Louis Armstrong, Al Jolson and Rodgers and Hart. The influence of *Show Boat* is considered.

WEEK 5—The Jazz Age continued. More on radio, recordings and finally talking pictures and the early stars and artists in the movie industry. Discussion of the songwriter/publisher migration from Tin Pan Alley to Hollywood, and the renaissance of popular music via the movies during the Great Depression (c. 1929-1938).

WEEK 6—The Flowering of American Pop Song and the Swing Era. Using extensive musical examples and slides, the work of Vincent Youmans, Gershwin, Cole Porter, Irving Berlin, Harry Warren, Rodgers and Hart, Dietz and Schwartz and others is analyzed; also a special unit on analyzing lyrics is introduced here, concentrating especially on Ira Gershwin, Lorenz Hart and Cole Porter. The swing era is introduced with sights and sounds of Benny Goodman, Duke Ellington and Glenn Miller bands, to name a few.

WEEK 7—The Great American Popular Singers, Part 1. The vocal styles and popularity of singers from Al Jolson through Bing Crosby and Billie Holliday to Frank Sinatra are treated; some technical concepts and discussion based on concepts Henry Pleasants presents in *The Great American Popular Singers* are discussed. Also discussed is the phenomenon of the singer superstar, primarily in the persons of Jolson and Frank Sinatra.

WEEK 8—*Oklahoma!* the "Integrated Musical," and World War II. Discussion here is a partial recap of the Broadway scene since the turn of the century, but mostly emphasis is placed on *Oklahoma!* and what it has meant to the development of contemporary musical theatre. The musical scene during the war years is also discussed and the events leading to the creation of BMI and broadcaster's strike of the '40s as well as other problems leading to the birth of rock; an extensive unit is presented here on country (hillbilly) music as well as an introduction to rhythm and blues as they existed in subcultures prior to the 1950s.

WEEK 9—The Birth of Rock 'n' Roll. The emergence of the DJ into power and the rise of rhythm and blues as the "sound of the city." Discussion of the rise of Elvis Presley, Chuck Berry and other leading figures in the early years of rock.

WEEK 10—The Rise and Dominance of Rock 1955-1960. Cover records, use of rock in movies and general reaction of culture to rising youth subculture are covered. The Folk Revival (which had earlier roots) is also discussed. Groups like the Weavers and more pop-oriented ones like Peter, Paul and Mary and the Kingston Trio as well as individuals, most notably Joan Baez and Bob Dylan, are featured.

WEEK 11—Rock 'n' Roll in the '60s. The work of the Beach Boys and Phil Spector are placed in context before the British Invasion and the role of the Beatles in developing a new wave in popular music. There will also be an introduction this week to the role of Dylan in the folk-rock movement.

WEEK 12—The Second Golden Age of Rock and Great American Popular Singers, Part 2. The majority of the time here will be devoted to discussion of "Rock, 1965-1970." Analysis of the "group phenomenon" and the great groups like the Byrds, Buffalo Springfield, The Lovin' Spoonful, the Hollies, the Rolling Stones, Cream, Traffic, etc.

WEEK 13—End of the Second Golden Age. Discussion of the politicization of rock, the breakup of the great groups, and reformation into the "supergroups"; introduction to the '70s with James Taylor, Linda Ronstadt, and the era of the solo artist.

WEEK 14—The '70s and Beyond. A look at the emergence of the female singer songwriter, the rise of country rock, disco, reggae, punkrock and the new wave; discussion of new technological advances which may have an impact on the future of popular music (like video discs).

Special Features

Paper Assignments. Two major papers will be assigned. The purpose of the papers is to encourage students to independently deal with some of the ideas covered in the course and apply concepts and tools discussed and used in the daily classroom work.

First paper. This essay (600-1100 words) treats some subject from the period 1900-1950. Some research is expected in the assignment. The student will be asked to relate a major musical figure or trend to some specific medium in an attempt to understand the dynamic of creativity. The student, for example, could discuss Max Steiner and film music in the 1930s; by doing this not only would he gain insight into the nature of film scoring but he would also discover how studio policy helped shape creative activity. Or the student could do a study of early opera recordings (c. 1900-1910) and discuss why this type of music was preferred over popular music by Victor and other recording companies.

Second paper. The second paper can be a bit more informal; in fact an informal essay may be preferable here. The second paper should deal with some aspect of popular music since 1950, preferably some aspect of rock music (this, however, is not hard and fast, primarily because one may have older students in this type of class who are not as close to the music as younger students are). In general, the paper can be a review of some important album, some important phase in rock, the stature of a rock superstar, or an analysis of the role of some medium in creating a musical trend. The only major requirement here is that the essay be more musically oriented, i.e. that the student discuss music first and foremost and personalities or media secondarily.

Tests. Tests will consist primarily of short answer and short essay questions; there will probably also be one long essay question on every test. Sample: Comparison/contrast essay:

Compare Cole Porter's "I Get A Kick Out of You" to Paul Simon's "America"; what does each say about the time period (era) in which it was written and what sort of values are communicated and reflected in the lyrics? (The lyrics, of course, would be included on the test.)

What type of singer was created and made popular by the advent and development of radio in the 1920s; why was this singer type so popular?

Bibliography:

Texts:

Goldstein, Richard. *The Poetry of Rock.* New York: Bantam Books, 1969. A basic anthology of rock lyrics from the early days (i.e. Chuck Berry) to acid rock.
Marcus, Greil *Mystery Train: Images of America in Rock 'n' Roll Music.* New York: E.P. Dutton

& Co., 1975. Analysis of rock music culture through a few major figures like Sly Stone, Elvis Presley and The Band.

Whitcomb, Ian. *After the Ball: Pop Music from Rag to Rock.* New York: Penguin Books, 1972. One of the finest and easiest to understand single volume histories of popular music.

There would also be assigned some contemporary musical comedy like *Fiddler on the Roof* to illustrate theory and practice in musical theatre.

Selected Background Readings:

Engel, Lehman. *Words With Music.* New York: MacMillan, 1972.

Feldman, David, ed. *Popular Culture Methods* 3 (1975?). This contains the best and most comprehensive bibliography of rock related materials.

Hodeir, Andrew. *Jazz; Its Evolution and Essence.* New York: Grove Press, 1956.

Lomax, Alan. *Folk Songs of North America.* New York: Doubleday; Dolphine Books, 1960, 1975.

Malone, Bill C. *Country Music, U.S.A.: A Fifty Year History.* Austin: Univ. of Texas Press, 1968.

Mussulman, Joseph Agee. *The Uses of Music.* Englewood Cliffs, N.J.: Prentice-Hall, 1974.

Pleasants, Henry. *The Great American Popular Singers.* New York: Simon and Schuster, 1974.

Shemel, Sidney and M. William Krasilovsky (ed. Paul Ackerman). *This Business of Business* 4th ed. New York: Billboard Publishers, 1979.

Spaeth, Sigmund. *A History of Popular Music in America.* New York: Random House, 1948.

Stearns, Marshall. *The Story of Jazz.* New York: Oxford University Press, 1958.

Toll, Robert C. *Blacking Up: The Minstrel Show in Nineteenth Century America.* New York: Oxford Univ. Press, 1974.

Wilder, Alec. *American Popular Song: The Great Innovators, 1900-1950.* New York: Oxford Univ. Press, 1972.

Timothy E. Scheurer
Division of Arts
Franklin University

American Studies 320
Television in American Culture
(3 credits—15 week semester)

Introduction

"Television in American Culture" is a permanent, junior-level overview course offered each semester in the American Studies Department. It is a course with a long and varied history, and the end-product of a synthesis of courses developed by David N. Feldman and Karen M. Stoddard. The American Studies Department here has consistently offered courses dealing with TV, beginning with television genre studies developed by Dr. Horace Newcomb in 1975; in 1978 the department formally instituted a Mass Media/Popular Culture emphasis for majors (one of several fields of interest majors may concentrate in) with "Television In American Culture" a prime, upper-level cornerstone for that course of study.

Offering two sections per semester, this course consistently draws a total enrollment of one hundred seventy-five students, necessitating a large-lecture approach in one section of 120 students and allowing a somewhat closer working situation in a section of 55 students. For each section, the overall thrust and objectives are the same: to explore the economic, artistic and social implications of American television, including an in-depth examination of daytime TV (a topic generally ignored or shortchanged in TV criticism and courses).

In the first part of the course, the business aspects of television are closely examined. Indeed, one primary object is to make the students realize that American television is a business first and an entertainment medium second, and that programming decisions rest almost entirely within a profit-motivated structure.

The second segment of the course deals with the mainstay of daytime TV—soap operas—as well as syndicated shows and game/quiz shows. The section on soaps included in this syllabus was first developed and taught by David Feldman while he was a student at Bowling Green State University in 1974; while working toward his doctorate at the University of Maryland, he taught a semester-long course entitled "Soap Opera and Daytime TV" in the American Studies Program at the College Park campus to enthusiastic students who consistently numbered 250 per semester. Having taken over the duties of teaching "Soap Opera and Daytime TV" for one year after Feldman left College Park to join N.B.C. in 1977, I incorporated a unit on soap opera into "Television In American Culture" when I began teaching at U.M.B.C. in 1978, and wish to acknowledge his contribution to the syllabus for this course.

The final segment of the course covers many aspects of prime-time fare—differing genres, news and sports, advertising, etc.—as well as the sociological impact of television on American society. What has TV done to change America? What would we be like without TV? What role will television play in our national future?

This course has one built-in advantage—almost all the students are television consumers of long-standing duration. By the end of the semester, hopefully, they leave as informed and knowledgeable critics of a medium which, for better or worse, touches all Americans in one manner or another.

Outline of Course

Part I. Business aspects of the American commercial television industry (4 weeks).
    A. Ratings
        1. How do Nielsen and Arbitron operate?
        2. The interrelationship of ratings, networks and producers.
    B. Demographics
        1. Who is the audience?
        2. What are the advertisers buying with their money?
    C. Programming/Counterprogramming
        1. Development of new programs
        2. Operation of network programming departments
        3. Programming/counterprogramming strategies—program flow, lead-ins, block booking, hammocking, etc.

The class information presented in Part I is largely technical and informational; this unit is followed by an objective examination and a short problem paper dealing with programming strategies for the Baltimore market.

Part II. Daytime Television (4 weeks)

From the beginning of the class to the end of this section, the class follows one soap opera on a weekly basis during assigned class time. This is absolutely essential so that the students share a common informational base, but also so that students can appreciate, through personal viewing, exactly what elements about soap operas inspire devotion and loyalty from regular viewers.

The use of soap operas as a major unit also works very successfully to orient students to the basically formulaic nature of commercial television programs, and Part II thus serves as an important transitional link to the later discussion of varying genres within Part III.

A. John G. Cawelti's Theory of Formula in Popular Entertainment.

B. History of Serial Form in Popular Entertainment
    1. Tracing the development and durability of the serial form in 19th century newspapers, "B" movies, radio and early television programming.

C. A Day on the Set of a Soap Opera
    1. Technical notes regarding actual production procedures: script production, sets, placement of actors/actresses, etc.
    2. Explanation of various jobs—producer, director, etc.

D. Discussion of inherent differences between daytime and prime-time programming.
    Differences in time, attitude, action vs. character development, etc.

E. Age and Sex Roles in Soap Operas

F. TV Game Shows
    Historical overview, including scandals of late 1950s up to current shows.

This second unit is followed by an objective and short essay examination.

Part III. Various Genres Within Prime-Time Programming (7 weeks)
    Alternatives to TV as we have always known it.

Within this unit, heavy use is made of representative examples of taped programs as they apply to lecture material. For example, when discussing television comedies, I show one tape of *I Love Lucy* and one of *Laverne and Shirley* to compare and contrast two shows, made twenty-five years apart, which illustrate quite vividly the strength (and consistency) of the television comedic format. Some people might question the use of class time to view tapes, but I have found this method preferable to assigning viewing time at home. Viewing in a classroom offers a unique situation which is conducive to critical and analytical examination of the programs; it is necessary to teach students how to *examine* TV, not just *watch* it. There is also the obvious advantage that the uniformity of the class experience insures that all students have equal access to required viewing, eliminating the many excuses of "My TV is broken," "I don't get that channel," etc.

A. Drama/Adventure
    Evolution of TV drama from close-up, live studio productions of the 1950s which emphasized characterization, to filmed series which emphasize action.

B. Comedy
    Tracing of major elements of domestic and situation comedies from the Fifties to current programs.

C. Children's Programming
    1. "Entertainment" vs. "Educational" programming
    2. PBS contributions

3. Advertising on children's shows
D. Children and TV violence
   1. Examination of available research (Gerbner & Gross, et al), most of which conflicts and contradicts, regarding effects of viewing violence.
   2. Special-interest groups which have formed—philosophies and objectives.
E. TV Advertising
   Since Part I deals so thoroughly with the interrelationship of advertising and television, this lecture deals with the content of the commercials themselves, particularly in terms of techniques being utilized, such as "snob appeal" as an emotional selling process, personification (such as the "Fruit of the Loom" Boys) which establishes artificial social relationships between the product and the viewer, etc.
F. TV News and Sports
   To what extent does television coverage alter the "reality" of real things? Can we trust what we see on the tube? This material deals specifically with the effects the medium itself has on the presentation of news events and coverage of professional sports.
G. Mini-series, docu-dramas, and made-for-TV movies. Commercial TV tries to expand its repertoire, with mixed results.
H. FCC Regulations; N.A.B. Code—anticipatory self-regulation; "Family Hour," etc.
I. PBS—an alternative to commercial TV
   1. Historical background on National Education Television
   2. Problems with PBS—management inefficiency, financial pressures, governmental interference, etc.
   3. Potential of public television in the U.S.
J. Cable TV/Pay TV/Satellite Transmission
   The future of TV as the communications and entertainment center of the home.

Throughout the third section, the underlying consideration is the social impact of American television, and its power to reshape our entertainment, politics and marketing. There are two in-class examinations during Section III, since the material covered is so extensive.

Special Features

Paper Assignments. The fact that this course is designed as an upper-level offering necessitates the writing of at least one problem paper in which the students have the opportunity to apply class material to realistic situations. If this course were taught to a significantly smaller class (no more than forty students), I would recommend more papers and fewer objective examinations as a better means of assessing student's abilities to integrate and utilize what they have learned.

Short Assignment Example: (6-8 pages; assignment originally developed by David Feldman)

Choose one weeknight's prime-time schedule and analyze what mass appeal and audience demographics each of the networks is aiming for. Assume that you have just been given the job of programming director for Channel 45 (a local independent station in the Baltimore market). You have been asked by your station manager to discuss the relative strengths and weaknesses of your shows versus the competition. Your manager couldn't care less about the artistic merit of your shows or of the competition's. He wants only to know how to get a bigger audience, perhaps a new demographic group. Most importantly, he wants to know whether changes should be made or whether he should stick with the same schedule for next session.

Your assignment is to file a report for the manager which should:

a) Analyze the strengths and weaknesses of your line-up vs.
   the competition's

b) suggest possible additions, deletions or substitutions in your line-up
   to strengthen your position (you needn't propose specific new shows but
   be precise about the *kind* of show you might want to replace an old one
   with and what type of audience it would be geared to).

c) be prepared for the manager to argue with every point of your report.
   Try to *prove* your case with as many examples and specific references
   to your shows and the competition's as possible.

A word of warning: this assignment might seem simple; if so, be forewarned. Millions of dollars are spent in research by the networks to provide the type of insight that you are asked to provide here. The major purpose of this assignment is to get you thinking about how shows (and whole days' or nights' line-ups) are designed to appeal to specific groups, and to recognize how different stations counter-program in order to maximize profits.

Bibliography

Texts

Barnouw, Erik. *The Sponsor.* New York: Oxford University Press, 1978.
Barnouw's book is an excellent, highly readable examination of the development of
   commercial television in the United States.
Brown, Les. *Television: The Business Behind the Box.* New York: Harcourt Brace Jovanovich,
   Inc., 1971.
Brown's book is an excellent account of the development of a television season,
   from proposals to actual air-play, from an insider's point of view. The only problem is that
   it is somewhat dated now (speaks of ABC as no. 3, for example) and students have
   a difficult time placing it in a proper time perspective.
Mankiewicz, Frank and Joel Swerdlow. *Remote Control: Television and the
   Manipulation of American Life.* New York: Ballantine Books, 1978.
Shanks, Bob. *The Cool Fire.* New York: W.W. Norton & Co., Inc. 1976.
Similar to the Brown book in format; again, television from the viewpoint of one
   who has worked closely within the structure.
Newcomb, Horace. *TV: The Most Popular Art.* Garden City, N.Y.: Doubleday, 1974, revised 1978.
   Very useful for any course which attempts to deal with television as a cultural force
   and art form.
Soares, Manuela. *The Soap Opera Book.* New York: Harmony Books, 1978.
   Do not be deceived by the simplistic title. This book offers solid analysis of soap operas
   as an art form; attempts to establish reasons for the success and durability of the form.

Background Reading:
Cawelti, John G. *Adventure, Mystery and Romance.* Chicago: University of Chicago Press, 1976.
Greenfield, Jeff. *Television: The First Fifty Years.*

Karen M. Stoddard
American Studies Department
University of Maryland, Baltimore County

English 400
America and the Movies: The 1930s and '40s
(3 credits—10 week quarter)

Introduction
   "America and the Movies: The 1930s and '40s" is one of several courses offered by the English Department under the heading of English 400: *Studies in Film.* As described in the University catalog, *Studies in Film* concentrates on "approaches to film; analysis of individual film styles, themes, genres, directors; esthetic and cultural significance of fiction and nonfiction films." *Studies in Film,* which was first offered in 1975, is listed by both the English and Speech Departments, and draws students from both departments; however, many students who enroll in the course are neither English nor Speech majors. All students must have previously taken at least one 3-credit course in film and be either a junior or a senior. These prerequisites are helpful because the instructor can count on the students having at least a basic film vocabulary and a certain amount of visual literacy.
   Besides "America and the Movies: the 1930s and '40s," other course offered under *Studies in Film* have been "Contemporary British Film," "Major Forms of American Film," "Howard Hawks," "Film Animation" and "Film Comedy." These offerings have attracted as many as 23 students ("America and the Movies") and as few as 12 ("Film Comedy"). A ten-dollar film fee, payable to the English Department, is required of all students in the course. These fees help defray the cost of renting films. (All film rentals are handled by the University's Media Resources Center, thus relieving the instructor and the Department of a great deal of paperwork.)
   Studies in Film is not a requirement for the English or Speech major, but it can be counted toward a major in either department; and any student in the University can use the course to help satisfy the Arts and Humanities requirement. Courses offered under the rubric English 400 are proposed by faculty in the English Department. Because of the nature of *Studies in Film,* only those faculty who had training in film propose courses. Course proposals are judged competitively by the Department's film committee and the curriculum committee, and both committees must recommend a proposal before the course can be offered. (Faculty in Speech rarely offer a course under *Studies in Film,* and Speech has its own method of selecting what course will be taught.) *Studies in Film* usually is offered twice a year. The course meets for two hours twice a week, in the afternoon so that screenings of lengthy films do not conflict with other courses.
   In offering "America and the Movies: the 1930s and '40s," I wanted to

examine thirties and forties Hollywood films that centered on personal aspiration, ambition and greed. I wanted to trace the success theme during this twenty-year period, and to attempt to account for the effects of the Depression, the war, and the post-war years on the cultural values and esthetic qualities in the films studied. I had several reasons for choosing the specific films shown in the course. The number of gangster films, social comment films, and *films noir* that centered on personal aspiration, ambition and greed was significantly large; such a grouping lent coherence to the course; and a study of the cultural values and esthetic qualities in these films was, I felt, basic to an understanding of American film styles during this period.

I hoped that our class discussions of these films would raise and attempt to answer several questions central to an examination of the success theme: Why, for example, if filmmakers were interested in portraying ambitious characters, do so many of these characters ultimately fail at being successful; why, in a country whose basic myth is that of unlimited possibilities for the individual, do these films opt for the status quo, for staying in one's place; why do women in films of this period often fail to achieve independence; or if they do achieve independence, why do they often become predators; and why, given the "peculiar authority photographs have in our culture" (as Michael Wood puts it), do films of the forties give the viewer the sense that things are not as they appear, that appearances are suspect, that motives and true character are hidden? If, as Andrew Bergman observes, the thirties was "a jittery society," and the forties, as Molly Haskell says, a time of paranoia, then perhaps these films, with their outlaw and deviant protagonists, their high-tension style of acting, and their squeezed-in world of narrow hallways and cramped, dimly lit rooms would tell us something about the society out of which they came.

Outline of Course

1. Introductory lecture on various approaches to the study of film, with emphasis on the social, sociological, genre and ritual approaches, film as popular culture; the Depression, the individual and the American Dream.
2. Reading: Warshow, *The Immediate Experience,* "The Gangster as Tragic Hero"; Bergman, *We're in the Money,* Introduction, "A Note on the Movie Industry and the Depression," "The Gangsters." Screening: *Little Caesar* (Warner Bros., 1930. Director, Mervyn LeRoy. 81 min.).
3. Reading: Nelson, "Warner Brothers' Deviants 1931-1933"; Bergman, "The Shyster and the City," "Some Anarcho-Nihilistic Laff Riots," "A Musical Interlude." Discussion: *Little Caesar.*
4. Reading: "The Motion Picture Production Code of 1930"; Bergman, "Warner Brothers Presents Social Consciousness." Screening: *I Am a Fugitive From a Chain Gang* (Warner Bros., 1932. Director, Mervyn LeRoy. 90 min.)
5. Reading: Bergman, "Back to the Earth," "The G-Man and the Cowboy," "The Mob and the Search for Authority, 1933-1937." Discussion: *I Am a Fugitive From a Chain Gang.*

6. Reading: Bergman, "A Solution to Environment: The Juvenile Delinquent."
   Screening: *Dead End* (United Artists, 1937. Director, William Wyler. 90 min.)
7. Discussion: *Dead End.*
8. Reading: Bergman, "Frank Capra and Screwball Comedy, 1931-1941," "Conclusions"; review Bergman, "The Shyster and the City."
   Screening: *Mr. Smith Goes to Washington* (Columbia, 1939. Director, Frank Capra. 127 min.)
9. Discussion: *Mr. Smith Goes to Washington.*
10. Reading: Kael, *The Citizen Kane Book,* "Raising Kane."
    Screening: *Citizen Kane* (RKO, 1941. Director, Orson Welles. 120 min.)
11. Midterm Examination.
12. Discussion: *Citizen Kane.*
13. Reading: Wood, *America in the Movies,* "The Price of Imagery."
    Lecture: War-time and post-war America.
14. Reading: Wood, "The Interpretation of Dreams."
    Screening: *Mildred Pierce* (Warner Bros., 1945. Director, Michael Curtiz. 111 min.).
15. Reading: Schrader, "Notes on *Film Noir.*"
    Discussion: *Mildred Pierce.*
Paper 1 due.
16. Reading: Wood, "America First."
    Screening: *The Best Years of Our Lives* (RKO, 1946. Director, William Wyler. 172 min.).
17. Reading: Warshow, *The Immediate Experience,* "The Anatomy of Falsehood."
    Discussion: *The Best Years of Our Lives.*
18. Reading: Wood, "Nice Guys Finish Last," "Ceremonies of Innocence."
    Screening: *Kiss of Death* (20th Century Fox, 1947. Director, Henry Hathaway. 98 min.).
19. Discussion: *Kiss of Death.*
20. Reading: Wood, "The Blame on Mame," "The Sense of the Past."
    Screening: *Nightmare Alley* (20th Century Fox, 1947. Director, Edmund Goulding. 111 min.).
21. Discussion: *Nightmare Alley.*
    Paper 2 due.
22. Final Examination.

Special Features
Sample Test Questions
1. Using Bergman's ideas about the role of authority in films of the 1930s, speculate on the absent father in so many thirties films. Illustrate with reference to specific films.
2. The newspaper has played a role in every film shown so far in the course. One of its roles is to advance the story quickly. Discuss at least two other roles the newspaper has played in the films you have seen this term.
3. Compare and contrast *Nightmare Alley* with either *Little Caesar* or *Citizen Kane.* Concentrate on the protagonists' origins, the size of their

ambitions, their relationships with women, their careers and their destinies.

Sample Paper Assignments

1. Write an essay in which you compare and contrast either the gangsters or the women in several films of the 1930s on the basis of their ambitions or aspirations; show how their ambitions or aspirations are conveyed through characterization and imagery. (This assignment could be, if the student wished, the basis for a longer paper due at the end of the term on the gangsters or the women in several films from the '30s and '40s.)

2. Frederick C. Crawford, board chairman of the National Association of Manufacturers, in an article titled "Getting Rid of the Women," published in *Atlantic,* June 1945, observed: "From a humanitarian point of view, too many women should not stay in the labor force. The home is the basic American unit." Write an essay which discusses the theme of *Mildred Pierce* (1945) and the film's iconography in light of Frederick C. Crawford's remarks, and speculate on the historical basis for the film's theme.

Bibliography

Texts:

Bergman, Andrew. *We're in the Money: Depression America and Its Films.* 1971; rpt. New York: Harper & Row, 1972. Sets forth the thesis that films of the thirties mirrored the society's tensions and concerns while keeping alive the myth of success.

Kael, Pauline. *The Citizen Kane Book.* 1971; rpt. New York: Bantom, 1974. Details Herman J. Mankiewicz's and Gregg Toland's collaborative efforts; includes also the shooting script and the cutting continuity of *Citizen Kane.*

Wood, Michael. *America in the Movies: or "Santa Maria, It Had Slipped My Mind."* 1975; rpt. New York: Dell, 1976. Sees films of the forties and fifties as shaping a mythology of their own, wherein hidden worries and concerns emerged indirectly.

Assigned Readings:

"The Motion Picture Production Code of 1930." In Olga J. Martin, *Hollywood's Movie Commandments: A Handbook for Motion Picture Writers and Reviewers.* 1937; rpt. New York: Arno Press & The New York Times, 1970, pp. 271-90. Written in 1930 by Martin Quigley but not enforced until 1934, the Code established principles which movie-makers were to follow in dealing with morality in films.

Nelson, Joyce. "Warner Brothers' Deviants 1931-1933." *The Velvet Light Trap,* No. 15 (Fall 1975), pp. 7-10. Argues that by punishing deviant characters in films, Hollywood deflected revolutionary impulses in the United States and thus denied the "reality" of individualism.

Schrader, Paul. "Notes on *Film Noir. Film Comment,* 8 (Spring 1972), 8-13. Defines *film noir* in terms of its "cultural and stylistic elements," its themes and phases.

Warshow, Robert. "The Gangster as Tragic Hero" and "The Anatomy of Falsehood." In *The Immediate Experience: Movies, Comics, Theatre, and Other Aspects of Popular Culture.* New York: Doubleday, 1962. "The Gangster as Tragic Hero" stresses the cultural and psychological needs fulfilled by the genre. "The Anatomy of Falsehood" argues that *The Best Years of Our Lives* is a pretentious film which evades political reality, distorts class differences and projects male passivity.

Reserve Texts:

Baxter, John. *Hollywood in the Thirties.* New York: A.S. Barnes, 1968. A studio-oriented approach to the decade's films.

Higham, Charles and Joel Greenberg. *Hollywood in the Forties.* New York: A.S. Barnes, 1968. A genre approach to the decade's films.

Selected Background Readings:

Altman, Charles F. "Towards a Historiography of American Film." *Cinema Journal,* 16, No. 2

(Spring 1977), 1-25. A classification and critique of thirteen approaches to film.

Friedan, Betty. *The Feminine Mystique.* New York: W.W. Norton, 1962. Argues that woman's role in the twentieth century emphasized fulfillment through male domination, sexual passivity and nuturing maternal love; see the chapter "The Mistaken Choice."

Haskell, Molly. *From Reverence to Rape: The Treatment of Women in the Movies.* New York: Holt, Rinehart & Winston, 1974. A chronological survey of the shifting images of women in films.

Lingeman, Richard R. *Don't You Know There's a War On? The American Home Front, 1941-1945.* New York: G.P. Putnam's Sons, 1970. A survey of American society and culture during the war years; see especially the chapters "Give Us the Tools," and "Will This Picture Help Win the War?"

Pells, Richard H. *Radical Visions and American Dreams: Culture and Social Thought in the Depression Years.* New York: Harper & Row, 1973. A wide-ranging analysis showing how the early decade's radical impulses and concerns were altered and transformed by the end of the decade.

Susman, Warren I. "The Thirties." In *The Development of an American Culture.* Ed. Stanley Coben and Lorman Ratner. Englewood Cliffs, N.J.: Prentice-Hall, 1970, pp.179-218. Argues that the thirties, rather than being an age of ideologies, was a decade in which the "idea of culture and the idea of commitment" were paramount.

Donald Dunlop
Department of English
Iowa State University

Popular Culture Courses
In Traditional Disciplines

Anthropology 280
Personal Anthropology
(3 credits—15 week semester)

Introduction

Personal Anthropology was designed in 1977 as part of a larger effort to increase enrollments and strengthen the undergraduate anthropology program at Illinois. As far as I am aware, I have invented the term "Personal Anthropology" but it is clear that there are similar courses elsewhere. I make no special claim for uniqueness. Personal Anthropology, however, has been taught for two semesters and it works: student response has been excellent. The course received a $1000 AMOCO undergraduate teaching and curriculum development award in 1978, and was written up in the Research and Commentary section of *Anthropology Newsletter* 20(8): 18-20, 1979. Not only has there been considerable local interest but I have received a large number of requests for information about the course from other anthropologists.

The design of Anthropology 280 stems from a critique of our traditional introductory course. Traditionally, cultural anthropology courses presented materials from primitive societies with the aim of developing in the student a cross-cultural comparative perspective. The purpose was to show that there are alternative solutions to common human problems. This perspective was considered a valuable corrective to ethnocentrism and to the belief that American ways and values were inherently better or more natural than those of other societies. Within this framework cultural anthropology prospered during the 1950s and 1960s.

The problem with such a course in the 1970s, however, is that most undergraduates have already learned these lessons. After Watergate, the Vietnam war, and the decline of American influence in the world, many undergraduates have become disillusioned with their own society. They know that there are alternate lifestyles and not just one establishment or "middle class" way that all segments of society must follow. Within their own lifetimes they have witnessed the overthrow of old ideas about the inferiority of blacks and women.

These changing perspectives have undercut the traditional humanistic lessons of the introductory course. Whereas in the past anthropology emphasized what was different in various cultures, the focus now has shifted from cultural diversity to a concern with universals, to what all human beings have in common. Whereas the point of the introductory course in the 1950s was to enhance awareness of the variety of cultures, the new course in the 1980s will stress the universality of the human experience. Anthropology 280 reflects this new emphasis on common humanity rather than on exotic differences, and what it has to say should be just as applicable to the life of a student in Urbana, Illinois, as to the Bushman of the Kalahari Desert.

There are other problems with the traditional approach. Most courses and textbooks are designed for professors, not students: they contain too much material that reflects professional concerns within the discipline rather than emphasizing those parts of anthropology most meaningful to the undergraduate. Rather than discuss Pueblo sacred clowns, for example, we can analyze Woody Allen and Steve Martin, those contemporary court jesters whose humor is so appealing to this generation. What anthropology has to say about rites of passage can be said just as effectively about fraternity initiations as about Nbembu ritual. Students can learn to do a structural analysis of myth by an examination of any contemporary text, be it a TV Western or Superman, without having to acquire the foreign data base necessary to understand the raw and the cooked in South American jaguar myth.

Personal Anthropology, then, came to the study of popular culture indirectly, by way of a critique of the traditional course. Its explicit aim was to relate anthropological concepts and methods to the students' everyday life situation. It makes anthropology a more personal experience in that it takes as its subject matter not just an amorphous American culture or even popular culture but specifically undergraduate campus culture and the world of the student. Concepts are used in ways that enable the student to develop a critical understanding of his/her position within society.

To abandon the cross-cultural perspective in introductory anthropology is revolutionary, as a comparative approach has been considered the very heart of our discipline. My rationale, however, is that the same theoretical points can be made just as effectively using ethnographic examples closer to home. My ultimate aim is for the students to develop a more reflexive view—which is really the essence of our discipline. Most students, and most people, do not reflect upon their society; they live in it, engage in actions to further their own interests, and advocate their own positions. Personal Anthropology encourages students to take their culture and society as objects of investigation, to penetrate the taken-for-granted, and it does so directly rather than by way of the Trobriand Islands.

The theory of Personal Anthropology is structuralism, symbolism and semiotics, combined with a focus on interpretation and processes of construction. This body of theory has some consistency and lends itself to the illumination of student life. The course is built around such concepts as image, communication, metaphor, myth, sign, interpretation, ritual, meaning and narrative structure because they seem to work so well together in teaching. It takes time to develop a new course, but working through Personal Anthropology has had a number of indirect benefits, not the least of which is that it has led me to make a synthesis of what had previously been a dispersed body of theory.

Outline of Course

I. Images and Communication
   A. The University as a Social System
      cognitive maps; mutual predictability; non-sharing.
   B. Interpretation and the Attribution of Meaning
      symbolic interaction; the interpretative act; the
      social construction of reality; the meaningful
      environment
   C. The Anthropological Experience: Fieldwork in Your
      Own Community; observation; participation; interviews;
      expressive culture; non-verbal communication; the
      ethics of field research; self deception.
   D. The Image of Women in Advertising
      Virginia Slims, "A Long Way to Go, Baby"; advertising
      as a symbolic form; conflicting images.
   E. Image of Women in Country Music: Loretta Lynn
      how to analyze a text; surface text and depth semantics;
      semiotics.
   F. Tourism, Kodak Culture, and Visual Images
      images in social life; the family album; the symbolically
      structured world of international tourism; tourist
      art.
   G. Campustown Bars
      social and symbolic structure; appropriate and
      inappropriate behavior.

II. Social Dynamics: Change and Liminality
   A. The Life Cycle as Metaphor
      social dramas; rites of passage; fraternity and
      sorority initiation.
   B. How to Study Social Change
      awareness of change; situational variability;
      revolutionary ideology creativity; new codes;
      prophets and artists.
   C. Liminality
      role reversals; institutionalized liminality on
      campus; rites of spring.
   D. Humor
      general aspects of humor; Woody Allen and Steve
      Martin; humor and society.

III. Myth, Ritual and Reflexity
   A. How to Analyze a Myth
      pseudo explanations; universality of myths; structural
      analysis.
   B. Narrative Structures
      the Western; the Detective Story; function of ritual
      and myth; Hansel and Gretel; transformation through
      comic books.
   C. Ritual
      professional football; metaphor in American culture;
      art and ritual as model; Memorial Day.

D. Graffiti
   gender differences; manifest and underlying meanings;
   restroom graffiti as political discourse.

This schematic outline covers only one part of the course, the formal lectures. Other components include presentation of audio-visual materials such as films, slides, and records; assigned and recommended readings; small weekly discussion sections (20-25 students) led by a teaching assistant; and individual conferences with the T.A. to work on student research projects.

Special Features

Each student takes an active role in the learning process by engaging in a series of four fieldwork projects. These are not isolated "exercises" to learn field "techniques" as an end in itself but rather are an organic part of the course in which field study of campus culture is closely tied to study of theoretical concepts.

One early student assignment, for example, was to draw a map of the university that included only those localities and physical places which were relevant in their lives, such as a dorm or the student union. Then they had to interview one person in the university unlike themselves—a secretary or faculty member—and to draw a similar map of someone else's meaningful places. Class discussion was devoted to a comparison of these "cognitive maps," and the conclusion emerged that participants in a social system occupy different slots and have different perceptions of the system.

The question was raised: What do we mean when we speak of the university community and to what extent is culture shared? This is an obvious formulation for us, but it has proven to be an effective teaching technique with undergraduates who usually have not given serious thought to their society or their own university as a system.

Other student field projects are adapted to the environment of Urbana—which I must admit is somewhat limited compared to Chicago or Los Angeles—but each project is directly related to theory. Student life in Illinois revolves around residential halls, campus bars, sports, music and film, but the projects could readily be modified to fit other geographical areas. The final project is an independent term paper, conceived and carried out in close consultation with the graduate student teaching assistant.

Personal Anthropology covers popular culture, campus culture and student life. Its focus is on the ethnography of students, utilizing structuralist-interpretive theory combined with student field study of their own life ways. Popular culture, nevertheless, is prominent in the course because it is prominent in the life of undergraduates.

Bibliography

I choose not to list any bibliography at this time as we are currently making a revision of the reading assignments, which the students, the teaching assistants and I agree are the weakest link in the course. The difficulty is that the theory of the course comes from such scholars as Levi-Strauss, Clifford Geertz, Anthony Wallace, Victor Turner, Terry Turner and

Roland Barthes—and they do not usually write for an undergraduate audience. The reading materials we are seeking must deal with student culture, must utilize the structuralist-interpretive conceptual framework, and must provide some genuine insights into the phenomena being investigated. Such readings are not easy to locate, and in practice most of the theory and applications are given in lecture and in the discussion sections.

Edward M. Bruner
Department of Anthropology
University of Illinois, Urbana-Champaign

English-Humanities 220:
American Literature and Popular Culture
"The American Depression and Its Creative Expression"
(4 credits—10 week quarter)

Introduction

I first offered "The American Depression and its Creative Expression" at Wittenberg University in 1975-76 and have twice offered it at University of Illinois, Chicago Circle in 1977-79. The course was initially designed to fit into an English elective series as an English-Humanities credit and continues to fulfill both English and Humanities requirements at the University of Illinois, Chicago Circle. The course is listed under "English-Humanities 220: American Literature and Popular Culture." This slot is filled each quarter by different English Department staff, three of whom were appointed in 1976-77 to begin a popular culture program within the English Department. Other English 220s have included "Approaches to Popular Literature," "American Science Fiction," "Jazz and American Literature in the 1920s," "Americans and the California Dream," "Sport and Game in American Fiction" and "Officer Friendly and Dirty Harry: Recent Detective Fiction." English 220 has a limit of 32 students per section and has averaged 20-25 students per class.

"The American Depression and its Creative Expression" is undeniably as close to a straight American Literature course as to a Popular Culture course. It is more accurate to say that it re-investigates the popular sources and subjects of mainstream literature. The American 1930s is an almost inexhaustible resource in fiction, music, art, ideology, style and folk culture. There was great experimentation in popular forms. Any ten week course must necessarily limit study to one particular focus to achieve any depth at all: the focus here is overly literary.

Outline of Course

A course on "The American Depression and its Creative Expression" presupposes the following:

1) That this time period can be approached as an organism for systematic investigation;

2) That there is a consistent crossing of influences in the period between literature and politics, literature and fine arts, literature and film,

popular literature and elite literature, fiction and documentary;

3) That such crossing of influences creates the tension that defines the popular forms of the decade;

4) That the urgency and energetic confusion of ideas in the decade will be conveyed through the popular forms of the decade;

5) That the expression of popular forms is the imaginative working through of both social themes and artistic imperatives.

WEEK I

Frederick Lewis Allen, *Since Yesterday*
Studs Terkel, *Hard Times*

Allen functions as a dictionary of the 1930s for the course, gives a short-hand history of the New Deal, profiles of leading personalities, the sweep of the decade—good, lively history marred by lack of an index.

Terkel functions as an encyclopedia for the course, dozens of personal testaments from all social classes and interests, models of oral history, public background for students engaged in studying the decade in its imaginative presentation as art. Introduction to subject documentary study—documentary as art. Suggestions of the rich and varied materials available to students.

WEEK 2

Nathaniel West, *A Cool Million*

West chronicles the American success story as really the American failure story a la Candide—a boy who starts with nothing and then loses even more. Physical grotesques, cartoon characterization, anger, urgency of West's satire. Real Alger books are distributed and discussed. John Cawelti's *Apostles of the Self-Made Man* is most helpful for background to the self-help ethic. Emphasis on West's assessment of the self-help ethic as obscene in hard times.

WEEK 3

Ernest Hemingway, *To Have and Have Not*

"Taking it," "A man alone ain't got no bloody fucking chance," pressures on major authors to confront the Depression. Hemingway the individualist adapting his themes to 1930s reality. Criticism of ideology of both left and right wing. The artist's praise of the free man. Adaptation of American naturalism to the Depression. Link to Chandler, Cain, McCoy. Suggested film: *I Am a Fugitive From a Chain Gang.* Suggested study: paintings of Hopper, the Soyer brothers, and Reginald Marsh to link with Hemingway's pictorial conception of prose and his social themes.

WEEK 4

John Steinbeck, *In Dubious Battle*

Mob psychology, social action, ideologies and their critiques. Characters with tags as spokesmen, Steinbeck as master social biologist, how to move masses of men, plight of group leaders and followers, the ethics of revolution. Suggested film: Fritz Lang's *Fury.*

WEEKS 5-7

William Stott, *Documentary Expression in 1930s America*
James Agee, Walker Evans, *Let Us Now Praise Famous Men*

The major unit of course work. Documentary prose and photography as art. Agee's cosmic conception of poverty and oppression. Transcendence of scene and imprisonment of artist by the scene. Liberal self-hatred and remorse. Suggested film: Pare Lorentz's *The River*. Focus on Margaret Bourke-White and the birth of *Life*. Focus on the Farm Security Administration photographers. Subjectivity vs. objectivity in photography. The ethics of photography. Documentary as an emerging art form. Discovery of rural America. Discovery of truly "American Studies."

WEEK 8

Nathaniel West, *The Day of the Locust* or
F. Scott Fitzgerald, *The Last Tycoon*

Shift of the American imagination to the West Coast and the dream factory. America's conception of itself as seen through entertainment cinema. American authors and the Hollywood screen-writing experience. The self-made man and his permutations in Hollywood. Suggested films: Preston Sturges, *Sullivan's Travels* (self-reflective Hollywood at its best); Frank Capra, *Meet John Doe, Mr. Smith Goes to Washington;* Orson Welles, *Citizen Kane*.

WEEKS 9-10

Student Projects in class—oral presentations (see Special Features).

Special Features

There are an hour exam and a final exam. Essay questions have included:

A. In the books we have read much attention is given to concepts of collective group action vs. individual action. Describe the strengths and contradictions of each course of conduct.

Based on the *evidence*, did the 1930s elevate or trivialize the individual? Did the 1930s heighten the interest in "mass man"? Positive interest? Negative interest?

Finally, aside from *Hard Times* (which you may use as contrast), in your opinion, is fiction a successful format in which to speak of such material?

B. What novelistic technique seems most successful in presenting the agony of the 1930s in the books we have read and WHY? Grotesque satire (West)? Sentimental individualism (Hemingway)? Evolution, biological determinism (Steinbeck)? If you had been an author in the 1930s what subject would you have investigated and in what style would you have written? (You may choose one style other than the above).

Student Projects

Student projects are a major part of the course (50% of the grade) and their presentation takes up the last two weeks of class time. Projects are stressed from the earliest class meetings and carefully monitored as to their development and scope. Students are not obligated to oral presentations but those whose projects might work well in visual and oral terms are strongly encouraged to perform by cajoling, the bullying of authority, and promise of extra credit. I urge students to make use of all sorts of media in presentation. These student presentations are unfailingly the highlight of each term, unquestionable learning experiences for the class and the instructor as well.

Students are encouraged to pursue topics that will move them away from the conventional literature term paper and toward imaginative use of media and community resources. A city such as Chicago is a living museum of architecture, art and *people* with vital links to the 1930s. Also, in the spirit of oral history and Terkel's *Hard Times,* students are urged to get their immediate family's account of the Depression not only for their own benefit but for possible incorporation into their research materials. A 1930s family chronology is suggested as a starting point.

Some projects undertaken by students in the course are as follows:

"My home town in the 1930s"
WPA projects in Springfield, Ohio
Magazine advertising and its evolution
Changing characters and ideas in science fiction
Edward Hopper's urban paintings
Chicago architecture in the 1930s
Bessie Smith and Fletcher Henderson
Political Cartooning in *The Masses* and *The Liberator*
Economic Conditions in Baseball
Art Deco Design in the 1930s
The Dionne Quintuplets as Popular Phenomenon
Women as Sex Sirens in 1930s Cinema

Bibliography

Course texts are listed in the week-by-week course outline. Selected reference works include:
Baigell, Matthew. *The American Scene: American Painting of the 1930s.*
Bourke-White, Margaret and Erskine Caldwell. *You Have Seen Their Faces.*
Cowley, Malcolm. *Think Back On Us.*
Hurley, Forrest Jack. *Portrait of a Decade.*
Kael, Paul. *The Citizen Kane Book.*
Kazin, Alfred. *On Native Grounds.*
Latham, Aaron. *Crazy Sundays: F. Scott Fitzgerald in Hollywood.*
MacLeish, Archibald. *Land of the Free.*
Madden, David, ed. *Proletarian Writers of the Thirties.*
———————————*Tough Guy Writers of the Thirties.*
Nye, Russel B. *The Unembarrassed Muse.*
Stryker, Roy. *In This Proud Land.*

Christian Messenger
Department of English
University of Illinois, Chicago Circle

Geomythography
(Geographic Myths as Popular Culture)

Introduction

"Geomythography," the study of geographic myths, has yet to achieve the status of a full-credit, catalog listed course. It is anticipated that such status will be attained during the 1980-1981 academic year. The course has evolved piecemeal over a period of many years, primarily as a result of this instructor's belief that the shattering of myths and misconceptions is an ideal teaching strategy to employ in introducing the subject matter of any geography course, regional, topical (e.g., physical, cultural, economic, historical), or methodological in nature. When used in this context, normal procedure has been to administer a true-false quiz (25 to 30 questions) during the first meeting of the class and to use the results as a point of departure for an introductory overview of the specific subject during one to three ensuing class periods. All questions are written in such a way as to reflect upon widely held misconceptions, i.e. based on such misinformation, the anticipated answer to each question is "true," whereas, in fact, all answers are false.

During the 1975-1976 academic year, the "myths" approach was adopted in the teaching of a senior-level "capstone" course for Social Studies Education majors at Oregon College of Education. It was team taught by a historian and myself; both instructors were involved in the course introduction and summary, and each held responsibility for approximately one-half of the teaching load and course content which, though oriented toward satisfying the needs of social studies educators, emphasized geographic and historical myths. Student response was extremely favorable; research involvement and class participation indicated quite clearly that the approach was highly successful in stimulating student interest, discussion and motivation. Further, the teaching strategy seemed well-designed for providing a meaningful means of integrating information and honing students' analytical skills.

Several practical considerations can be cited in support of a myth-oriented geography course (the same factors would pertain to the use of myths as the organizational framework for the teaching of any social science, and perhaps other disciplines as well):

1) the course may be tailored to any level of instruction by simply directing instruction, topics, the depth of analysis, and student assignments to the appropriate capability level;

2) the use of myths as an organizational focal point for instruction can easily be adapted to any time-frame, i.e., from a relatively brief introductory segment to an entire term;

3) the approach provides an ideal means by which a broad spectrum of geographical subjects and information can be introduced and studied within a meaningful organizational context which provides ample opportunity for the crossing of traditional disciplinary boundaries, e.g., anthropology, history, economics, political science, geology; inherent within this flexibility is an excellent opportunity for the team-teaching of interdisciplinary courses;

4) the study of myths affords both faculty and students maximum flexibility in pursuing topics of individual interest and academic concern by simply selecting those myths which are most appropriate to the desired subject area or learning experience;

5) there are no limitations on class enrollment other than those which may be imposed by the need for open discussion and oral student reports.

Though not yet classroom tested, it is assumed that "Geomythology" would be an ideal course not only for departmental majors, but as a service course for non-majors with little or no academic work in the discipline. Certainly, it would stimulate more interest among non-majors and those students still in search of an academic field of study than would many of the lower division courses presently being offered by most departments.

Outline of course
It would be presumptive to recommend or suggest any rigid outline for a course in Geomythography. Rather, each instructor should develop a series of topics which represent areas of individual academic interest and knowledge, and are designed to fulfill a desired set of instructional objectives. As presently structured, my own outline of major topical headings reads as follows:

I. Orientation and Introduction:
  a) The nature of geography; geography as a social-
     physical-temporal science which integrates knowledge
     pertaining to the variable phenomena of the earth's
     surface in a spatial context.
  b) The origin, nature and perpetuation of geographic myths.
II. A Potpourri of Myths:
  a) Selected geographic myths drawn from geographic and popular
     literature.
  b) The myth of academic disciplines and problems inherent in
     the compartmentalization of knowledge and research
     methodology.
III. Myths Relating to the Physical Earth and Natural Environmental
     Conditions:
  a) Beliefs held from antiquity to present day on such conditions as
     the earth's origin, antiquity, shape, size, place in the universe,
     movements, climatic zones, seasons, ecumene, terra incognita,
     distortions found within all map projections, etc.
IV. Geographical Exploration and Myths Pertaining to Place:
  a) The importance of myths in exploration and discovery.
  b) Analysis of place-related myths from Mediterranean antiquity,
     e.g., the Land of Punt, Atlas, Mountains of the Moon,
     Amazons, the Lost Continent of Atlantis, the Four
     Quarters of the Earth, the Seven Seas, Australis, Thule,
     Prester John, mythical islands of the Atlantic, etc.
  c) The Age of Discovery, including consideration of such topics as
     the nature of discovery, place names to lure (e.g., "Greenland"
     and "Cape of Good Hope"), El Dorado, Seven Cities
     of Gold, the Fountain of Youth, the Strait of Anian
     and Island of California, etc.
V. The Nature of Human Behavior and Cultural Achievement:
  a) Brief survey of the spatial and temporal distribution of human
     life styles and technological achievement.
  b) Analysis of various "determinants" of human achievement
     which have been cited as factors accounting for
     differences in levels of cultural achievement, e.g.,
     race, climate, economic, sexual, teleological,
     environmental and cultural determinism.
VI. Man in the Environment:
  a) The nature of the man-environment relationship.
  b) Selected myths relating to population growth, overpopulation,
     food and famine, natural resources, the role of science
     and technology in providing for human needs, etc.

VII. Man's impact on the Physical Environment: Natural vs. Human-induced Environmental Change:
   a) Man as an ecological agent, e.g., the human impact on vegetation patterns, weather and climate, animal life, soils, etc.
   b) Selected environmental issues, with emphasis on environmental change induced by contemporary vs. early man.
VIII. Environmental Perceptions:
   a) The nature and origin of attitudes relating to the quality of environment and place.
   b) Analysis of selected examples including: early Mediterranean views of Northern Europe; changing American attitudes of such environments as the Great Plains, the "Sun Belt," California. the urban and rural milieu, etc.
IX. The Myth of Regions:
   a) The nature of geographical regions (arbitrary designations).
   b) Regional stereotypes.
X. Summary, Conclusions and Review of Geographical Myths.

Special Features

Evaluation closely adheres to course objectives which are designed to achieve the following pedagogical results: 1) the integration of knowledge, skills and concepts from within the various sub-fields of geography and of geographical understanding with fundamental information and methodological practices of cognate disciplines; 2) to familiarize the student with a variety of references and research techniques; 3) to encourage the development of attitudes and beliefs based on scholarship and understanding, rather than accepting information at face value and without question; 4) acquisition of experience in skillfully and thoughtfully formulating, articulating and defending attitudes, beliefs and perceptions; and 5) the organization of both thoughts and material into some useful form.

Specific means of evaluating class achievement will, of necessity, vary on the basis of the students' academic level, time available and student enrollment. To date, all evaluation has been based on criteria other than examinations, i.e. assigned written and oral reports; class participation; the preparation of a well-organized notebook containing class notes, copies of student reports, bibliographic references, articles and clippings pertaining to myths, and any other information which the student wishes to present— all of which is organized in such a way as to allow the easy retrieval of information in an organizational framework which will be most useful to the individual; and a final written term research paper devoted to an in-depth analysis of a "major' myth or mythical theme (e.g., environmental determinism, the significance of myths in North American exploration, the American Indian as "noble savage" and guardian of the natural environment, myths relating to the institution of slavery in the Americas, etc.).

Each major topic is introduced and concluded with a lecture-discussion; the majority of time spent on each theme is devoted to brief student reports and class discussion relating to these reports. For each topical heading, students are asked to do one of two things: either select a subject from those listed on a class hand-out (pre-selected by the instructor as myths best illustrating a particular theme) upon which they will prepare a brief report, or write a short essay on one philosophical position selected from those listed.

Bibliography
Very few geographical works are devoted to geographic myths, per se. By necessity, most research activity must utilize books and periodicals relating to a particular geographic location, culture, environmental element or some other specific topic or theme. Both the instructor and students must be resourceful in seeking appropriate literature. The following references can serve as an overall thematic point of departure:

Arthur H. Doerr, "Geographic Myths," in *Methods of Geographic Instruction,* ed. John W. Morris (Waltham, Mass.: Blaisdell Publishing Co. 1968), pp. 25-33.

Charles F. Gritzner, "Sharpening the Teeth of Some Old 'Saws'," *Journal of Geography,* 76 (September/October 1977), pp. 186-188.

Preston E. James, "On the Origin and Persistence of Error in Geography," *Annals of the Association of American Geographers* 57 (March 1967), pp.1-14.

Charles F. Gritzner
Department of Geography
South Dakota State University

Sociology 210
Sociology of Popular Culture
(15 week semester)

Introduction

"Sociology of Popular Culture" was developed in the summer of 1974 with support from an Improvement of Instruction Grant from the University of Iowa's Counsel on Teaching. I have taught the course annually, first at the University of Iowa and since 1976 at Skidmore College. I originally designed the course for the sophomore level, but it has evolved into an upper-level course taken primarily by juniors and seniors. Since I have always been able to limit enrollments to a manageable 35 students, the course "closes" with upper-level students who register first. All students take the course as an elective, although sociology and American studies students count it toward their majors. Sociology of Popular Culture attracts a diverse group of students, but has special appeal to sociology, American Studies, anthropology and art majors.

By design this popular culture course has a very special and somewhat narrow emphasis. Unlike most sociology of popular culture courses, it stresses a critical theory approach to and develops only a "negative critique" of popular culture. That is the course deliberately eschews a celebration of popular culture to focus instead on the role of popular culture in the inhibition and control of forces and tendencies that could fundamentally transform contemporary industrial society into a significantly less repressive social order.

Sociology of Popular Culture is intended to stimulate and sharpen students' critical understanding of the social and historical contexts in which their lives are embedded. The course addresses the following sets of questions paralleling the central issues of sociological interest identified by C. Wright Mills in *The Sociological Imagination* (New York: Grove Press, 1959):

1) What principal taste cultures comprise popular culture in America? In what ways are these taste cultures similar and dissimilar and how are they interrelated? What interrelationships exist between popular culture and the American social structure? How does popular culture affect and how is popular culture affected by religion, the polity, the economy and other social institutions? 2) What are the social bases of the development of popular culture? How does popular culture contribute to the sociological and historical distinctiveness of the contemporary American experience? In what ways does popular culture inhibit, foster, and shape social change? How is popular culture itself changed and affected by changes in the social structure? 3) How does popular culture affect the development of personalities of kinds of "human nature" in America? In what ways are men and women selected and formed, liberated and repressed, made sensitive and blunted by popular culture? What kinds of "human nature" and "character" are revealed by popular culture? How does popular culture expand and restrict the alternatives available to men and women in the construction of the biographies?

This course does not devote as much attention to such aspects of popular culture as youth culture and black culture as many other popular culture courses do. The emphasis is very strongly on middle-class culture, the culture with which most of my students and I are engaged. I have found, to my surprise, that emphasis on a negative critique of popular culture is well received by students, even those who initially enroll in the course expecting a celebration of popular culture. I am careful, however, to explain this emphasis very early in the course. I also find that students have little difficulty with a critical theory approach to popular culture although many students have difficulty reading primary materials in critical theory and fairly formal lectures are necessary to supplement readings on critical theory. I rely most heavily on Herbert Marcuse's work because students find it much more "accessible" than the work of other critical theorists such as Theodor Adorno and Walter Benjamin.

Students have received Sociology of Popular Culture favorably at both the large state university and small liberal arts college at which I have offered it. Students have evaluated the course positively on formal "objective" and essay evaluations and have "voted with their feet" by "closing" the course early in registration. Informal feedback has also been extremely favorable. Students report in particular that the course sensitizes them to issues and concerns of which they had been unaware.

Outline of Course
I. Administratrivia, introduction and sensitization to popular culture (1/2 week)
   A. General definition and discussion of popular culture.
      I do not explicitly define popular culture or distinguish between it and folk culture or high culture until Herbert Gans' concepts of taste cultures and taste publics are introduced in Part III.
   B. The significance of popular culture in our lives.
      Consideration of the roles of popular culture in individual lives using C. Wright Mills' concept of "the sociological imagination," or the ability to understand one's historical role and to grasp the interconnections of biography and history within society.
   C. The sociology of popular culture.
      Consideration of both the distinctiveness and the similarities of a *sociological* approach to popular culture and potential contributions of a sociological approach to other, especially humanistic, approaches.

    D. One sociological approach to popular culture: critical theory. General overview of the origins, development and objectives of critical theory, with special emphasis on the differences of this approach from "mainstream" sociological approaches and the special focus of this approach.

II. A critical theory approach to contemporary industrial society. (2 weeks)

    A. Some assumptions: Sigmund Freud and civilization. Examination
       of Freud's notions of the relationship between repression
       and civilization.

    B. Some possibilities: Herbert Marcuse and America.

    Consideration of critical theorists' (especially Marcuse's) elaboration of Freudian arguments about repression and civilization, including notions of the possibilities of nonrepressive societies and both positive and negative critiques of contemporary societies.

    C. Some problems: America as a one-dimensional society. Development of a negative critique of industrial society, with special attention to "repressive tolerance," the cooptation of dissent and affluence as social control.

III. Taste cultures and taste publics. (2 weeks)

    A. Overview of Herbert Gans' "liberal" approach to culture.

    B. The concepts of taste cultures and taste publics.
       Examination of the dimensions and determinants of taste
       public membership, especially social class and education.

    C. General, broad description of major American taste
       cultures and publics.

    D. The meaning of "popular culture" in Gans' approach
       to taste cultures.

    E. The implications of popular culture for the vitality
       of high culture and folk culture. Discussion of the
       "affirmative" tendences of popular culture and the "critical"
       or "negative" functions of high culture and folk culture.

IV. Some social contexts of popular culture. (2 weeks)

    A. Technology and popular culture. Examination of the
       interrelationshps between technology and popular
       culture, with special emphasis on their historical
       developments.

    B. The constraint of time and popular culture. Discussion
       of the conservative approach to time offered by Sebastian
       de Grazia and its compatibility with the radical approach
       of critical theory, with special attention to the
       distinction between free time and leisure.

    C. Alienation and popular culture. Discussion of popular
       culture and the increase in alienation from self and
       decrease in alienation from society.

V. Negative critiques of specific elements of popular
       culture. (5 weeks)

    A. Contemporary language. The role of language in dissent
       from the existing social order.

    B. Popular heroes, villains and celebrities. The social
       significance of heroism and the decline of heroes

and the rise of celebrities.
- C. Contemporary folklore. The decline of folklore, the rise of "fakelore," and attempts to create a new vitality for folk cultures.
- D. Popular wishes, fantasies and dreams. Popular culture and the erosion of imagination, with special attention to the use and abuse of astrology.
- E. Popular culture and children. The special difficulties of popular culture for children, especially the destruction of play through programmed activities, toys and dolls.
- F. The special medium: television. The special effects of television compared with other media, especially on imagination, play and social interaction.
- G. Packaged environments. The manipulation of physical environments for social control.
- H. A case study: McDonald's Is Your Kind of Place. An in-depth analysis of McDonald's that reflects points A through H, with special attention to the "politics of hamburger."

VI. Popular culture and the arts. (1 1/2 weeks)
- A. A critical theory approach to art. Discussion of the critical nature of art and its ability to negate and transcend the social order within which it is created.
- B. The social class basis of art.
- C. The role of art in political and social dissent, including its limitations.
- D. The destruction of art in contemporary industrial societies: popular art and elite art.

VII. Living inside popular culture. (1 1/2 weeks)
This section is devoted to selected student reports/presentations of term projects involving "immersions" in particular taste cultures.

VIII. Sociology and popular culture: overview and prospects. (1/2 week)
Consideration of the contribution of the sociological study of popular culture to a revitalization of humanistic sociology.

Special Features

1. **Course Projects and Paper Assignments.** I usually assign one term-long project and paper assignment asking each student to seek out and immerse him/herself in a taste culture with which he or she has had little or no previous experience. In effect, students are asked to engage in small-scale ethnographic research. The assumption underlying this assignment is that by learning about others and their social context, we can better understand ourselves and the social context within which our own lives are embedded. Most students submit written reports of their projects, but some have prepared interesting photo essays or films. Particularly well-done projects of general interest are presented to the class near the end of the semester. Examples of projects over the past few years range from skydiving to encounter groups to fundamentalist churches to taverns to stockcar racing. A detailed guide to projects is given very early in the course

126   Popular Culture Studies in America

and is available on request.

2. **Examinations.** I have come to favor distributing about eight essay questions well in advance of an exam and then selecting one or two questions on the day of the in-class exam. All questions are designed to have students integrate and/or apply course content.

Essay question example:

The political implications of music have long been debated. Twenty-five centuries ago Plato warned in *The Republic* that "any musical innovation is full of danger to the whole State, and ought to be prohibited. . . when modes of music change, the fundamental laws of the State always change with them." In short, Plato suggested that changes in music lead to broader social changes.

Assuming that you share Plato's concerns with preventing "social change," would you ban such musical innovations as jazz and rock music and Beethoven's Ninth Symphony? Why or why not? Extending Plato's remarks to other aspects of popular culture, would you ban astrology? Heroes? Folklore? Why or why not?

3. **Films.** Since I find that films in the classroom tend to be "low yield" and to aggravate student slack-jaw, I use few in my courses. A few films, however, have proven useful in Sociology of Popular Culture. I show three surreal films—"Time Piece," "Passing Days" and "No. 00173"—back-to-back on the first day of class to introduce major course themes and to help "break through the established reality" and get in the proper frame of mind for the course. "Of Time, Work, and Leisure" describes Sebastian de Grazia's work in much too simplistic and romantic terms (despite de Grazia's own role in the film), but it does manage to capture some of the spirit if not the rigor of his analysis. Dennis Lanson's "Crock of Gold" is a short, amusing and thought-provoking look at McDonald's that fits in well with this course.

Bibliography

I have assigned various readings to students in Sociology of Popular Culture. The following books have generally worked well. Asterisked items are used in the present offering of the course. A more detailed bibliography, including articles, is available on request.

*Boas, Max and Steve Chain. *Big Mac: The Unauthorized Story of McDonald's.* New York: New American Library, 1977. A useful, irreverent and readable account of "Your kind of place" and its economic and political underpinnings and implications.

Carpenter, Edmund. *Oh, What a Blow That Phantom Gave Me!* New York: Bantam, 1974. An aphoristic, McLuhanesque account of electronic media; the first half is excellent for sensitizing students to the impact of media on society and culture and the importance of the seemingly mundane.

Denisoff, R. Serge and Richard Peterson (eds.) *The Sounds of Social Change.* Chicago: Rand McNally, 1972. A well-integrated set of readings that worked well when I placed greater emphasis on music than I do now.

*Gans, Herbert J. *Popular Culture and High Culture.* New York: Basic Books, 1974. Although Gans fails to adequately address many issues raised by critical theory, critical theory itself must now address issues raised by Gans; his work fits well into my course.

Huebel, Harry Russell (ed.). *Things in the Driver's Seat.* Chicago: Rand McNally, 1972. Its title correctly suggests the theme running through its selections.

Kando, Thomas M. *Leisure and Popular Culture in Transition.*
St. Louis: C.V. Mosby, 1975. Kando's work both addresses
many critical theory issues and provides summaries of popular
culture studies important to students.

*Lewis, George H. (ed.). *Side-Saddle on the Golden Calf.*
Pacific Palisades, Ca., 1972. A well-edited reader much
enjoyed by students; I find that selections fit surprisingly
well into my course if I carefully select and order them.

*Real, Michael R. *Mass-Mediated Culture.* Englewood Cliffs,
N.J.: Prentice, Hall, 1977. Real's approach to and case
studies of selected examples of popular culture works quite
well in my course, although students require some explanations
of Real's arguments.

*Shrank, Jeffrey. *Snap Crackle and Popular Taste: The
Illusion of Free Choice in America.* New York: Delta, 1977.
Its subtitle is more descriptive than its title and suggests
its compatibility with a critical theory approach to popular
culture.

William S. Fox
Department of Sociology
Skidmore College (N.Y.)

Popular Culture Courses
in Specific Topics

American Studies 325
The Train in American Culture
(3 credits—3 week summer session)

Introduction

"The Train in American Culture" was developed as an experimental traveling course for the summer of 1978 and was offered again in 1979 with minor changes. The goal was to explore the once powerful but now fading influence of railroads in American life through the experiential approach of holding classes both on the train and in stopover cities particularly rich in railroading. This approach allowed us to recreate epic moments and explore cultural situations in an immediate, dramatic way, thus bringing America's lost world of railroading to life.

The course satisfies university general education requirements and is one of many from which majors can choose in completing their American Studies degree. Its appeal seems to be somewhat limited in that it demands a substantial commitment of summer time and a willingness to travel many miles. Thus far, enrollment has just met spaces available. It has been successful, however, in drawing media attention and personal queries from all over the country; each summer the enrollment has been a national rather than a local one. Given the enthusiasm of students who have participated, and changing popular sentiment toward trains today, demand may well increase in the future.

Many practical difficulties accompany teaching the course, especially if one is concerned with making the trip as inexpensive, comfortable and academically coherent as possible. One must juggle Amtrak's now sparse schedule against the most interesting cities to visit, the appropriate time to spend there, and students' unfailing desire to have free time for sightseeing. One must balance theme, place and knowledgeable people to meet there. It is sometimes difficult to consider subjects in a logical classroom order. For inexpensive rates in reasonable hotels, it is necessary to reserve rooms months in advance, well before class enrollment and breakdown by sex is known. Although accommodation problems can be reduced by limiting enrollments, hotel arrangements may have to be negotiated at the last minute.

The course suffers recognition problems common to popular culture courses. Despite popular enthusiasm, it may be suspect in university settings as just a train ride for which students get credit. Although students spend almost twice as much time in class as they would during a regular semester's course, and although structured classtime is enriched by the opportunity to meet train travelers and workers, by fulltime access to the instructor and other students, and by all that students can learn from over 6000 miles of rail travel and the chance to explore distant cities, there is no denying that this is a trip.

Despite these difficulties, the rewards are extraordinary. Most college students grew up in communities without trains, and most are unaware of what railroads have meant to American life. Not only do they learn from this dramatic, intensive experience of train travel a great deal about their own culture and railroads' place in it, but they also learn that through train travel they can gain a new appreciation of the diversity of America; they learn how to interpret what they see; and they better understand how popular culture reflects and recreates American institutions. This is only one version of a course which could be either shorter or longer, oriented to one region, one route, or one city; for the train offers many unique possibilities for exploring America.

Outline of Course

PART I. INTRODUCTION TO AMERICAN RAILROADING AND TO THE COURSE.
   Day 1. The Influence of Trains in Expressive Culture.
      A. Slide lecture on development and variety in station architecture.
      B. Slide lecture on trains in American painting. Machine in the garden theme. Popular art (calendars, Currier & Ives, etc.) as source.
      C. First session on railroad music: Great Train Songs (e.g. "Washbash Cannonball," "Orange Blossom Special," "Rock Island Line"). Why and how commemorated; train sounds as musical devices.
      D. Railroads in film: view, as example, Buster Keaton in *The General.*
      E. Personal folklore: sampling varied individual perspectives on trains through talks by a hobo and a railfan.
   Day 2. Travel background.
      A. Introduction to Amtrak (goals, political difficulties, etc.) at headquarters.
      B. Introduction to early railroading and railroads' link to technological progress (in communications, bridge, track, brake and locomotive design, in adoption of Standard Time zones) at the B & O Railroad Museum in Baltimore.

PART II. RIVERS, RAILROADS AND THE GROWTH OF CITIES.
   Day 3. Arrive Cincinnati in the morning.
      A. Walking tour and lecture on the banks of the Ohio River: Cincinnati as a river/steamboat city; rivers as lifelines south; seen through city grid plan, early architecture and dramatic place on the river.
      B. Transformation of city life by railroads: walking tour

of late 19th century railroad renaissance areas; visit
to now-vacant Union Terminal.

PART III. THE RAILROAD AS WORKPLACE.
  Day 4. Depart Cincinnati for Chicago.
    A. Class session on board: Labor history; drama and danger
       of early railroad work; workers as popular heroes;
       work in popular music (including track-laying and
       rail-tamping songs; blues and country ballads about work
       and workers such as John Henry).
    B. Class with sleeping-car porter in Pullman suite: How
       railroad work has changed; the significance of the
       recently-absorbed Brotherhood of Sleeping Car Porters
       as a Black union.
  Day 5. Railroad work in Chicago.
    A. Walking tour of Pullman Village (a total working and
       living community constructed by George Pullman for his
       workers) with Dr. Tom Schlereth.
    B. Visit the modern railyard facilities of the Santa
       Fe Railroad for tour of operations.

PART IV. RAILROADING AND THE WEST.
  Day 6. Depart Chicago for Seattle. Classes on board.
    A. The great rail barons (enriched with board game "Rail
       Baron").
    B. Railroad's impact on the Northwestern states.
  Day 7. Railroad Heroes (such as Casey Jones, Railroad Bill)
         and their music.
  Day 8. Railroads and Seattle (just before arriving there).
  Day 9. Field trip to restored logging camp, influence of
         railroads on the industry.

PART V. THE TRAIN IN THE CITY.
  Day 10. Arrive San Francisco. Field trip to Cable Car Museum/Barn;
          class on early urban rail technology.
  Day 11. Development of urban railroading: Visit Municipal Railway
          Shops and BART.

PART VI. THE FIRST TRANSCONTINENTAL RAILROAD.
  Day 12. Depart San Francisco for Ogden, Utah. Class on board
          (while traveling through the Sierra Nevadas) on Chinese
          workers building the Central Pacific.
  Day 13. Visit Golden Spike National Park, where Central Pacific
          met Union Pacific in 1869, preserved and reenacted daily.

PART VII. RAILROADS AND THE FUTURE.
  Day 14. Travel from Ogden to Pueblo, Colorado on the Denver & Rio
          Grande Railroad, last non-Amtrak passenger service in the
country.
  Day 15. Visit Transportation Test Center (a desert facility for railroad
          innovations).

PART VIII. RAILROADS IN MIDWESTERN LIFE TODAY.
Day 16. Arrive Kansas City. Kansas City as Railroad City.
    A. Visit Smoky Hill Railroad Museum of old, elegant passenger cars.
    B. Visit Missouri Pacific freight yards.
    C. Meet with local Railway Historical Society for presentation of homemade train films and memorabilia: timetables, tickets, prints, postcards, etc.
Day 17. Travel from Kansas City to St. Louis.
    A. Class on board: 19th century passengers' travel accounts; the peculiar quality of passenger interaction on trains today.
    B. Meet in St. Louis with Missouri Pacific Chief Special Agent of railroad police.

PART IX. THE DECLINE OF AMERICAN RAILROADS.
Day 18. Visit now-abandoned St. Louis depot. Depart for New Orleans. Stopover in Effingham: the continuing place of trains in small town life. Class on board: What happened to trains? The role of nostalgia in promoting the automobile against the train.

PART X. THE RAILROAD AS METAPHOR.
Day 19. Final class in New Orleans on railroad as metaphor in poetry and music.

Special Features.
Journals. It is difficult to manage course assignments in a normal way. Students are expected, however, to do background reading each day which will help them interpret what they see and to facilitate discussion. (For example, as they travel from Cincinnati to Chicago they read biographical sketches of Debs and Randolph for their class on labor history; as they travel from Chicago to Seattle they read of Sitting Bull's resistance to the Northwestern railroads.) In daily journals, students synthesize readings, classroom and travel experiences. The best journals reflect that students grow more and more sensitive to the meaning of what they see: for example, early in the course they learn that depots were once built as gateways to the city, and many react to those they see abandoned as an expression of that historical moment. When they reach Cape Horn, many see beyond the spectacular ascent the remarkable feat of Chinese railroad builders there. Journals also give students the opportunity to incorporate informal learning from travelers they talk to and the cities they explore. While they can include personal experiences which make them meaningful travel diaries, the focus must be academic.
Oral Presentations. 5% of each student's grade is based on a short presentation given in the last class session, comparing music and poetry for the ways in which railroad imagery is invoked there as metaphor: for love, loneliness, home, heaven, the modern industrial complex, the past, etc. Taped collections of popular songs are available for students to listen to and discuss during the trip, and this final participatory session seems to be an effective way to close: for it shows how railroading lives on in popular

culture.

Final Exam. Upon returning home, students complete a 10-15 page exam to be mailed to the instructor. Because the journal has stressed immediate daily learning, the exam questions tend to be integrative. One sample question is: "It may be that to understand railroads is to understnd America. Discuss this proposition with specific reference to any two of the following: nostalgia, the machine in the garden, heroism, the frontier, government and business, or work."

Bibliography

TEXTS

Brown, Dee. *Hear That Lonesome Whistle Blow.* New York: Holt, Rinehart & Winston, 1977.
  Historical account, stresses activities of 19th century rail barons and railroads' impact on Native Americans. Firsthand accounts of 19th century travelers.
McPherson, James and Miller Williams. *Railroad: Trains and Train People in American Culture.*
  Interdisciplinary collection including historical and biographical articles, poetry, song lyrics, photographs, folklore, explanation of train signals, etc.
Whitman, Walt. "Passage to India."
  Invokes 19th century hopes for transcontinental railroad; railroads west as a route to the Far East.

Selected Background Reading:

Belasco, Warren. *Americans on the Road.* Cambridge: MIT Press, 1979.
  Popular Culture sources illuminating the displacement of the train by the automobile.
Bryant, Keith L. "Cardinals, Castles and Roman Baths: Railway Station Architecture in the South." *Journal of Urban History,* Feb. 1976, pp. 195-230. Overview of southern depot architecture, station's role in southern cities.
Carwardine, William. *The Pullman Strike.* Chicago: Charles Kerr, 1973.
  Pullman Village minister's account of living, working conditions culminating in strike.
Dorson, Richard M. "The Career of 'John Henry'." *Western Folklore,* 24:3, pp. 155-163.
  Origins of the legend and ballad; nature of his heroic appeal.
Hoffius, Steve. "Railroad Fever." *Southern Exposure* V:1, pp. 47058. Railroads in southern culture and folklore; why southerners love and hate trains.
Klamkin, Charles. *Railroadiana.* New York: Funk and Wagnalls, 1976. Amply illustrated guide to railroad collectibles: timetables, lanterns, sheet music, many more.
Marx, Leo. *The Machine in the Garden.* New York; Oxford University Press, 1964. Good background for ideas influencing train's presence in expressive culture.
Meeks, Carroll. *The Railroad Station.* New Haven: Yale University Press, 1956.
  Overview of changing architectural styles; how to identify them in sample stations.
Ogburn, Charleton. *Railroads: The Great American Adventure.* National Geographic Society, 1977. Enthusiastic photo-history; focus on hoboes and workers.
Taylor, George R. *The Transportation Revolution.* New York: Rinehart, 1951.
  How cities turned from dependence on rivers to railroads. (Additional guides for students include several publications by Amtrak, especially the booklet *Background on Amtrak,* free U.S. railroad maps distributed by Union Pacific and such popular publications as *Trains* magazine.)

Brett Williams
American Studies Program
The American University

American Studies 498
Culture and Society in American Humor
(3 credits—15 week semester)

Introduction

"Culture and Society in American Humor" examines humor as an index to and as an influence on our values, attitudes, dispositions and concerns. The rationale for the course is based on the prevalence of humor in virtually every society in the world, and upon its universal roles as an acculturation device, as a means of articulating socially approved and disapproved belief and behavior, as a licensed expression of dissent, of alternative models, and as an influence on public mood and temper. From the colonial period to the present, American humor can be examined as one perspective on practically everything of importance, including the nature and viability of democracy, the definition of national character, regionalism versus national unity, sex-marriage-family roles, race and ethnicity, social class conflict, political ideology, the pros and cons of progress and technology, and a host of other more specific issues and subjects. Humor has frequently been cited as central to American life; studying it provides an excellent opportunity to explore who we are and why we believe and behave as we do.

The course is multidisciplinary and multigeneric, exploring humor from perspectives which include historical, psychoanalytic, sociological, anthropological, aesthetic and ideological. Sources for study are drawn from literature (both elite and popular), journalism, the graphic arts, the theater, various popular entertainment forms (e.g. vaudeville, burlesque, the revue), standup comedy, the broadcast media, and such "folk" and quasi-folk materials as graffiti, bumperstickers, t-shirts, posters, joke-fads and so forth. Attention is given to recurring archetypal characters such as the Wise Fool, or the Little Man, or the Termagant Wife, to changing stereotypes, to humor as a possible source of particular social and political issues, to humor as a possible source of insight into the spirit of the era, and to questions of the significance of varying personal and small-group differences in the perception and appreciation of humor.

First offered in 1971 as a Graduate Seminar, the course has been taught as a lower-level and an upper-level elective, and as an option for the humanities requirement of our General University Requirements. The course is organized as a lecture/discussion colloquium, offered every semester, and made available to the entire university population without prerequisite or other requirement (the course number suggests that it is for juniors and above). Registration is closed at fifty-five students and is usually filled. The American Studies faculty has warmly and unanimously supported the course, and despite a few informal snide remarks made by colleagues in other departments, there has been no university objection or interference. Many students take the course as an elective, and they assume from the title that it will be the easy, amusing "Mickey-Mouse" course that administrators fear, and unfortunately too often associate with popular culture offerings. Considerable time and effort is devoted, during the first two class sessions, to explaining the rationale for the paradox of "taking humor seriously," to discussing the often-cited notion that because

analyzing humor ruins its effect, it shouldn't be done, and in justifying
course requirements that are equal qualitatively and quantatively to those
of other upper-level courses.

Outline of Course
Responsibilities: Two hourly examinations; a final examination. Note: the
course sometimes requires several essay reviews, or thorough, analytic,
evaluative accounts of primary sources. Class participation is a factor in
the consideration of final grades. Both lectures and class discussion are
employed.
   I. Introduction: defining humor, consideration of the major theories
explaining its origin, motives and functions, discussion of the role of humor
in culture and society. Read introduction to Veron, essays by Rubin and
Kronenberger in Veron. Optional additional reading in Feibleman,
Goldstein and McGhee, and Chapman and Foot recommended (see reading
list).
   II. Native American Humor: discussion of Wise Fool character
(anthropological and pre-American appearances), colonial humor, Yankee
"folk" humor, Southwestern humor. Read appropriate sections of Veron
and Blair (both introductory material and selections)—don't overlook
Rourke essay in Veron.
   III. Literary Comedians, Local Color, Mark Twain: read appropriate
materials in Blair and Veron.
   IV. Minstrel Theater, Vaudeville, Silent Films—the "new humor":
read Agree in Veron; films will be shown in class.
   V. The "golden age" of American Humor: readings in White,
assignments in magazines of the 1920s and 1930s, discussion of the "little
man" character, the battle of the sexes, college humor, screwball comedy,
romantic comedy.
   VI. Modern American Humor:
      a) Readings in Veron—"black humor" defined and discussed
(don't overlook the Hassan essay in Veron)—optional additional reading: a
novel by one of the authors classified as a "black humorist" in the class
lecture.
      b) The comic strip—slide presentation, historical overview,
consideration of humor strips in local newspapers (read Berger essay in
Veron).
      c) The standup comedian—reading in material handed out in
class, tape presentation, assignments from concern opportunities (if
available) and/or recordings.
      d) Film—lecture, assignments of films currently playing locally,
lecture/discussion of theatrical comedy, popular entertainments.
      e) Radio and television: read essay by Newcomb in Veron,
assignments of television programs, primarily sitcoms.
      f) Discussion of "folk" and "quasi-folk" humor—joke fads,
bumperstickers, graffiti, t-shirts, posters, etc.
      g) Consideration of recurring tradition and changes in motifs,
themes, and characteristics of American humor since the beginning.
   Summary discussion of the significance of American humor to
American Studies.

Special Features
Sample question on first examination:
    Discuss any three (3) of the following pieces as *satire,* explaining what they criticize, from what perspective the attack is made, and what the significance of the attitudes and opinions expressed might be to our understanding of the American culture and society of the times.
    a) Artemus Ward (C.F. Browne), "Among the Free Lovers" (Veron, 82-84).
    b) Mr. Dooley (F.P. Dunne), "Mr. Dooley on Reform Candidates" (Veron, 94-96).
    c) Mark Twain, "The Facts Concerning the Recent Resignation" (Blair, 522-527).
    d) Oliver Wendell Holmes, "Contentment" (Veron, 75-77).

Sample Question on second examination:
    Discuss the cynical treatment of the "American Dream" (peace, prosperity, progress, property, marriage and family) in four (4) of the following sources:
    a) "George F. Babbitt Starts the Day"
    b) "The Parable of the Family Which Dwelt Apart"
    c) "Christmas Afternoon"
    d) "Glory in the Daytime"
    e) "Fables for our Time"
    f) the silent film comedy

Sample final examination question
    Washington Post critic Tom Shales has written, "We are living in the age of the devalued laugh. One can understnd a society seeking refuge from pain and strife in escapist froth. But at some point the lust for yocks and titters, and the entertainment industry's eagerness to appease that lust, gets a little pathological. Our incredible surplus of comedy suggests that seldom have so many people been so desperate for so much escape." Comment on Shales' observation from the perspective of the humor-materials you have examined this semester, and from the perspective of the history and the traditional motives and functions of American humor. Is the dominant trend in contemporary American humor "escapist"? If so, why? Is this entirely new?

Bibliography
Texts: Veron, *Humor in America*
        Blair, Walter, Native American Humor
        White, E.B. and Katherine, *A Sub-Treasury of American Humor* (abridged ed.)
Additional assignments are made from current newspapers, magazines, broadcasts and other sources.
Additional reading (optional)
Humor theory:
Feibleman, James. *In Praise of Comedy*
Goldstein, J. and P. McGhee, *The Psychology of Humor* (essays)
Chapman, A. and H. Foot, *Humor and Laughter* (essays)
———, *It's a Funny Thing, Humor* (essays)
Collections by Corrigan, Lauter, several books by Leonard Feiberg, many introductions to satire as a genre. See bibliography in Chapman and Foot, *It's a Funny Thing, Humor.*

American Humor:
Blair, Walter and Hamlin Hill, *America's Humor: from Poor Richard to Doonesbury*
Bier, Jesse, *The Rise and Fall of American Humor*
Yates, Norris, *The American Humorist: Conscience of the Twentieth Century*
Rubin, Louis, *The Comic Imagination in American Literature* (collection).

Lawrence E. Mintz
American Studies
University of Maryland, College Park

Women's Studies 408G
Women and Popular Culture
(3 Credits—10 Week Quarter)

Introduction
"Women and Popular Culture" was originally developed in 1978 as a senior seminar in Women's Studies at the University of Oregon. It was offered to 40 students. Many of them were enrolled in the Women's Studies Program and received credit toward requirements for a Women's Studies Certificate. Other students took the course as an elective to satisfy course requirements in the humanities. This course has been offered in a revised form, emphasizing popular literary materials, for sophomores in the English Department at Bowling Green State University.

In part, this course has a remedial objective. Women's creative roles in popular culture often have been trivialized, ignored completely, or understood only in relation to male-defined standards. Women's roles as consumers of popular culture have yet to be fully understood. By focusing exclusively on women and popular culture, it is hoped that women's contributions will be given proper recognition, and women's status will be subjected to close scrutiny.

This course also provides students with the opportunity to develop skills as cultural analysts. They are encouraged to formulate an articulate, personally-meaningful, critical perspective on the culture in which they are enmeshed. In no sense is this course value-free; rather, its very existence presupposes a concern with the politics of culture, a critique of sexism, and an interest in women's status in society.

Outline of Course
Throughout the quarter, women's roles in popular culture are surveyed. Central considerations include identifying those forms of popular culture which are directed primarily toward women; examining the ideological content of popular culture as it relates to women; and, studying the complex interactions between women as objects and consumers of popular culture. Students are encouraged to analyze the politics of popular culture—sexual, economic, and otherwise—to determine whose interests are served by the images and values which are represented.

The course is organized into four topics, which provide a general framework for study:
1. Images of Women in Popular Culture (3 weeks)
Subjects: Advertising, Fashion and Pornography.
Through surviving images of women in advertising, popular

stereotypes are identified. Race, class, ethnicity and regionalism are considered in relation to sex as categories of analysis. Turning to the history of advertising and mass production, readings focus on the transformation of women's labor in the family from a production to a consumption orientation.

Both fashion and pornography are central forces in defining sexual roles and standards within a culture. Fashions such as foot-binding, corsets, shoes, cosmetics and "cosmetic" surgery are discussed, as forms of social expression and control.

The topic of women and pornography has been approached through a fieldtrip to an Adult Bookstore, to the movies, and through common readings. Many issues emerge: women's roles as erotic objects, student attitudes toward pornography, and, unavoidably, the relationship between sexuality and violence against women that is depicted in pornography. Strategies for eliminating media violence against women are discussed.

2. Women as Consumers of Popular Culture (3 weeks)
   Subjects: Women's Magazines, Supermarkets, Television.

Women's taste in entertainment is considered in relation to women's work in the family and in the paid labor force. The form and content of magazines, television game shows and soap operas are analyzed. Shopping is considered both as a chore and as an important cultural event for women. Romance novels are used to discuss the ideology of Love, and its meaning in women's lives.

3. Women Working in Popular Culture (2 weeks)
   Subjects: Publishing, Music and Film Industries.

Women's status as workers in the publishing industry is analyzed, considering sex-segregation, stratification and discrimination. The positions of women at all levels of the industry are considered. Biographies of "stars" in the music and film industries offer insights into the complex and contradictory position of successful women in a male-dominated culture.

4. Women Shaping Popular Culture (2 weeks)
   Subjects: Feminist News-Journals, Recording Companies and Fiction.

The course is concluded by examining those forms of popular culture which have been controlled by women and which intentionally adopt a feminist perspective. The journalistic ethics of a news-journal are considered; the organization of labor and the training programs within a women-owned recording company are examined; and the relationship between aesthetics and ideology in a feminist novel is analyzed. Final class sessions are devoted to a discussion of the media and social change: strategies for media reform, the social function of sub-cultures (e.g., feminist) and the viability of cultural separatism.

Special Features

Student evaluations are based on three individual papers and on one group project/presentation. Two of the papers are analyses of women's role in a form of popular culture; one, a traditional item directed toward women, the other, an item with a feminist approach. In the third paper, the student is expected to formulate his or her own perspective on the politics of women's role in popular culture, considering women's status as workers and as consumers, their images in the culture and the role that popular culture plays in women's lives. Group projects are organized according to the special interests of class members, addressing topics not otherwise covered. Projects are designed primarily for in-class presentation rather than as written works, although an outline or summary of each project is expected. In the past, groups have covered such topics as sexism in children's books, disco dancing, images of women in country western lyrics and the history of women's fashions.

I. Basic Reading List: Women and Popular Culture

Clausen, Jan. "The Politics of Publishing" in *Sinister Wisdom.*

Ehrenreich, Barbara and Dierdre English. "The Manufacture of Housework," in *Socialist Revolution* 5(4) (Oct.—Dec., 1975).

Ewen, Steuart. *Captains of Consciousness: Advertising and the Social Roots of Consumer Culture.* New York: McGraw-Hill, 1976.

Firestone, Shulameth. *The Dialectic of Sex: The Case for Feminist Revolution.* New York: Morrow, 1970. Chapter 6 on "Love" is particularly insightful (pp. 126-155).

Galana, Laurel. "Toward a Womanvision," in Galana and Covina, eds. *The Lesbian Reader.* Oakland, California: Amazon Press, 1975.

Janus, Noreene Z. "Research on Sex-Roles in the Mass Media: Toward a Critical Approach." In *Insurgent Sociologist* 7(3) (Summer, 1977), pp. 19-31. Includes a useful bibliography.

Jong, Erica. "The Artist as Housewife—The Housewife as Artist," in F. Klagsbrun, ed. *The First Ms. Reader.* New York: Warner Paperback Library, 1974, pp. 111-122.

Parrent, Joanne and Susan Rennie. "The Tyranny of Women's Clothes," in *Chrysalis* 2, pp. 91-97.

Piercy, Marge. *Women on the Edge of Time.* New York: Knopf, 1976.

A Redstocking Sister. "Consumerism and Women," in Gornick and Moran eds. *Women in Sexist Society.* New York; Basic Books, 1971.

Russ, Joanna. "What Can a Woman Do? or Why Women Can't Write," in S.K. Cornillion, ed. *Images of Women in Fiction.* Bowling Green, Ohio: Popular Press, 1974, pp. 3-10.

Russell, Diana E.H. and Susan Griffin. "Hypatia's Column: On Pornography," in *Chrysalis* 4 (pp. 11-17). See Lynne Bronstein's letter and Russell's response in *Chrysalis* 5.

Tax, Meredith. "Introductory: Culture is not Neutral: Whom Does it Serve?" in L. Baxandall, ed. *Radical Perspectives in the Arts.* Harmondsworth, England: Penguin, 1972.

Weibel, Kathryn. *Mirror, Mirror: Images of Women Reflected in Popular Culture.* Garden City, N.J.: Anchor Books, 1977.

Weinbaum, Batya and Amy Bridges. "The Other Side of the Paycheck: Monopoly Capital and the Structure of Consumption," in *Monthly Review* 28(3) (July-August, 1976).

West,Celeste. "The Literary-Industrial Complex," in *Chrysalis* 8, pp. 95-103.

II. Additional Resources for Studying Women and Popular Culture

1. A harlequin-type Romance novel
2. A True Confessions-style magazine
3. Feminist periodicals, such as:
   a. *Chrysalis:* a magazine of women's culture
      Woman's Building, 1727 North Spring Street
      Los Angeles, California 90012 (since 1977)
      Two year index in *Chrysalis* Vol. 9
   b. *Heresies: A Feminist Publication on Art and Politics*
      Box 766 Canal Street Station
      New York, N.Y. 10013 (since 1977)
   c. *Media Report to Women: What Women are Doing and Thinking about the Communication Media*
      3306 Ross Place, N.W.

Washington, D.C. 20008
d. *Off Our Backs:* A Woman's News-Journal
1724 20th Street, N.W.
Washington, D.C. 20009 (since 1970)
Indexed in *New Periodicals Index.*
e. *Paid My Dues:* Journal of Women and Music
P.O. Box 11646
Milwaukee, WI 53211
III. Relevant Women's Magazines
1. Of General Interest
Brides (1935), circulation 253,215
Cosmopolitan (1901) and *Cosmopolitan El Espanol*
Essence (1970), circulation 500,000
Farm Wife News (1971)
Lady's Circle (1963), circulation 600,000
McCalls (1870), circulation 7.5 million
Ms. (1972), circulation 400,000
National Business Woman (1919), circulation 170,000
New Dawn (1976), circulation 350,000
New Woman (1971), circulation 200,000
Phyllis Schlafly Report (1957)
Seventeen (1944), circulation 1.5 million
Viva (1973)
Woman (1966), circulation 161,000
Women's World (B'nai B'rith, 1951), circulation 157,000
Working Woman (1976)
2. Home Economics Emphasis
Better Homes and Gardens
Family Circle
Journal of Home Economics
Woman's Day
3. Interior Design and Decoration Emphasis
Apartment Life (1969)
Better Homes and Gardens (1922)
House and Garden (1901)
House Beautiful (1896)
Redbook's Easy Decorating (1976)
Residential Interiors (1975)
Sunset Ideas for Improving Your Home (1973)
4. Fashion Emphasis*
Body Fashions/Intimate Apparel (1913)
Glamour (1939)
Harper's Bazaar (1867)
Mademoiselle (1935)
Modern Bride (1949)
Simplicity Home Catalogue (1967)
Vogue (1892)
Vogue Patterns (1915)
Women's Intimate Apparel Buyers (1951)
Women's, Misses and Jr. Dress Buyers (1951)

Women's, Misses and Jr. Sportswear Buyers (1951)
Women's Wear Daily
*See medical journals and pharmaceutical trade publications for additional
information on women and drugs, cosmetics, etc.

Gail Lee Dubrow
Women's Studies Program
University of Oregon

Popular Culture 426
American Popular Entertainments
(4 credits—10 week quarter)

Introduction
"American Popular Entertainments," a senior level course, is required
of all Popular Culture majors. Minors may elect the course as part of their
program, and it also satisfies part of the general education requirement in
humanities. PC 426 is offered once every second year and draws students
from a variety of disciplines. The course is particularly attractive to
students with majors in health, physical education and/or recreation. The
usual enrollment is from twenty-five to thirty-five. At least one of two basic
courses in Popular Culture studies is a prerequisite.

Popular Culture 426 is an important part of the major in Popular
Culture. Unlike most courses in the curriculum, the mass media are *not*
examined in American Popular Entertainment. Rather, the focus is on such
diversions as board games, popular theater, circuses, camping, hunting,
fairs, pinball and electronic games, toys (both children's and adults'), night
clubs and discos, gambling, resorts, participant and spectator sports,
family reunions, office picnics—in short, any non-media activity in which
people entertain and amuse themselves either in groups or individually.
Class discussions, presentations, and student assignments all illuminate
the meaning of entertainments in a complex society.

A primary objective of the course is to demonstrate to the students that
there are useful approaches to the study of popular culture other than the
examination of the mass media and traditional written sources. For
example, the students might be asked to examine a small group ritual (i.e.
playing cards). Most of the material they gather for this study will be in the
form of interviews with participants and copious notes based on their own
participation. Or, students visit a county fair or similar event and attempt
to examine the manner in which their participation is structured by the
organization of space in and around the event. Or, they might study a
photographic collection which records an event in the past. They would
then compare and contrast their impressions of the past event with their
visit to a similar contemporary event. In a limited form they will begin to
realize that the *experience* and *perception* of the participant is an important
element in the study of popular entertainments.

A second major objective of the course is the examination of popular
entertainments as a reflection of cultural continuity and change. The
premise is that diversions reflect and/or shape certain basic myths, beliefs
and values which Americans hold or have held in the past. To accomplish

this objective an extensive examination and comparison of two similar events which are widely separated in time will help the students formulate hypotheses related to how American culture has changed and how it has remained the same over the time period.

A final objective is to provide students with an understanding of how entertainments function in the lives of the participants, what they mean to various cultural groups, and why they are important to popular culture studies. For example, students will be able to explain how small group diversions are used to foster group cohesion. They will understand that regional variations in entertainment forms reflect regional differences in basic cultural beliefs and myths. Entertainments will be characterized as a means to provide individuals with a sense of self-worth in a rapidly changing, mobile society. Entertainments are also an important force in defining the meaning, importance and sense of community in various institutions such as churches, businesses, industrial organizations and state and national political institutions. Entertainments also provide group identity for ethnic groups.

Outline of Course

PART I. "A History of American Entertainments: An Overview" (3 weeks)

A. Introduction: Theories of Play and Work and Their Relationship.

B. Entertainments Among the Early Settlers. This unit describes the types of entertainments which were popular among the early settlers in New England and Virginia. Emphasis is on the tendency of these early settlers to limit the bounds of play to variations of work (communal harvesting), religion (community worship) and social and oral lessons (public floggings, execution sermons).

C. American Entertainments Grow in Sophistication. This unit examines the rise of spectator sports, popular fads (bicycling), professional theater, the circus, carnivals, fairs and amusements parks. The primary focus is on the 19th century, and developing amusements are studied as antecedents to modern entertainments. A connection is made between two developing forces in American life and shifts in styles and means of entertainments—urbanization and industrialization.

D. Into the 20th Century. Discussion moves into the modern era, and a number of important topics are discussed: entertainment as "big business"; entertainment as an active and involving enterprise which provides a distinctly different experience than the mass media; the role of entertainment in a society where work plays less and less a part in individual lives; the need for more forms of entertainment as individuals gain more discretionary leisure time.

This segment of the course includes a short paper comparing a modern entertainment form with an earlier equivalent (i.e. comparison of a modern amusement park with a "pleasure garden"), and culminates with a one-hour written examination. A research paper of 10-12 pages is assigned during the second week.

PART II. "Entertainments as Popular Rituals" (4 weeks)

A. Rituals are defined as any regularly repeated and structured activity which embodies cultural values, myths, beliefs and attitudes.

B. Individual Diversions. The class examines activities which normally or *occasionally* involve a single participant. Jogging, exercise, and crossword puzzles are discussed as individual pastimes which also potentially lead to self-improvement. The stress here is on the traditional American fear of "wasted time," though this point can be made elsewhere. Hobbies, such as stamp or beer can collecting, are discussed as individual activities which provide the participants with both a sense of accomplishment and the potential to meet others. Students discuss the relationship between the selection of individual entertainments and the work a person normally does.

C. Family and Small Group Entertainments. Discussion centers on "card clubs," board games, family Thanksgiving and Christmas celebrations and traditions, Tupperware parties, picnics, reunions, etc., as providers of small group unity and identity.

D. Entertainments for Relatively Large Groups. Spectator sports, organized amateur sports, national, regional and local celebrations (Fourth of July, community "Sesquecentennial" and other celebrations), parades, exhibitions, "home shows," "auto shows," and ethnic festivals are potential topics. The manner in which these entertainments celebrate and affirm major cultural beliefs is examined.

Students submit a short paper on a small group activity *or* a short paper on an entertainment event designed for a large group. There is a one hour written examination at the conclusion of this part of the course.

PART III. "Entertainment and Culture" (2 weeks)

A. Entertainment in the Great Outdoors. Students read Frederick Jackson Turner's "Frontier Thesis." Next, 20th century entertainments such as camping, backpacking, hunting and fishing are discussed. Students examine the implications of modern "wilderness" experiences in terms of Turner's assertion that the frontier was *the* crucial shaping force in American history. Turner was incorrect, but the ideal of the "rough, wilderness experience" in a mechanized, relatively comfortable, and modern society is a manner of celebrating such traditional American virtues as ingenuity, individualism and self-sufficiency.

B. Entertainment and Cultural Change and Continuity. This unit is an in-depth study of two similar entertainment events which are widely separated in time. An effort is made to include all the approaches developed in the course; various facets of the events are studied in terms of their individual, small group and large group rituals. The cultural history of the events is developed. A multitude of audio-visual aids are used. Newspaper, magazine, diary, and photographic accounts of the events are considered and compared. Students are told that the two events will illustrate how American beliefs and lifestyles have changed and how they have remained the same over a period of time. One class studied the 1876 Centennial and the 1976 Bicentennial celebrations. Another approach to the same material might be thematic. The class could scrutinize changing attitudes toward blacks as reflected in entertainments during various periods (i.e. the minstrel show and how it changed, the portrayal of blacks in popular theater, black participation in sports from Jack Johnson through the Negro baseball leagues, to the National Basketball Association and Muhammad Ali).

PART IV. Student Presentations. (1 week)

Each student is assigned ten to fifteen minutes to present the findings of a research paper (10-12 pages). Each student is responsible for preparing a one page outline and abstract for distribution to class.

The course concludes with a one-hour in-class written examination and a brief take-home examination.

Special Features

PAPER ASSIGNMENTS. Two short papers are designed to provide experience in analyzing popular entertainments. Both are developed around major topics which are discussed at length in the classroom. The longer paper is designed to allow the students to apply most of the approaches and theories presented in the course. The long paper also serves as an important means to touch on a number of entertainment forms which are not discussed in class. The sharing of ideas and findings during the final week of the course provides the students and instructor with an opportunity to review the major topics of PC 426.

Short Paper Example:

The class spends half an hour playing a parlor game in the classroom. The game, "Facts in Five," is structured to allow any number to participate, so it is ideal for this purpose. After the game the instructor and students discuss the game's influence on the participants, how it structures interaction, how it stimulates certain types of discussion and discourages others. Students are then assigned the task of entertaining two to six friends for an evening. The group is to participate in one of the following activities: playing cards, playing a board game, playing charades, or playing a parlor game. Students then write a brief, analytic paper (3-4 pages) which describes how the activity structures the interaction of the players. They are also to suggest at least two ways the group might be expected to act differently if viewing television had been the dominant activity.

Long Paper Example:

During the second week of the course students are provided with a list of dozens of entertainments and diversions which will not be discussed in PC 426. Each student is to prepare a research paper of 10-12 pages which provides a detailed analysis of an activity selected from the list. All of the activities have been around for a number of years, and all have earlier antecedents (examples: roller skating, yachting, bowling, vacationing, building models). Each research paper must include the following information: 1) origin and *brief* history of the entertainment form; 2) description of the ritual aspects of the form; 3) discussion of participants; 4) explanation of why people participate (i.e. what satisfaction is to be derived from the entertainment?); and 5) an hypothesis which suggests what cultural beliefs are represented in the entertainment. While the instructor will help each student select appropriate resources, each student should make an effort to include as many of the following materials as possible:

Interviews with participants
notes taken while participating
newspaper, magazine and other accounts

photographic records, past and present
diaries, letters and similar sources.

FIELD TRIPS. Ideally this course would include two or more field trips to
entertainment events. For this reason it is best to offer the course in the
Spring and Fall, though campus activities occur all year. Events might
include style shows, parades, fairs, a local disco, collegiate events, or even a
rummage sale. Such field trips enhance class discussion of group
entertainments.

TAKE—HOME EXAM. Half of the final examination is of the take-home
variety. The text book used for the first half of the course is Foster Rhea
Dulles' *A History of Recreation.* The subtitle of the book, *America Learns to
Play,* suggests Dulles' thesis. He postulates that *the* major characteristic of
American entertainment is that Americans had to *learn* to amuse
themselves because of, among other things, the frontier experience and the
Protestant work ethic. The students are to use as many of the materials
presented in the course as possible to develop their own concise, plausible
and cogent "Theory of American Entertainments." The only restriction is
that they may not use the Dulles thesis. While they might argue almost
anything, success on this assignment requires that the theory be firmly
grounded in materials presented in class. Each student should also discuss
a multitude of entertainments in support of the thesis.

Bibliography.
TEXTS:

Dickson, Paul. *The Mature Person's Guide to Kites, Yo-Yos, Frisbees and Other Childlike
Diversions.* New York: New American Library, 1977. A provocative discussion of numerous
diversions, including related materials such as rules for various frisbee games, information
on making kites and model airplanes.

Dulles, Foster Rhea. *A History of Recreaton: America Learns to Play.* New York: Appleton-
Century-Crofts, 1965. The finest available survey history of American recreation.

Other required readings: Students also read a variety of materials on reserve at the library. These
readings are usually fairly current articles dealing with various facets of entertainment. I
also require that they read one issue of *Amusement Business,* one issue of an outdoor or
camping magazine (*Field and Stream* works well), and one sports book, usually an
autobiography of a disgruntled star (i.e. Lanze Rentzel, *When All the Laughter Died in Sorrow*). A
weekly entertainment supplement to the daily newspaper would also be a useful text.

Selected Background Readings:

Brightbill, Charles K. *Man and Leisure: A Philosophy of Recreation.* Westport, Conn.:
Greenwood Press, 1961. Brightbill's "philosophy" explores the relationship of recreation to
numerous other aspects of culture.

Kando, Thomas M. *Leisure and Popular Culture in Transition.* St. Louis: C.V. Mosby Co., 1975.
Kando's provocative discussion centers on the period after World War II.

Matlaw, Myron, etc. *American Popular Entertainment.* Westport, Conn.: Greenwood Press, 1979.
An indispensable collection of 25 essays and a superb bibliography.

Peacock, James L. *Rites of Modernization: Symbolic and Social Aspects of Indonesian
Proletarian Drama.* Chicago: Univ. of Chicago Press, 1968. Don't let the title throw you—
this is a useful study of a popular entertainment form and its relationship with culture.
Peacock's approach can be used to help explain everything from garage sales to demolition
derbies.

Selected Issues of *Journal of Popular Culture:* The *Journal* has published several useful "In-
Depth" sections. Three which are especially helpful are Volume VI (3), Winter 1972,
"Circuses, Carnivals, and Fairs in America"; Volume VIII (2), Fall 1974, "Sports: A Social

Scoreboard";
   and Volume XII (3), Winter 1978, "Musical Theater."

Christopher D. Geist
Department of Popular Culture
Bowling Green State University

Humanities 270
Popular Culture and Political Consciousness
(3 credits—10 Week Quarter)

Introduction
   This course was first offered in winter quarter, 1979, as a section of a variable-content, sophomore-level humanities course, "Contemporary Ideas," which students can take as one means of fulfilling a university humanities requirement. This was the first course I had taught explicitly in popular culture, although for several years I had been incorporating elements of this course in my composition and semantics classes and had edited an issue of *College English* on "Mass Culture, Political Consciousness, and English Studies" in April 1977. About forty students enrolled; the course was well received by both students and administration, and present plans are to repeat it at least once a year. The following year I added a second Humanities 270, "The Semantics of Contemporary Public Discourse," which was a sequel to this course in its specific emphasis on the semantic dimensions of news reporting, advertising, and mass-mediated popular entertainment.
   Popular (or mass) culture is perhaps the most influential socializing force in the United States today. Its critics assert that it is also among the most powerful agencies for political indoctrination and social control. Despite its all-pervasive presence in our collective and individual lives, relatively little academic study has been devoted to the influence of popular culture and mass media on political consciousness, largely because such study does not fit neatly in any one conventional academic department. This course, then, is an interdisciplinary approach to the humanistic aspects of the relations between mass culture and mass consciousness.

Outline of Course
   Class sessions combine lecture and discussion, along with some monitoring of records and TV and application of theoretical perspectives to current films, TV shows, etc.
   The following topics are considered, not necessarily in this order, and with a good deal of overlap among them.
   1) Popular versus mass culture.
   2) Mass culture and mass society.
   3) Culture and social class; the relation between taste cultures (highbrow, middlebrow, lowbrow), socioeconomic class, and political ideology in the producers and audience of popular culture as well as in its subject matter.
   4) The relation of the world portrayed in popular culture to social reality and real-life values and priorities. Images in mass media of various social classes, women and minorities, government and politicians, the

military and police, professions and occupations, science and technology.
   5) The mind-numbing, pacifying effects of TV and other mass media.
   6) Political ideology in popular culture; explicit or implicit attitudes toward:
      Capitalism, socialism, communism, fascism, conservativism, liberalism, radicalism;
      Wealth and poverty, social inequality, status quo vs change;
      Sociopolitical power and authority, the State;
      Business vs. labor, environmental issues;
      Nationalism and war,
      Competition vs. cooperation.
   7) Political implications of the portrayal of violence, crime and sex in mass media.
   8) Political implications in advertising.
   9) The political economy of the culture industry.
Course Schedule:
Week 1 Introductory survey.
   2 Sports; the Super Bowl.
   3 Media images vs. reality: stereotypes, celebrities and authorities, Disneyland, tourist attractions, fantasy, diversion, commercial-land.
   4, 5 Television and films.
   6 Popular music, radio. (Midterm examination)
   7, 8 Print media: magazines, newspapers, popular books, comic books and strips.
   9 Mass-mediated politics, news, religion.
   10 Summary: possible alternatives to mass culture toward a true popular culture.
   11 Final examination.

The following quotations are distributed the first class meeting and form a point of reference for discussion throughout the term.

We shall show them that they are weak, that they are only pitiful children, but that childlike happiness is the sweetest of all. They will become timid and will look to us and huddle close to us in fear, as chicks to the hen. They will marvel at us and will be proud at our being so powerful and clever, that we have been able to subdue such a turbulent flock of thousands of millions. They will tremble more weakly before our wrath, their minds will grow fearful, they will be quick to shed tears like women and children, but they will be just as ready at a sign from us to pass in laughter and rejoicing, to happy mirth and childish song. Yes, we shall set them to work, but in their leisure hours we shall make their life like a child's game, with children's songs and innocent dances.

Fyodor Dostoevsky, "The Grand Inquisitor,"
Chapter in *The Brothers Karamazov* (1880)

What's finished is the idea that this great country is dedicated to the freedom and flourishing of every individual in it. It's the single, solitary human being who's finished. Because this is no longer a nation of independent individuals. This is a nation of two hundred-odd million, transistorized, deodorized, whiter-than-white, steel-belted bodies, totally unnecessary as human beings and as replaceable as piston rods....
   We are no longer an industrialized society; we aren't even a post-industrial or technological society. We are now a corporate society, a corporate world, a corporate universe. This world is a vast cosmology of small corporations orbiting around large corporations who, in turn, revolve around giant corporations, and this whole endless, eternal, ultimate cosmology is expressly designed for the production and consumption of useless things.

Howard Beale, in *Network,* by Paddy Chayefsky (1976)

The spectacle is the continuously produced and therefore continuously evolving pseudo-reality, predominantly visual, that each individual encounters, inhabits and accepts as public and official *reality,* thereby denying as much as is possible, the daily private reality of exploitation, pain, suffering and inauthenticity he or she experiences.

> Norman Fruchter, "Movement Propaganda
> and the Culture of the Spectacle" (1971)

People who watch television the most are unread, uneducated, untraveled and unable to concentrate on single subjects more than a minute or two.

> Producer of "Top 40 Stories" local TV newscasts,
> quoted in *San Francisco Examiner,* March 16, 1975.

We sophisticates can listen to a speech for a half hour, but after ten minutes the average guy wants a beer.

> President Richard Nixon, as quoted by his former
> speechwriter, William Safire, in *Before the Fall.*

Resolved, that the National Council of Teachers of English support the efforts of English and related subjects to train students in a new literacy encompassing not only the decoding of print but the critical reading, listening, viewing, and thinking skills necessary to enable students to cope with the sophisticated persuasion techniques found in political statements, advertising, entertainment, and news....

> Resolution passed by National Council
> of Teachers of English, November 1975

Special Features

Rather than writing papers, students are asked to keep a class journal, to be turned in at two or three points during the term. The journal is used for afterthoughts on each class period, comments on required and recommended readings, and applications of ideas from the class to daily monitoring of popular culture—TV programs, films, newspapers and magazines, ads, popular music, radio, current best-selling books, sports, tourism, etc.

Sample midterm exam question:

Write an essay summarizing the pro's and con's of the argument that mass culture (as opposed to popular culture) just gives the people what they want. Support the various lines of argument with applications to specific fields of mass culture, including—but not restricted to—at least two of the following: the Superbowl and other televised sports, Disneyland or other tourist attractions, TV commercials. Make specific references to arguments presented by each of the following—Real, Cirino, Fiedler, MacDonald, Brantlinger—supplemented by recommended readings and your own observations.

Sample Final Exam Question (take-home exam):

One of the main arguments made by critics on both the political left and right is that mass culture (and the mass society of which it forms an integral part) is tending more and more toward social-cultural conformity and unquestioning support for the established order. Write an essay enumerating and analyzing examples and patterns drawn from the readings and class discussions that substantiate this argument, along with opposing examples representing cultural diversity and critical questioning of the status quo in the United States. Try to maintain a reasonably objective, balanced and unemotional tone in which you are trying to summarize arguments pro and con rather than taking sides.

Bibliography

Texts:

Real, Michael. *Mass-Mediated Culture* (Englewood Cliffs, N.J.: Prentice-Hall, 1977.
  Introductory and concluding chapters survey theoretical positions of critics of mass and popular culture, while other chapters apply these critical perspectives to current topics such as the Superbowl, Disneyland, televised medical dramas, Billy Graham-style religion, and political campaigning.
Cirino, Robert. *We're Being More Than Entertained.* Honolulu: Lighthouse, 1977.
  A study of the political implications in the content and institutional structure of American mass media, in which media messages are analyzed for their explicit or implicit support of conservative, liberal, socialist or libertarian ideology.
Weibel, Kathryn. *Mirror, Mirror: Images of Women Reflected in Popular Culture* (Garden City, N.J.: Anchor, 1977).
  Historical survey of stereotypes of the social role of women in fiction, TV, movies, women's magazines and fashion.
Chapple, Robert and Reebee Garafalo. *Rock 'n' Roll Is Here to Pav* (Chicago: Nelson-Hall, 1977).
  Marxist analysis of the politics and economics of the popular music industry over the course of the twentieth century.
Fiedler, Leslie A. "Towards a Definition of Popular Literature," in *Superculture,* C.W.E. Bigsby, ed., Bowling Green, OH.: Popular Press, 1975.
  Refutation of the distinction between high and popular culture and of critics who claim that mass culture manipulates and debases popular taste.
Macdonald, Dwight, excerpts from "Masscult and Midcult," in Macdonald, *Against the American Grain* (New York: Random House, 1961).
  Classic expression of the distinction between mass and popular culture and of the appeal of mass culture to the lowest common denominator.
Brantlinger, Patrick, "Giving the Public What it Wants," *Public Doublespeak Newsletter,* III, 2, 1976.
  Refutation of defenses of the culture industry that claim it simply reflects popular tastes rather than determining them.
Gitlin, Todd, "The Televised Professional," *Social Policy,* November/December 1977.
  Argues that the idealization of professionals on TV dramas, as well as their depiction through stereotyped, fixed dramatic formulas and formal structures, fosters passivity, dependency and legitimation of the established social order in the minds of the audience.

Recommended Readings:

Daniel Boorstin, *The Image*
Fyodor Dostoevsky, "The Grand Inquisitor"
Herbert Gans, *Popular Culture and High Culture*
Rose K. Goldsen, *The Show and Tell Machine*
Paul Hoch, *Rip Off the Big Game*
Aldous Huxley, *Brave New World Revisited*
James Michener, *Sports in America*
Michael Novak, *The Joy of Sports*
Robert Sobel, *The Manipulators: America in the Media Age*
Benjamin Stein, *The View from Sunset Boulevard*
College English, April 1977, issue on Mass Culture, Political Consciousness and English Studies.

Donald Lazere
Department of English
California Polytechnic State University

History 397
American Popular Cultural History, 1900-1945

Introduction

"American Popular Cultural History" has been offered as an upper division course in the Department of History at the State University of New York at Buffalo since 1969. The course serves as an elective for History majors and other students as well. For those in non-Social Sciences areas (i.e. Engineering, Mathematics, English, etc.) it can be used to fulfill what is called Distribution credit (32 semester hours of courses outside the major area). In 1969, the first semester American Popular Cultural History was offered, 151 students enrolled in both day and evening sections. Since that time, the registration has been between 25 and 76 students per offering. Generally this course is offered every other year in day school and in the alternative years in the evening division. The present author has taught this course since its inception.

While the course is currently numbered on the third year level, it is open to any student, generally sophomore to senior. There is, as is typical of most courses in the Department, no formal prerequisite, but most students have had at least a survey course in American history. Most of the students have been juniors and History majors. Probably if the course was numbered on the 100 level, the enrollment would be higher. In 1980 the University will require a General Education component and there is the possibility of increased enrollment since there will be a requirement in the area of social sciences.

The main objective of the course is to get the students to understand the complexities of the period 1900-1945, from the turn of the century to the end of the Second World War, and to identify the currents and trends that together comprise the spirit of each period within this time frame. This course treats popular culture as a valid branch of historical study. Traditionally, little attention has been paid to such topics as those mentioned below in the "Outline of Course" section. The social historian's task is to uncover the tastes, manners, habits and interests of people. Since, by definition, he is concerned with man's everyday existence—his reading material, what he wears, his amusements, how he earns a living, and all-in-all, in his "grassroots" existence—such a course is pertinent. In his attempts to attain relevance—to utilize experiences in order better to comprehend contemporary life, as well as to shed scholarly light on the past itself—the social historian must cross boundaries between disciplines and this course offers such an opportunity. Because the subject matter deals with topics from the areas of history, economics, sociology, science, education, religion, literature, art, music and theatre and the "lively arts," the course has interest for a broad spectrum of student interest.

This course originated because the instructor realized that popular culture was one obvious area of history to which students had the least academic exposure, one in which they were very interested, but one in which they had little if any understanding. Their previous exposures to American history emphasized political, diplomatic and economic topics, but items of everyday life were so taken for granted that they little understood that this is history too. Also, the author realized that the treatment of popular culture topics provided another dimension which helped to spark student interest in history that rightly or wrongly was all-too-often flagging. In other words, this was something new to many. Incidentally, this same thinking prompted the successful inclusion of such topics in survey courses in general American history.

Outline of Course
Specifically this course attempts to interpret popular culture as a vital part of American history and as an indicator of the attitudes and values of the American people. The specific aspects of this culture to be studied include the mass entertainment media such as motion pictures, radio and popular music; mass-produced literature such as newspapers and popular magazines, comic books and strips, pulp fiction, and best-selling novels; recreational outlets and sports; intellectual values; family issues and evolving life styles, especially that of youth, women and minorities.
Introduction
Popular Culture, Popular Cultural History (1 week)
The End of American Innocence, 1900-1914 (3 weeks)
New Immigrants. The New Women. A New Affluence. Literature—High and Low (including journalism). Intellectual Values—Religion, Science, Education. Mass Leisure—The Automobile, The Saloon, The Circus, The Chautauqua. The Outdoor Life and Sports. The Movies. Vaudeville and Burlesque. Popular Music.
The Great War, 1914-1920 (2 weeks).
The end of the "Good Old Days." The Home Front at War. The Witch Hunt. The Legacy of War.
The Roaring Twenties, 1920-1929 (4 weeks).
Tensions of the Times. Radicalism, Bootleggers, Criminals, the "Revolt" of Youth, Women and the Intelligentsia. Mass Entertainment. Jazz, Sports, Radio, Movies, Literature, Art. Boom and Bust. The New Industrial Ethos.
The Lean Years, 1929-1939 (3 weeks).
Depression Mentalities and the Era of Social Significance.
Leisure and Escape—Art, Music, Sports, Movies, Radio, The Stage, Journalism.
Intellectual Values—Science, Literature, Education.
A World at War, 1939-1945 (2 weeks).
Preparedness and Patriotism.
The G.I. Way of Life.
Domestic Adjustments—Rationing, Housing, War Plants, Juvenile Delinquency, Racism
Escapism and Cultural Expressions—The Stage, Movies, Radio, Music.
The Life of the Mind—Education, Science, Literature.
NOTE: 1. There are special lectures on the following topics
by University specialists, i.e. "Jazz in the 1920s and
1930s," "Dance in the 20th Century," "The Comic Strip
and Comic Book."
2. Tours of several old homes in the Buffalo area
representative of early 20th century architecture are
scheduled, i.e. a Frank Lloyd Wright house.
3. There is a mid-semester examination covering the period

1900-1920. The final examination, while including the
earlier material tested on the mid-semester examination,
emphasizes the 1920-1945 period.
4. Movies and records are used almost weekly. See below (Special Features).

Special Features
Paper Assignments
   The subject of popular cultural history easily lends itself to a wide
variety of options. The project can be practically anything related to the
course with which both professor and student can agree and together set the
standards. A non-written project will need an introductory statement.
Where there should be something written for each project, it is probable that
oral interviews with participants and/or witnesses will be a main course.

Possible Options
1. Oral history—interviews (taped, filmed or written) with analysis.
      Sample research projects: Recollections of a "flapper" or "sheik"
   of the 1920s; Depression victims; Participants in World War
   II—soldier, plant worker; Emigres to Buffalo; Gangs; Black migrant;
   A Buffalo actor; Participant in a cultural institution, an
   athletic or social club, a "Y" or Jewish Center, religious
   community or organization, a sports team; Bar patrons; A cleric.
2. A study of how a periodical or periodicals treated a given subject—
   a person or topic.
3. How the music of one or several eras reflected the history of that time.
4. Family history—relating family history to a period (or several periods
   covered in this course). Possible topics—how grandparents and
   parents met, homes and neighborhoods, occupations, economic status,
   daily routines, religion, schooling, discipline in town, leisure
   time activities.
5. A study of a fictional "hero," i.e. The Shadow, Tarzan, Frankenstein,
   Charlie Chan, Lone Ranger, Nancy Drew, Frank Meriwell, etc.
6. And for those whose interests are best served by the more traditional
   research paper, such topics as: One related to the Motion Picture industry
   in the '20s and '30s, i.e. public reaction to movies, study of impact of a
   "star" or several "stars." One related to radio in the '30s and '40s, sports,
   women, youth, popular literature, music.

   An essential feature of this course is movies and records which
illustrate specific or general cultural trends of the 20th century. Selected
movies have been shown including:
The Great Train Robbery (the first movie supposedly with a story line).
The Birth of a Nation and *Tolerance* (Griffith epics)
Bubbling Over (1934 Black Musical)
Documentaries, i.e., *William S. Hart, Story of Serials,* abbreviated versions
of *Dr. Jekyl* and *Mr. Hyde, Phantom of the Opera,* Metropolis.

Records, part of which are played in class, include:
Music of the early 20th century—i.e. Victor Herbert, John Phillip Sousa, miscellaneous popular tunes involving romantic, rural nostalgia, ethnic-immigrant commemorations, etc.
World War I music—i.e. "Oh What a Lovely War" (a British musical about the futility of war), typical World War ballads (i.e. "Over There," "My Buddy," etc.)
The '20s in Song and Words—i.e. a Broadway show such as "No, No Nanette"; Prohibition ballads, songs celebrating the Sacco-Vanzetti case
The '30s in Song and Words—i.e. "Hard Times" (voices of Depression-affected Americans), "Sunshine Songs of the Great Depression," "Pins and Needles" (social significance proletarian musical), "Movies records" (i.e. actual voice tracks of the Marx Brothers, monster movies, Hollywood musicals; miscellaneous radio shows on record).
World War II—"Big Band" music, Historic Voices and music of World War II.

There are also many records that have been put on tape and which are available for optional listening in the University's Language and Learning Laboratory.

Examinations

Except for "relationship" questions all tests are of the essay type with the emphasis on comparisons and relating different epochs of the 20th century. The mid-semester examination when not one of the "take-home" variety, is 75 minutes, and the final, three hours.
Typical Examination Questions:
1. Explain concisely the relationship between the two items in each
   of fifteen of the following:

> "The Jazz Singer," "The Gold Rush"
> Elbert Hubbard, Frank Merriwell
> Bernarr McFadden, Henry Luce
> Izzy Einstein, Texas Guinan
> American Student Union, Ma Perkins
> Aimee Semple McPherson, Billy Sunday
> Jimmy Walker, Al Smith
> David W. Griffith, Mack Sennett
> Paul Whiteman, Benny Goodman
> Al Capone, Charles A. Lindberg
> V Mail, Superman
> Jack Armstrong, John Dillinger
> "Flapper," "It"
> Pola Negri, Irene Castle
> Bruce Barton, "Tex" Rickard
> *Saturday Evening Post, Reader's Digest*
> Mae West, Margaret Sanger
> Chautauquas, Florenz Ziegfeld
> Bill Mauldin, Rosie the Riveter
> Babbitt, Penrod
> Flash Gordon, Orson Welles
> Busby Berkeley, *Scarface*
> Edgar Rice Burroughs, Zane Grey
> "Cutting a Rug," "The Black Bottom"

2. After reading Lingeman, contrast two of your experiences during the Vietnam war with two comparable images he presents pertaining to World War II.

3. In this exercise you are not being asked to demonstrate your powers of memory recall, nor your capacity for factual material but rather upon your ability to think about and interpret materials studies. Draw upon readings (in addition to Doctorow), movies, records and lectures. There will be premium for lucid organization and presentation. The length of your response should not exceed six (6) typewritten, double-spaced pages. Pages should be stapled and decent margins should be provided. Each page should be numbered.

E.L. Doctorow's evocation of the early years of this century in *Ragtime* is done with "a voice that veils irony in nostalgia and deceptive simplicity. He invests a great deal of effort in being true to the details and nuances of the period, while at the same time constantly reminding his readers that this was ...[a] chunk of time in which everything was in transition, in a state of becoming...." Using some of the themes and characters in *Ragtime* as points of departure, examine selected aspects of the new popular culture that was emerging in the first two decades of the 20th century and if possible how they continued development or how they could be characterized after World War I.

4. Assume you are home for Winter recess and discussing with your parents your courses for the past semester. When you mention American Popular Cultural History and say that it concerns such things as movies, comics, radio, sports, music, etc., they are outraged. What might be your rejoinder? Include your feelings on why the course was a serious approach to understanding the American experience, and how it helped illuminate the past in ways tradional courses did not. Pay attention to how several examples of popular culture evolved or changed during the period 1900-1945. Use specific illustrations from material covered. You will be evaluated on the basis of how well I think you convinced your parents as well as by the facts you cite and your analysis. If you agree with your parents, be objective and specific in your feelings, but also, in your response, be sure to cite illustrations as called for above.

Bibliography

Class readings are taken from the following selected list:

Allen, Frederick L., *Only Yesterday,* N.Y.: Bantam, 1957; and *Since Yesterday,* N.Y.: Bantam, 1972. A brilliant overview of the social-political-economic scene in the 1920s and '30s respectively.

Berger, Arthur A., *The Comic-Stripped American,* Baltimore, Penguin, 1973. An examination of the message and impact of selected comic strips.

Bergman, Andrew, *We're In The Money,* N.Y.: Harper's, 1972. An examination of the Depression's impact on 1930s movies.

Doctorow, E.L., *Ragtime,* N.Y.: Random House, 1976. A novel depicting popular life before World War I.

Goulart, Ron, *An Informal History of Pulp Magazines,* N.Y.: Ace, 1972. A discussion of such pulp heroes as The Shadow, Doc Savage, Tarzan, etc.

Harmon, Jim. *The Great Radio Heroes,* N.Y.: Ace, 1967; *The Great Radio Comedians,* Garden City, N.Y.: Doubleday, 1970. A nostalgic view of two aspects of radio's golden age.

Lingeman, Richard. *Don't You Know There's a War Going On?* N.Y.: Paperpack Library, 1976. An overview of the effects of World War II on the American domestic scene.

Lord, Walter, *The Good Years,* N.Y., Bantam, 1969. A breezy account of social life 1900-1914.

Loos, Mary, *The Beggars Are Coming*, N.Y.: Bantam, 1974. A fictional
representation of the establishment of the movie industry.

Lupoff, Dick & Don Thompson, eds.*All in Color for a Dime*, N.Y.:
Ace, 1970. A description of the comic strip and comic book phenomenon.

Plesur, Milton, ed. *Intellectual Alienation in the 1920s*, Lexington,
Mass.: D.C. Heath & Co., 1971. A collection of articles, both
primary and secondary, which examine both literary and other
unhappiness as well as contentment with the American 1920s.

MacDonald, J. Fred, *Don't Touch That Dial!*, Chicago: Nelson-Hall,
1979. The newest and best analysis of the radio and its impact.

Terkel, Studs, *Hard Times*, N.Y.: Pocket Books, 1970. An
excellent oral history as told by Depression survivors.

Warshow, Robert, *The Immediate Experience: Movies, Comics, Theatre,
and Other Aspects of Popular Culture*. N.Y.: Atheneum, 1970. An
excellent collection of this perceptive critic's analysis of movies
and other aspects of popular culture.

n.b. Any reputable survey text in American history is recommended for background.
    At times I have assigned various novels that reflect the *Zeitgeist*, i.e. Sinclair, Upton, *The Jungle;* Dos Passos, John, *Three Soldiers;* Fitzgerald, F. Scott, *This Side of Paradise;* Steinbeck, John, *The Grapes of Wrath*; Mailer, Norman, *The Naked and the Dead*.

Selected background reading.

Browne, Ray B. et al, *Heroes of Popular Culture*, Bowling Green, Ohio: Popular Press, 1972.

Hamel, William M., ed., *The Popular Arts in America: A Reader*. N.Y.: Harcourt, Brace,
Jovanovich, 1972.

Nachbar, Jack, et. al., *The Popular Culture Reader*. Bowling Green,Ohio: Popular Press, 1978.
    A collection of articles that comprise an excellent introduction to the study of popular culture.

Nash, Roderick, ed., *The Call of the Wild, 1900-1916*, N.Y.: Braziller, 1970.

Nye, Russel B., *The Unembarrassed Muse: The Popular Arts in America*, N.Y.: Dial Press, 1970.

Sklar, Robert D., *The Plastic Age, 1917-1930*, N.Y.: Braziller, 1970.

Milton Plesur
Department of History
SUNY/Buffalo

American Studies 050:284
Freud in America
(2 credits—second 7 weeks of 14-week semester)

Introduction

"Freud in America" was designed as a mini-course to be held one night a week during the second half of the 1978 spring semester. At that time the course served to fulfill distribution requirements for all Douglass College students or could be used to provide credits toward completion of the American Studies major. The course was intended to allow students to study the cultural imperatives shaping the popularization and distortion of Freudian doctrine in the United States via an interdisciplinary consideration of psychology, social history, popular literature, drama and film. Initially the course met with resistance from the psychology department when members of that department mistakenly believed that we would be teaching Freudian theory *per se*, but that opposition evaporated when it became clear that Freud in America would concern itself with the cultural impact of Freudianism. In fact, when students in the course were polled with regard to their previous familiarity with actual Freudian texts, none of them, including the psychology majors, had read any. So far the course has been taught once, to an enrollment of thirty-five students drawn from the several campuses of Rutgers University in New Brunswick. It served to acquaint many non-majors with American Studies methodology and to familiarize students with the cultural significance of Freudianism, a useful pedagogical function given the behaviorist orientation of many of the University's psychology department.

Outline of Course
  I. Introduction
    A. Discussion of pervasiveness of Freudianism in American popular culture.
    B. Reasons for popularity of Freudianism in America.
      1. Americans modified Freudian theories and techniques to adapt them to a far more optimistic outlook than Freud had intended.
      2. Erosion of other traditional sources of authority in open, mobile society.
      3. In America psychoanalysis used as therapy for victims of American cult of success.
      4. Introduction of Freudian thought coincided with American rebellion against restrictions of prevailing mores and rise of the "new woman."
      5. Americans unusually prone to seeking expertise to solve personal problems.
    C. The Nineteenth Century Context of Freudianism: the Failure of Somatic Medicine.
      1. Increasing late 19th century concern with "neurasthenia," nervous disorders which seemed to be inevitable price of advancing civilization.
      2. Rigidifying Victorian sexual code frustrated basic human needs in interests of decorum, propriety, respectability.
      3. Failure of somatic medicine to provide cures for neurasthenia and for sexual disorders associated with "civilized" morality.
      4. Arrival of Sigmund Freud to lecture at Clark University in 1909 coincided with crisis of the somatic style of medicine; Freud offered more viable explanation of nervous disorders.
  II. Initial Impact of Freudian Theory.
    A. Comparison of reception of Darwinian theory and Freudian theory in America.
    B. Discussion of Freud's own perceptions of the introduction of his doctrines to an American audience as chronicled in his *On the History of the Psychoanalytic Movement* (1914).
  III. Popularization of Freudianism in the Teens.
    A. As a result of optimistic misinterpretations,

Freudian doctrine appealed to some mind cure
practitioners, academic psychologists disheartened
by failure of somatic medicine, and to Edwin B.
Holt and other child psychologists who hoped to
adapt Freudian insights for application to adjustment
therapy.
B. Greenwich Village bohemians and racicals adopted
Freudianism as a liberating doctrine.
1. Ignored Freud's belief sublimation essential
to civilization.
2. Freudianism distorted to justify sexual experimentation
and free love arrangements.
3. Failure of Village radicals to fuse Marxism
and Freudianism, thereby permitting strands of
political and psychological radicalism to disentangle
in the postwar era.
IV. Freudianism in the Twenties
A. Popularization of Freudianism coincided with
revolution in morals and greater social freedom
for women.
B. Impact of Freudianism upon literature, music,
advertising, film; Herbert Brenon's 1926 film
Dancing Mothers shown in class.
C. Decline in popularity of Freudian explanations
coincides with onset of the Great Depression; economic
issues seem more urgent than psychological ones.
V. The Forties and the Feminine Mystique.
A. Presentation of Betty Friedan's critique of the
renewed popularity of Freudianism in the post-World
War II era.
1. Provided a rationale for demanding that women
retreat from the world of work into motherhood and
domesticity.
2. Biological determinism used to explain new woman
problem in such works as Marynia Farnham and Ferdinand
Lundberg's *Modern Woman: The Lost Sex* (1947) and
Helene Deutsch's *The Psychology of Woman: A
Psychological Interpretation* (1944).
3. Emphasis on individual adjustment rather than social
reform.
B. Analysis of influence of Freudianism and feminine
mystique on 1948. Anatole Litvak film *The Snake
Pit* shown in class.
VI. Impact of Freudianism in Modern America.
A. Discussion of responses of Freud's female followers,
such as Helene Deutsch and Karen Horney, and modern
feminists, such as Juliet Mitchell, Elizabeth Janeway
and Margaret Mead, to Freud's theories of femininity
and female sexuality.

B. Discussion of radical critiques of Freudianism by left wing Freudians such as Wilhelm Reich, Geza Roheim, Herbert Marcuse, Norman O. Brown.

Special Features

Paper Assignment: The course seeks to develop the critical and analytical abilities of the students. The writing requirement consists of a three to five page critical paper on one of the two films, *Dancing Mothers* or *The Snake Pit,* shown in class. The paper is to analyze the elements of popularized Freudianism present in the film chosen. How does the film treat such issues as normality, sexuality, feminine role prescription, therapy and the need for social order? Using the required reading, the students are to place the film within its social context and explain the reasons for its particular interpretation of Freudianism. A detailed question sheet is supplied for each film.

Sample questions for *Dancing Mothers* (1926):

1. What is the significance of the fact that the film begins with a scene on the steamship returning from Europe? What was the popular American image of Europe during the Twenties?
2. What is the social universe of this film? Why does it confine itself to members of a single class?
3. From their behavior aboardship, what can one infer about the relationship between Hugh Westcourt and his daughter Catherine (Kittens)?
4. Why does Westcourt's wife Ethel (Buddy) absent herself from her family's activities? What model of womanhood does she represent?
5. How does Hugh Westcourt compare to the traditional Victorian image of the father? On what does he model his behavior?
6. The actress Clara Bow, who portrays Kittens, was known in her day as the "It Girl." What image of sexuality does she portray? How does this image relate to popularized Freudianism during the Twenties?
7. Why does Ethel Westcourt introduce herself to Gerald Naughton as Yvonne de Bressac? What is the significance of her posing as a French woman? What does speaking French represent?
8. What is the significance of Kittens clutching the book *Dante and Beatrice* while she is dead drunk?
9. Why does Ethel resist appeals from her family to return to her traditional maternal responsibilities?
10. How does *Dancing Mothers* relate to Charlotte Perkins Gilman's view of the place of monogamy in the world of sexolatry?

Final Examination: the final test consists of a comprehensive essay exam in which the students are required to answer two out of the four questions posed.

Test example:

Karen Horney wrote in "Problems of Marriage" (1932): "The generations preceding ours demanded too much renunciation of instincts. We, on the other hand, have the tendency to fear it excessively." How well does Horney's analysis apply to the American reception of Freudianism in the early decades of the twentieth century? How effective as a tool was Freudianism in undermining Victorian civilized morality? Does Horney's analysis correspond to Frederick J. Hoffman's view of American writers like Floyd Dell, Sherwood Anderson and Waldo Frank in *Freudianism and the Literary Mind* (1957)? How does it compare with views of contemporary critics of Freudianism like George Sylvester Viereck, Viola Paradise, Grace Adams, Eleanor Rowland Wembridge and Charlotte Perkins Gilman? Were Americans who argued that repression was unhealthy accurately reflecting Freudian theory or distorting Freudianism for their own ends?

Bibliography

Texts:

Freud, Sigmund. *The History of the Psychoanalytic Movement and Other Papers.* New York: Macmillan, 1972. Freud's own history of the introduction of psychoanalysis to the United States, preceded bv a provocative essay by Philip Rieff on the perils accompanying the rise of psychoanalytic professionalism and orthodoxy.

Hoffman, Frederick J. *Freudianism and the Literary Mind* 1957: reprinted Baton Rouge, La.: Louisiana State University Press, 1967. Insightful analysis of distortions accompanying popularization of Freudianism in America and its adoption by American writers.

Strouse, Jean, ed. *Women and Analysis: Dialogues on Psychoanalytic Views of Femininity.* New York: Dell Publishing Co., Inc./A Laurel Edition, 1974. Excerpts treating the issues of femininity and female sexuality from the writings of Freud, his followers and modern feminists.

Robinson, Paul A. *The Freudian Left: Wilhelm Reich, Geza Roheim, Herbert Marcuse.* New York: Harper & Row/Harper Colophon Books, 1969. Stimulating attempt to set Freudianism in the context of a revolutionary tradition.

Other Texts:

Matthews, F.H. "The Americanization of Sigmund Freud: Adaptations of Psychoanalysis Before 1917." *Journal of American Studies,* I (April, 1967), 39-62.

Burnham, John Chynoweth. "Psychiatry, Psychology and the Progressive Movement." *American Quarterly,* XII (Winter, 1960), 457-465.

Repplier, Agnes. "The Repeal of Reticence." *The Atlantic Quarterly,* CXIII (March, 1914), 297-304.

Glaspell, Susan and George Cram Cook. *Suppressed Desires* (1915). Reprinted in Bennett Cerf and Van H. Cartmell, eds. *Thirty Famous One Act Plays.* Garden City, N.Y.: Garden City Publishing Co., 1942. pp. 327-341.

Adams, Grace. "The Rise and Fall of Psychiatry." *The Atlantic Monthly,* CLIII (Jan., 1924), 82-92.

Kuttner, Alfred B. "Nerves." pp. 427-442 in Harold E. Stearns, ed., *Civilization in the United States: An Inquiry by Thirty Americans.* New York: Harcourt, Brace, 1922. "Is Psycho-Analysis a Science?"
Forum, LXXIII (March, 1925), 302-320.

Paradise, Viola. "The Sex Simplex." *Forum,* LXXIV (July, 1925), 108-111.

Gilman, Charlotte Perkins. "Toward Monogamy." pp. 52-56 in Freda Kirchwey, ed., *Our Changing Morality: A Symposium.* New York: Albert & Charles Boni, 1924.

Watson, John B. "The Myth of the Unconscious: A Behavioristic Exploration." *Harper's Magazine,* CLV (Sept., 1927), 502-508.

Williams, Frankwood E., M.D. "What are Parents For?" *The Survey,* LVII (Dec., 1, 1926), 307-309, 335.

Wile, Ira S., M.D. "As Children See It." *The Survey,* LVII (Dec. 1, 1926) 312-313, 335.

Wembridge, Eleanor Rowland. "Petting and the College Campus." *The Survey,* LIV (July 1, 1925), 393-395.

Friedan, Betty. *The Feminine Mystique.* 1963; reprinted New York: Dell Publishing Co., 1965. Chapter Five: "The Sexual Solipsism of Sigmund Freud," pp. 95-116; Chapter Eight: "The Mistaken Choice," pp. 174-196.

Selected Background Reading:

Haller, John S. and Robin M. Haller. *The Physician and Sexuality in Victorian America.* Urbana: University of Illinois Press, 1974. Details social conservatism of medical profession in treating 19th century neurasthenia, especially feminine nervous disorders.

Hale, Jr., Nathan G. *Freud and the Americans: The Beginnings of Psychonalysis in the United States, 1876-1917.* New York: Oxford University Press, 1971. Excellent scholarly analysis of the collapse of somatic medicine and the subsequent popularization of Freudian theory in the United States.

Ruitenbeck, Hendrik M. *Freud and America*. New York: Macmillan Co., 1966. Sexist and somewhat superficial survey of the impact of Freudian thought on American art, education, child rearing practices, religion; occasionally insightful.
child rearing practices, religion; occasionally insightful.

Shakow, David and David Rapaport, eds. "The Influence of Freud on American Psychology." *Psychological Issues*, Vol. IV, No. 1, Monograph 13 (1964). Special issue comparing reception of Darwinian and Freudian theory, detailing historical background of Freudian theory, and surveying its impact on American psychology.

Leslie Fishbein
American Studies Department
Douglass College
Rutgers/The State University of New Jersey

History 357
History of the American Family and Sexual Mores
(3 Credits—10 Week Quarter)

Introduction

Since coming to Radford University in 1961 I had taught American Social History with a small part of the course devoted to Victorianism and the question of censorship and pornography. During the sixties it became obvious that the "sexual revolution" was becoming a critical area of national social development and especially a significant part of the lives of the students at Radford. Because of certain local school conditions, the climate at the institution made it impossible to offer a course involving sexual mores. By 1974 there was a complete change in administration, and the atmosphere at the university was very conducive to innovative courses and new teaching techniques. Thus this course was developed and approved by administration action during the spring of 1976 and offered for the first time in the winter of 1977.

This course is offered two times each year and in summer school every other year. No other instructor in the department feels qualified to teach the course. The university, which is on the quarter system, has maintained a consistent policy of small classes. The normal enrollment in survey courses is a maximum of forty, and the normal enrollment in upper level classes is between 15 and 25. The average enrollment in this class has been 26 students since the winter of 1977 with 36 students the highest number enrolled.

The course is an elective, not part of the university general education requirements, and is open to any student who has had any six hours in history, either American or World. The course thus far has served as a "service" course; i.e., at least half the students every quarter have been non-history majors. The three hours credit of the course do count toward a history major and/or state certification requirements for teaching history.

Thus far the course has been very important to the department in that the large enrollment has consistently brought up the department's upper level course average enrollment. Because of the "service" nature and student enrollment, the course has been enthusiastically supported by both the department and the administration. The instructor has requested quarterly evaluation of the class by the students, and this has produced periodic needed changes in both reading materials and classroom procedures.

The course has proved beneficial to most students because of the comprehensiveness of the material. The overwhelming majority of students have told they knew nothing of many areas studied (e.g. sex customs in earlier times and Victorianism), and very little about many others (e.g. transsexualism and multifaceted aspects of pornography). In addition two sex tests given by permission of publishers to each student (they do not count as a grade) have proved very helpful to students in helping them to realize how much they do not know about the full range of human sexuality. The students have also indicated to me that they feel the extensive bibliography provided each one will prove valuable in the future. The stated objective of the course at the outset is the hope of acquainting each student not only with an indication that most aspects of the "sexual revolution" have gone on for centuries, but also to suggest various viewpoints of modern problems so each student can think and make intelligent decisions on his or her own.

Outline of Course:
Unit One: Historical development of sexual customs and mores.
Readings: "Medieval Sexual Behavior," in G.R. Taylor, *Sex In History,* Chpt. 2. "Ten Historical Sex Hangups," *Playboy,* February 1979. Passout sheet on the Indian philosophy of Tantra.

Unit Two: Colonial family, child-rearing, women, marriage customs, and sexual attitudes.
Readings: "Infancy and Childhood," "Puritans and Sex," in M. Gordon, *The American Family In Social-Historical Perspective* (2nd ed.), chpts. 9, 17. Passout sheet on bundling.

Unit Three: Early 19th century and Victorian America. The Oneida Community.
Readings: "The Cult of True Womanhood," "The Female World of Love and ritual: Relations between Women in Nineteenth-Century America," "The Spermatic Economy," "What Ought to Be and What Was: Women's Sexuality in the Nineteenth Century," in Gordon, chpts. 15,16,18,19. "Awful Letters, I, II," "Comstock's Yokes," in Hal Sears, *The Sex Radicals,* chpts. 5,8,10. "This Was Sex," in *Hustler,* September 1978. "From Maidenhead to Menopause: Sex Education for Women in Victorian America," *Journal Of Popular Culture,* VI, 1, 49-70. "Dr. Kellogg's Plain Facts for Old and Young" in *Playboy Philosophy,* Vol. 3, pp.135-147. "The Parlor," in *American Heritage,* October 1963 pp.54-64. "Victorianism," in *This Fabulous Century* 1870-1900, pp.186-199. "Another View of Love," in *This Fabulous Century* 1900-1910, pp.166-167. Passout sheet on "Little Rollo."

Unit Four: The 1920s: A breakdown in morals? Ben Lindsay and Companionate Marriage. Miss America contests. Hollywood and sex. The 1930s: Sally Rand.

Readings: "Women," in *This Fabulous Century* 1910-1920, pp.28-41. "Miss America Contests," in *This Fabulous Century* 1920-1930, pp.252-253.

MID TERM EXAMINATION

Unit Five: The Sex Researchers: from Havelock Ellis to the 1980s.
Reading: "Sex Research," L. Kirkendall, *The New Sexual Revolution,* chpt. 5.

Unit Six: "Situation Ethics" and the "New Morality." Premarital sex. Adultery. State sex laws.
Reading: "Many Sex Laws an Invasion of Privacy," in L. Ramer, *Your Sexual Bill of Rights,* chpt. 9. "How New Ideas About Sex Are Changing Our Lives," in J. Delora, *Intimate Life Styles,* pp.80-86. A Karlen, "The Sex Revolution is a Myth," *Saturday Evening Post,* December 28, 1968. "Religion and the New Morality," (panel discussion), *Playboy,* June 1967.

Unit Seven: Sex education: Home and Schools. *The Sex Knowledge Inventory* (Family Life Publications). *Sex Knowledge Test* (Sexology Corporation).

Unit Eight: Birth control, sterilization and abortion. A local obstetrician-gynecologist and a specialist in abortion counseling will both conduct sessions with this unit.
Reading: "Aborting a Fetus: The Legal Right, The Personal Choice," in E. Morrison, *Human Sexuality,* pp. 300-302, 312-315.

Unit Nine: Homosexuality and bi-sexualism.
Readings: Walter Wink, "Biblical Perspectives on Homosexuality," *Christian Century,* Nov., 7, 1979, pp. 1082-1086. "I Am a Lesbian and I Am Beautiful," in DeLora, *Intimate Life Styles,* pp. 212-215.

Unit Ten: Transsexualism, Transvestism, Prostitution, and Strippers.
Readings: "The Transsexuals," *Newsweek,* Nov. 22, 1976, pp. 104-105. "Stripteasing: A Sex-Oriented Occupation," in J. Henslin, *Studies in the Sociology of Sex,* pp. 294-296.

Unit Eleven: Alternate life styles to the family. Group sex.
Readings: "The More the Merrier," "The Future of the Family," in DeLora, *Intimate Life Styles,* pp. 320-326, 398-402. E. LeShan, "The family is *NOT* Dead," *Woman's Day,* August 7, 1979, p. 26. W. Tucker, "4 in a Bed," *New Woman,* July 1971, pp. 74-77.

Unit Twelve: Other aspects of the sexual scene since World War II: Artificial insemination. Massage parlors. Bestiality. Dildoes, vibrators, and other sexual aids. Catalogs. Incest. Gigolos.
Readings: "Bestiality, the Ultimate Taboo, Comes Out into the Open," *Hustler,* Feb., 1976, pp. 35-36. T. Tiede, "Incest Leads Child Abuse Stats," *Burlington County (N.J.) Times,* Dec. 2, 1977, p. 7.

Unit Thirteen: Pornography, obscenity and censorship. Slide presentation on pornography. Court decisions. Presidential Commission Report. Thorough analysis of passout sheets on pornography and crime and censorship and outline of major censorship cases.

Readings: R. Rist, *The Pornography Controversy*, Chs. 4-8, 10-14. "Nude Journalism," *Journal of Popular Culture*, IX, 1, 153-161. "The Whore vs. the Girl Next Door," *Journal of Popular Culture*, IX, 1, 90-94. "The Playmate of the Month: Naked But Nice," *Journal of Popular Culture*, VIII, 2, 328-336.

Special Features

The course is a combination of lecture and class participation. Lectures are given periodically throughout the course; e.g. on historic sexual customs and current medical positions on such aspects of the modern scene as homosexuality and transsexualism. Class participation is largely accomplished through three methods: 1) discussion of library reading assignments and various passout sheets distributed throughout the quarter on such topics as bundling and pornography; 2) psychodramas which are used during discussion of the "new morality" and transsexualism; 3) small group "buzz" sessions. The class is usually broken up into small groups to discuss the issue of homosexuality: is it a "sin" or a "mental disorder," should homosexuals be allowed to teach in the public schools, etc.?

At the beginning of the unit on pornography the class is shown a set of 80 slides ranging from art exhibits in the British Museum and pictures from marriage manuals to pictures from *Hustler* magazine and *Fetish Times*. Before the presentation students are asked to think on such questions as: "What constitutes pornography? Is there any difference between museum objects and pictures from 'Girlie' magazines? Are pictures on venereal disease or dead mutilated bodies in Vietnam "obscene," especially if they are published in a magazine like *Hustler*?

There is a mid-term examination and a final examination, which covers the last half of the quarter. The mid-term is an essay examination usually with one required question involving the reading assignments. For the final examination the students are given a choice of either an essay exam or 55 identification questions over terms and persons. Students are given both exams to read and may answer either one. Choice questions are on all essay exams, and on the identification exam any five may be omitted.

A 15-minute conference is required of all students to go over the mid-term in detail. The purpose is to be sure that 1) the student understands all comments made on the exam by the instructor; 2) the student feels the grade evaluation is a fair one; and, if not the grade may be raised provided the student can fully justify an interpretation on the exam misunderstood by the instructor; 3) the student knows where he or she stands gradewise at this point in the course. Each student is required to re-read the exam questions and relevant material before the conference so an intelligent exchange can take place. The mid-term is an incomplete grade until the conference is held, and no student can take the final exam until such a conference has been completed. The conferences are scheduled within 48 hours of the return of the mid-term.

While neither a book report not a term paper is absolutely required, each student is urged to do one or the other (and a majority of students usually do so). Otherwise it may be noted that the entire grade depends on the mid-term and final. A special book report form is used which puts emphasis on the student's analysis of the thesis of the book and his or her reaction to that thesis. The book report may count 10% of the final grade. A term paper may carry the equivalent of an hour examination and must be thoroughly researched and well-written, utilizing all proper research tools.

Sample question from a final examination: One of the great social issues of our time for many people is whether or not there is a relationship between pornography and crime. In a concrete essay discuss the issue. Show a clear knowledge of the Presidential Commission report as well as various viewpoints reflected in the passout sheets.In the *The Pornography Controversy* pornography is spoken as a "raging menace or a paper tiger?" Explain what is meant by this question and relate it to the question at hand. Conclude your essay with a statement of *your* position at this time and why you hold it.

Bibliography
Textbooks
Ditzim, S. *Marriage, Morals, and Sex in America.* New York: Norton, 1953. Detailed study of how men and women felt about each other during our history.
Gillette, P. *An Uncensored History of Pornography.* Los Angeles: Holloway House, 1965. Concise and popular history with excellent period bibliography.
Gordon, M. (ed.) *The American Family in Social-Historical Perspective.*
  New York: St. Martin's, 1978, 2nd. ed. Essays on aspects of the American family, sexual and otherwise, from the colonial period to the present. (Course text)
Rist, R. (ed.) *The Pornography Controversy.* New Brunswick: Transaction, 1977. Essays on aspects of the problem, including the Presidential Commission Report. (Course text)

Selected Background Reading:
Brecher, E. *The Sex Researchers.* Boston: Little Brown, 1969. Discussion of the major sex researchers from Havelock Ellis to Masters and Johnson.
Broun, H. *Anthony Comstock.* New York: A.C. Boni, 1927. Biography of the most important 19th century American in regard to obscenity and pornography.
Cable, Mary. *American Manners and Morals.* New York: American Heritage, 1969. Popularly written pictorial account of how Americans have behaved and misbehaved.
Friedman, L. *Obscenity.* New York: Chelsea House, 1978. Complete oral arguments before the Supreme Court of major obscenity cases.
Kinsey, A. *Sexual Behavior of the American Male; Sexual Behavior of the American Female.* Philadelphia: W.B. Saunders, 1948, 1953. The classic studies in American sexual behavior.
Sears, H. *The Sex Radicals: Free Love in High Victorian America.* Lawrence, Kansas: Regents Press, 1977. Comprehensive study of the major figures, male and female, who opposed the prevailing Victorian standards and ideas.
Taylor, G.R. *Sex in History.* New York: Harpers, 1954. Concise study of sexual ideas and customs in history, largely the Judeo-Christian tradition.

Edward D. Jervey
Department of History
Radford University

Introduction to Appendices

Appendix A

    This appendix lists specific titles of Popular Culture courses covered in the survey (as reported in Part 1) and shows the departments of the institutions where these courses are being offered. In some cases only the course title is given because additional information was not reported. Courses are arranged according to 18 major categories and are divided by state.

    As a result of a different editing process used to construct the appendix, the number of courses under each category deviates slightly from the figures in Part 1. Fewer cross-listings of one course under two or more categories appear here. In several categories there are more courses than were reported in earlier sections. This discrepancy occurs because courses being offered at ten additional schools gathered in a later case study are included.

Appendix B

    This appendix lists the schools surveyed and the contributors who supplied the information. The number behind the state name denotes the number of courses surveyed in that state. The number in parentheses behind the listing of each school indicates the number of courses in a particular school.

164

Appendix A

Science Fiction

Alabama
SCIENCE FICTION (u). English. Auburn University.
FANTASY AND SCIENCE FICTION (u). English. Spring Hill College.
SCIENCE FICTION (u). English. University of South Alabama.

Arizona
SCIENCE FICTION (u/g). English. University of Arizona.

Arkansas
SCIENCE FICTION (u/g). English. Henderson State University.

California
SCIENCE FICTION (u). English. California State University—Fullerton.
SCIENCE FICTION (u). English. California State University—
    Northridge.
SCIENCE FICTION (u). English. Palomar College.
SCIENCE FICTION (u). English and Comparative Literature; and
    HUMANS, CULTURES, AND SCIENCE FICTION (u).
    Anthropology. San Diego State University.
SCIENCE FICTION AND FANTASY (u/g). English. San Francisco State
    University.
SCIENCE FICTION (u). Humanities and Social Sciences. Harvey
    Mudd College.
LITERATURE OF SCIENCE FICTION (u). English and Modern
    Languages. California State Polytechnic University.
SCIENCE FICTION (u). English. University of California, Berkeley.

Colorado
LITERATURE OF SCIENCE FICTION (u). English. University of
    Southern Colorado.
SCIENCE FICTION (u). English. University of Colorado.

Connecticut
SCIENCE FICTION (u). English. University of New Haven.

Florida
SCIENCE FICTION (u). Literature; and PHYSICS OF SCIENCE
    FICTION (u). Physics. University of Central Florida.
FANTASY, FREUD, AND SCIENCE FICTION; and MEN,
    MONSTERS, AND GODS: THE LITERATURE OF SCIENCE
    FICTION AND FANTASY (u). Language and Literature.
    University of North Florida.
SCIENCE FICTION (u). English. Florida Atlantic University.

Georgia
SCIENCE FICTION (u). English. Augusta College.
SCIENCE FICTION (u). English. Georgia Institute of Technology.
SCIENCE FICTION (u). English. Southern Technical Institute.
HISTORY OF SCIENCE FICTION (u). English. Georgia State University.
SCIENCE FICTION (u). Special Studies. Mercer University.

Illinois
SCIENCE FICTION (u). English. Augustana College.
SCIENCE FICTION AND FANTASY (u). English. Bradley University.
SCIENCE FICTION (u). English. DePaul University.
SCIENCE FICTION (u). English. Illinois Wesleyan University.
SCIENCE FICTION (u). English. Mundelein College.
SCIENCE FICTION (u). English. Northern Illinois University.
SCIENCE AND SCIENCE FICTION (u). English/Physics. Southern
    Illinois University.

Indiana
SCIENCE FICTION (u). English. Indiana State University, Terre Haute.
RECENT WRITING: SCIENCE FICTION (u). English; and
POPULAR CULTURE: SCIENCE FICTION (u). English. Indiana
    University/Purdue University at Indianapolis.
SCIENCE FICTION (u). Humanities. Indiana University, Southeast.
AMERICAN BESTSELLERS (u). American Studies. University of
    Notre Dame.

Iowa
SCIENCE FICTION (u). English. Drake University.
TOPICS IN POPULAR CULTURE: SCIENCE FICTION (u). English;
    and MODERN LITERATURE: SCIENCE FICTION (u). English.
    Iowa State University.

Kentucky
SCIENCE FICTION (u). English. Murray State University.
SCIENCE FICTION AND UTOPIAN LITERATURE. Literature.
    Northern Kentucky University.

Louisiana
SCIENCE FICTION STUDIES (u). English. Louisiana State University.

Maryland
SCIENCE FICTION AND GLOBAL/U.S. FUTURE ALTERNATIVES
    (u). Political Science. Goucher College.
THE WORLD OF SCIENCE FICTION (u). English. Western Maryland
    College.
MODERN FANTASY AND SCIENCE FICTION (u/g). English.
    University of Maryland, College Park.

Massachusetts
SCIENCE FICTION (u). English. Emerson College.

SCIENCE FICTION (u). English. Northeastern University.
SCIENCE FICTION (u). English. Southeastern Massachusetts
University.
SCIENCE FICTION (u). English. Westfield State College.

Michigan
SCIENCE FICTION (u). English/World Literature. Grand Valley
State College.
SCIENCE FICTION (u). Humanities. Michigan Technological University.
SCIENCE FICTION (u). English; and
SCIENCE FICTION (u). Sociology. Central Michigan University.

Minnesota
SCIENCE FICTION (u). English. Mankato State University.
SCIENCE FICTION (u). English. College of St. Thomas.
SCIENCE FICTION (u). English. University of Minnesota,
Morris.

Missouri
SCIENCE FICTION (u). Language and Literature. Missouri Southern
State College.
READINGS IN THE OCCULT AND SCIENCE FICTION (u). English.
Southeast Missouri State University.
SCIENCE FICTION (u). English. Stephens College.
SCIENCE FICTION AND FANTASY LITERATURE (u). Humanities.
University of Missouri, Rolla.

Montana
SCIENCE FICTION (u/g). English. University of Montana, Missoula.

Nebraska
FANTASY AND SCIENCE FICTION (u). English. University of
Nebraska.

New York
SCIENCE FICTION (u). Comparative Literature. Fordham University,
College at Lincoln Center.
SCIENCE FICTION (u). English. Long Island University.
GOVERNMENT: SCIENCE FICTION (u). Government; and
CHEMISTRY: SCIENCE FICTION (u). Chemistry. Skidmore College.
SCIENCE FICTION AND SOCIAL FACT (u). General Studies. SUNY
at Binghamton.
SCIENCE FICTION (u). General Studies. SUNY at New Paltz.
SCIENCE FICTION (u). Center for the Study of Human Dimensions of
Science and Technology. Rensselaer Polytechnic Institute.
SCIENCE FICTION (u). Humanities. School of Visual Arts.
SCIENCE FICTION (u). English. SUNY at Fredonia.

North Carolina
SCIENCE FICTION AS SOCIAL SCIENCE (u). Social Sciences. North

Carolina Wesleyan College.
SCIENCE FICTION (u). English. Western Carolina University.
SCIENCE FICTION (u). English. University of North Carolina at
Wilmington.

Ohio
SCIENCE FICTION (u). Popular Culture. Bowling Green State University.
INTRODUCTION TO SCIENCE FICTION (u). English. Ohio State
University.
POPULAR LITERATURE: SCIENCE FICTION (u). English. Miami
University, Hamilton.
SCIENCE FICTION (u). English. University of Dayton.
SCIENCE FICTION (u). English; and PHYSICS IN SCIENCE
FICTION (u). Physics. Youngstown State University.
POPULAR CULTURE: SCIENCE FICTION (u). English. Miami
University.

Oklahoma.
SCIENCE FICTION AND FANTASY (u/g). English. Oklahoma State
University.
SCIENCE FICTION AND FANTASY (u/g) English. Southwestern State
University.

Oregon
SCIENCE FICTION AND FANTASY (u). English. Oregon State
University.
SCIENCE FICTION (u). English. Southern Oregon State College.

Pennsylvania
SCIENCE FICTION (u). English. Pennsylvania State University,
University Park.
SCIENCE FICTION (u). English. Cabrini College.
SCIENCE FICTION (u). English. Lehigh University.

South Carolina
SCIENCE FICTION (u). English. University of South Carolina,
Aiken.
SCIENCE FICTION (u). English. University of South Carolina, Columbia.
SCIENCE FICTION (u). English. Clemson University.

South Dakota
SCIENCE FICTION (u). English. Black Hills State College.

Tennessee
SCIENCE FICTION AND FANTASY (u). English. Middle Tennessee
University.
SCIENCE FICTION (u). English. Tennessee Wesleyan College.

Texas
SPECULATIVE FICTION IN POPULAR CULTURE (u). English. Austin
College.

SCIENCE FICTION (u). English. Texas Christian University.
SCIENCE FICTION AND FANTASY (u). English. Trinity University.
SCIENCE FICTION (u). English. West Texas State University.
SCIENCE FICTION (u). English. Rice University.
SCIENCE FICTION (u). English. East Texas State University.

Utah
SCIENCE AND FANTASY FICTION (u). English. Utah State University.

Vermont
SCIENCE FICTION (u). English. College of St. Joseph the Provider.
SCIENCE FICTION AND FANTASY LITERATURE (u). English.
   University of Vermont.

Virginia
READINGS IN SCIENCE FICTION (u). Interdisciplinary Studies.
   University of Richmond.
RELIGION AND SCIENCE FICTION (u). Philosophy and Religion.
   George Mason University.

West Virginia
SCIENCE FICTION (u). English. West Liberty State College.
SCIENCE FICTION: CONCEPTS AND CONSEQUENCES (u).
   Freshman Studies. Bethany College.

Wisconsin
UTOPIAN AND SCIENCE FICTION LITERATURE (u). English.
   Milwaukee Area Technical College.
SEMINAR IN SCIENCE FICTION (u). English. Northland College.
SCIENCE FICTION (u). English. University of Wisconsin, River Falls.
SPECULATIVE FICTION (u). English. University of Wisconsin, Stevens
   Point.
HELLS AND HEAVENS IN SCIENCE FICTION (u). English. University
   of Wisconsin, Superior.
SCIENCE FICTION: VISION OF THE FUTURE (u). English. University
   of Wisconsin, Whitewater.

Detective Fiction

Alabama
THE DETECTIVE STORY (u). English. Spring Hill College.

California
MYSTERY NOVEL (u). Comparative Literature. UCLA.
DETECTIVE FICTION (u). English. California State University,
   Fullerton.
MYSTERY AND MURDER IN FICTION (u). English. Immaculate Heart
   College.
SHERLOCK HOLMES (u). English and Comparative Literature. San
   Diego State University.

Connecticut
DETECTIVE FICTION (g). English. University of Hartford.

Florida
TOLKIEN AND FRIENDS (u). Language and Literature; and
  NOVELS OF MYSTERY AND SUSPENSE (u). Language and
  Literature. University of North Florida.
DETECTIVE FICTION (u). English. Florida Atlantic University.

Georgia
DETECTIVE FICTION (u). English. Georgia Institute of Technology.

Illinois
DETECTIVE FICTION (u). English. Augustana College.
MYSTERY AND DETECTIVE FICTION (u). English DePaul University.
DETECTIVE HERO IN POPULAR FICTION AND FILM (u). English.
  Mundelein College.
DETECTIVE FICTION (u). English. Northern Illinois University.
DETECTIVE FICTION (u). English. Southern Illinois University.

Indiana
DETECTIVE FICTION (u). English. Indiana State University, Terre
  Haute.
POPULAR CULTURE: DETECTIVE FICTION (u). English. Indiana
  University/Purdue University at Indianapolis.
DETECTIVE, MYSTERY AND HORROR FICTION (u). English. Indiana
  University Southeast.

Iowa
MANOR HOUSES AND MEAN STREETS: THE DETECTIVE IN
  FICTION (u). American Studies. Grinnell College.
POPULAR CULTURE: DETECTIVE FICTION (u). English. Iowa State
  University.

Kentucky
MYSTERY AND DETECTIVE FICTION (u). English. Murray State
  University.

Louisiana
DETECTIVE FICTION (u). English. Louisiana State University.

Maryland
MYSTERY NOVELS (g). English. Morgan State University.
POPULAR NOVEL: DETECTIVE (u/g). English. Western Maryland
  College.

Massachusetts
DETECTIVE STORY (u). American Studies. Brandeis University.
DETECTIVE STORY (u). English. Southeastern Massachusetts
  University.

Michigan
DETECTIVE FICTION (u). English-World Literature. Grand Valley
   State College.

Minnesota
DETECTIVE NOVEL (u). American Studies. St. Olaf College.
THE ANNALS OF CRIME: DETECTIVE FICTION (u/g). English; and
   PARTNERS IN CRIME: A.C. DOYLE'S HOLMES AND WATSON
   (u/g). English. College of St. Thomas.

Missouri
DETECTIVE FICTION (u). English. University of Missouri, Rolla.

Nebraska
DETECTIVE FICTION (u). English. University of Nebraska.

New Jersey
DETECTIVE FICTION (u). English. Fairleigh Dickinson University.
DETECTIVE FICTION (u). English. St. Peter's College.

New York
MYSTERY AND DETECTIVE FICTION (u/g). English. University of
   Rochester.
DETECTIVE FICTION (u). English. Colgate University.
DEVELOPMENT OF DETECTIVE GENRE (u). Humanities. School of
   Visual Arts.
THE DETECTIVE NOVEL (u). English. SUNY at Fredonia.

North Carolina
DETECTIVE FICTION (u). English. University of North Carolina,
   Wilmington.

Ohio
DETECTIVE FICTION (u). Popular Culture. Bowling Green State
   University.
POPULAR CULTURE: DETECTIVE FICTION (u). English. Miami
   University.

Oklahoma
DETECTIVE FICTION (u). English. University of Oklahoma.
MYSTERY AND DETECTIVE FICTION (u/g). English. Southwestern
   State University.

Oregon
DETECTIVE CRIME NOVELS (u). English. Oregon State University.
DETECTIVE FICTION (u). English/Criminology. Southern Oregon
   State College.

Pennsylvania
POPULAR DETECTIVE FICTION (u). English. Gannon College.
DETECTIVE FICTION (u). English. University of Scranton.

Tennessee
DETECTIVE FICTION (u). English. Tennessee Wesleyan College.

Texas
DETECTIVE AND SUSPENSE FICTION (u/g). English. Texas Christian
    University.
DETECTIVE FICTION (u). English. Rice University.

West Virginia
COWBOYS, GANGSTERS, AND PRIVATE EYES (u). Freshman Studies.
    Bethany College.

Wisconsin
DETECTIVE FICTION (u). English. University of Wisconsin,
    River Falls.
MYSTERY LITERATURE (u). English. University of Wisconsin,
    Stevens Point.

Popular Literary Genres

Alabama
POPULAR LITERATURE (u), English. Auburn University.
TOPICS IN POPULAR LITERATURE (u). English. University of
    Southern Alabama.

Arizona
POPULAR LITERATURE (g). English. Northern Arizona University.

Arkansas
POPULAR LITERATURE (u). English. Arkansas State University.

California
LITERATURE AND POPULAR CULTURE (u). English. University of
    California, Berkeley.
POPULAR FICTION (u). English. California State University,
    Fullerton.
AMERICAN POPULAR LITERATURE (u). Comparative Literature; and
    SPECIAL GENRES (u). English; and THE MYSTERY NOVEL (u).
    Humanities. UCLA

Colorado
SPECIAL TOPICS (u). English. USAF Academy.
POPULAR LITERATURE TOPICS (u). English; and SEMINAR IN
    POPULAR LITERARY GENRES (g). English. Western State
    College.

Connecticut
NARRATIVE FORMULAS IN FICTION AND FILM (u). English.
    University of Connecticut, Storrs.

Delaware
POPULAR FICTION (u). English/History. University of Delaware.

Florida
STUDIES IN CONTEMPORARY FICTION (g). English. University of Central Florida.
POPULAR LITERATURE AND SOCIAL ISSUES (u). Language and Literature. University of North Florida.

Illinois
POPULAR AMERICAN LITERATURE (u). English. Augustana College.
POPULAR FICTION (u). English. DePaul University.
SPECIAL TOPICS IN LITERATURE (u). English. Illinois Wesleyan University.
TOPICS IN LITERATURE (u). English. Mundelein College.
SCIENCE AND DETECTIVE FICTION (u). English. Northern Illinois University.
POPULAR LITERATURE IN AMERICA (u). American Studies. Southern Illinois University.

THE WESTERN IN FILM AND FICTION (u). English. Bradley University.

Indiana
DETECTIVE, MYSTERY AND HORROR FICTION (u). English— Indiana, Southwest.
POPULAR LITERATURE (u). English. Indiana State University.

Iowa
POPULAR LITERATURE (u/g). English. University of Iowa.

Kansas
POPULAR LITERATURE (u). English. Baker University.

Maryland
POPULAR NOVEL (u/g). English. Western Maryland College.

Michigan
CURRENT TOPICS IN LITERATURE (u). English. Oakland University.
POPULAR LITERARY GENRES (u). English. Michigan State University.

Minnesota
POPULAR LITERARY GENRES (u). English; and THE WESTERN (u). English. Mankato State University.
TOPICS IN ENGLISH AND AMERICAN LITERATURE (u/g). English. University of Minnesota.
THE HORROR STORY (u). Language and Literature (u). Missouri Southern State College.

Nebraska
POPULAR LITERATURE (u/g). English. Kearny State College.

New Jersey
POPULAR LITERATURE. English. Fairleigh Dickinson University.

New York
POPULAR LITERARY GENRES (u). Humanities. Fordham University,
   College at Lincoln Center.
MODERN FICTION: POPULAR GENRES (u). English. SUNY at New
   Paltz.

North Carolina
GENERAL FICTION (u). English. University of North Carolina,
   Wilmington.

Ohio
TOPICS AND GENRE (u), English; and INTRODUCTION TO
   POPULAR LITERATURE (u). Popular Culture; and
   POPULAR LITERATURE (u). Popular Culture; and
   POPULAR LITERATURE GENRES (u/g). Popular Culture.
   Bowling Green State University.
CONTEMPORARY FICTION (g). English. Youngstown State University.
POPULAR GENRES (u). English. Miami University.
POPULAR GENRES (u). English. Wright State University.
SPECIAL LITERARY TOPICS (u). English. Findlay College.

Oklahoma
CREATIVE WRITING CONFERENCE: POPULAR GENRES (u). English
   and Creative Studies. Central State University.

Oregon
POPULAR LITERARY GENRES (u). English. Oregon State University.
POPULAR LITERARY GENRES (u). English. Southern Oregon State
   College.

South Dakota
TOPICS IN POPULAR LITERATURE (u). English; and WESTERN
NOVEL
   (u). English. Black Hills State College.

Tennessee
THE WESTERN NOVEL (u). English. Tennessee Wesleyan College.

Texas
SPECIAL TOPICS IN FICTION (u). English. Abilene Christian
   University.
TOPICS IN POPULAR LITERATURE (u). English. Dallas Eastfield
   College.

POPULAR LITERATURE (u). English. North Texas State University.
TOPICS IN POPULAR LITERATURE (u). English, Classics,
Philosophy. University of Texas, San Antonio.
THE WESTERN (u/g). English; and THE GANGSTER IN FILM
AND FICTION (u). English/Radio-TV-Film. Texas Christian
University.

Virginia
TOPICS IN POPULAR LITERATURE (u). American Studies. Lynchburg
College.

West Virginia
COWBOYS, GANGSTERS AND PRIVATE EYES (u). Freshman Studies;
and THE WESTERN (u). English. Bethany College.

Wisconsin
THE CONTEMPORARY NOVEL (u). English. University of Wisconsin,
Whitewater.
MYSTERY LITERATURE (u). English—Stevens Point.

Literature—other Course Types

Arizona
AMERICAN WAR LITERATURE (u/g). English; and WOMEN IN
LITERATURE (u/g). English. University of Arizona.
POPULAR CHRONICLES (u). American Studies. Northern Arizona
University.

Arkansas
AMERICAN ETHNIC LITERATURE (u/g) English. Henderson State
University.

California
CONTEMPORARY SOCIAL ISSUES (u). English; and UTOPIAN
LITERATURE (u). English; and EPIC LITERATURE (u).
English. Palomar College.
AMERICAN POPULAR HUMOR (u). American Studies; and
AMERICAN COMIC WRITERS (u). English/American Studies.
San Diego State University.
LITERATURE OF MYTH AND ORAL TRADITION (u). English; and
LITERATURE AND SOCIETY (u). English; and
SEXUAL STANCES IN MODERN FICTION (u). Humanities;
and INTRODUCTION TO SPECIAL GENRES (u). English; and
WOMEN IN FRENCH LITERATURE (u). French. UCLA.

Colorado
LITERATURE OF PSYCHIC PHENOMENA (u) English. University of
Southern Colorado.
IMAGES OF WOMEN IN LITERATURE (u). English. University of
Colorado.

Connecticut
LITERATURE FOR ADOLESCENTS (u). English; and THE GENESIS
   OF AMERICAN LITERARY MYTHOLOGY (u). English;
   and AFRO-AMERICAN NARRATIVE (u). Center for Afro-
   American Studies and English. Wesleyan University.
CHILDREN'S LITERATURE (u). English; and NINETEENTH
   CENTURY CHILDREN'S BOOKS (u). English; and
   CHILDREN'S LITERATURE AND THE MEDIA (g). English.
   University of Connecticut.

Delaware
CULTURE OF THE 1960's (u). English. University of Delaware.

Florida
ETHNIC LITERATURE IN AMERICA (u). English; and MEDIA
   AND POPULAR LITERATURE (g). English. University of Central
   Florida.
AMERICAN LITERARY MOTIFS (u). Language and Literature; and
   STUDIES IN POPULAR CULTURE (u). Language and Literature;
   and GOING NOWHERE: RECENT AMERICAN LITERATURE (u).
   Language and Literature. University of North Florida.
LITERATURE OF FANTASY (u). English. Florida Atlantic University.

Georgia
LITERATURE OF SPORTS (u). English. Georgia Institute of Technology.

Hawaii
SPORTS AND LITERATURE (u). American Studies. University
   of Hawaii.

Illinois
THE LITERATURE OF WALKING (u). English. Augustana College.
COMEDY IN FILM AND FICTION (u). English and Foreign Languages;
   and GOTHIC IN FILM AND FICTION (u). English; and
   FANTASY LITERATURE (u). English; and AMERICAN HEROES
   English. Bradley University.
ETHNIC LITERATURE (u). Humanities. DePaul University.
LITERATURE AND FILM (u). English. Northern Illinois University.
AMERICAN CHARACTER (u). English; and AMERICAN HUMOR
   AND SATIRE (u). English; and SOCIAL—CULTURAL
   FACTORS IN CONTEMPORARY BLACK LIFE (u).
   Sociology; and SONG AND POETRY (u). English and
   Music. Southern Illinois University.

Indiana
AMERICAN BESTSELLERS (u). American Studies. University
   of Notre Dame.
WOMEN IN LITERATURE (u). English; and LITERATURE OF
HORROR
   (u). English; and FEMININE LITERATURE (u). English.
   Indiana University/Purdue University at Indianapolis.

WOMEN IN LITERATURE (u). English. Indiana University—Southeast.

Iowa
SELECTED TOPICS IN POPULAR CULTURE (u). English; and
STUDIES IN ETHNIC LITERATURE: AMERICAN INDIAN
(u). English; and CONTEMPORARY AFRO—AMERICAN
LITERATURE (u/g). English. Iowa State University.

Kentucky
FILM AND LITERATURE (u). English; and LITERATURE
OF SUPERNATURAL (u). English; and LITERATURE OF
FARM AND VILLAGE (u). English; and KENTUCKY LITERATURE
(u). English; and WESTERN AMERICAN LITERATURE (u).
English; and LITERATURE OF AMERICAN INDIAN (u). English;
and MINORITY LITERATURE (u). English. Murray State
University.
CONTEMPORARY LITERATURE (u). Comparative Literature; and
IMAGES OF WOMEN IN LITERATURE (u). English; and
BASEBALL LITERATURE (u). English. University of Kentucky.

Louisiana
LITERATURE OF THE SUPERNATURAL (u). Languages. Northwestern
State University.
THE FIFTIES (u). English. Louisiana State University.
AMERICAN HUMOR (u). English; and COMMUNICATION
AND CULTURE (u). English. University of
Southwestern Louisiana.

Massachusetts
AMERICA OBSERVED (u). English; and WOMEN AND
LITERATURE (u). English. Emerson College.
SMALL TOWN IN AMERICAN LITERATURE (u). English; and
LITERATURE OF AMERICAN WEST (u). English. Merrimack
College.
LITERATURE OF THE '60s AND '70s (u). English; and
CHILDREN'S LITERATURE (u). English; and THE LITERATURE
OF SPORTS (u). English. University of Lowell.

Michigan
LITERATURE AND FILM (u). English; and SEMINAR IN
AMERICAN LITERATURE AND CULTURE (u). English.
Michigan State University.
WITCHCRAFT TRADITION IN LITERATURE (u). English.
Central Michigan University.

Minnesota
NINETEENTH CENTURY POPULAR FICTION (g). English; and
CONTEMPORARY AMERICAN NOVELS: FICTIONS OF THE '70s
(u). English. College of St. Thomas.

BESTSELLERS OF THE '60s AND '70s (u). English. University
of Minnesota, Morris.

Nebraska
POLICEMAN AS FICTIONAL HERO (u). English; and
ANALYSIS OF ROCK LYRICS (u). English; and
BESTSELLERS (u). English; and LITERATURE
AND MASS MEDIA (u). English; and POPULAR
LITERATURE (u). English. University of Nebraska.

New Jersey
SATIRE, CARICATURE AND FARCE (u). English; and
BLACK AMERICAN LITERATURE (u). English; and
MULTI—ETHNIC LITERATURE IN AMERICA (u). English.
Rider College.

New York
WORDS AND IMAGES: PRINT (u). English; and
BALLAD REVIVALS (g). English. SUNY at New Paltz.
THE IDEA OF PROGRESS IN AMERICA (u). English; and
LITERATURE OF THE HOLOCAUST (u). English. Colgate University.
WOMEN IN LITERATURE (u). English; and
CONTEMPORARY URBAN WRITERS (u). English; and
AMERICAN MINORITY LITERATURE (u). English. Herbert H.
Lehman, CUNY.
THE IMAGE OF BLACKS IN AMERICAN LITERATURE (u). English;
and WOMEN AND VICTORIAN LITERATURE (u). English.
Vassar College.
FANTASY AND THE MODERN LITERARY FAIRY TALE (g). English.
SUNY at Buffalo.

North Carolina
CHILDREN'S LITERATURE (u). English; and LITERATURE
FOR ADOLESCENTS (u). English. University of North
Carolina, Charlotte.
LITERATURE OF THE SUPERNATURAL (u). English. University
of North Carolina, Wilmington.

North Dakota
STAR TREK (u). English; and WOMEN AND LITERATURE (u).
English. University of North Dakota.

Ohio
STUDIES IN POPULAR FICTION (u). English. University of
Dayton.
WOMEN IN LITERATURE (u). English; and SELECT TOPICS
IN JOURNALISM (u). English; and CONTEMPORARY
FICTION (g). English. Youngstown State University.

AMERICAN FRONTIER AND WESTERN LITERATURE (u). English; and GREAT CONTEMPORARY ISSUES (u). English. Kent State University.
MAGAZINES AND AMERICAN CULTURE (u). Popular Culture. Bowling Green State University.

Oklahoma
WESTERN LITERATURE (u). English; and SPORTS IN LITERATURE (u). English. University of Oklahoma.

Oregon
AMERICAN SPORTS LITERATURE (u). English. Oregon State University.
AMERICAN HISTORY THROUGH NOVELS (u). History. Southern Oregon State College.

Pennsylvania
AMERICAN LITERARY UTOPIAS (u). English; and MUSIC AND WORDS (u). General Programs, Music, and English. Haverford College.
AMERICAN HUMOR (u). Widener College.
LITERATURE OF THE OCCULT (u). Comparative Literature. Pennsylvania State University, Abington.

South Dakota
LITERATURE OF THE AMERICAN WEST (u). English; and MYTHOLOGY AND LITERATURE (u). English. South Dakota State University.

Tennessee
POPULAR LITERATURE OF THE 20TH CENTURY (g). English; and AMERICAN HUMOR (u). English; and LITERATURE AND FILM (u). English. Middle Tennessee University.
SUPERSTITION, SCIENCE, AND MYSTICISM (u). Tennessee State University.
GOTHIC FICTION (u). English; and BESTSELLERS (u). English. Tennessee Wesleyan College.

Texas
SPORTS AS LITERATURE AND PHILOSOPHY (u). English/Philosophy; and GHOSTIES, GHOULIES, BEASTIES (u). English; and FANTASY AND LITERATURE (u). English; and BEAT LITERATURE (u). English. Dallas Eastfield College.
THE AMERICAN BESTSELLER (u). School of Arts and Humanities. University of Texas, Dallas.
AMERICAN SPORT FICTION (u). English. Texas Christian University.

Utah
MAJOR AMERICAN THEMES (u). Utah State University
THE LITERATURE OF THE AMERICAN WEST (u). English; and

LITERATURE OF THE LATTER-DAY SAINTS (u). English;
and AMERICAN ETHNIC LITERATURE (u). English.
Brigham Young University.
STUDIES IN FORM LITERATURE (u/g). English. University of Utah.

Vermont
WOMEN IN LITERATURE (u). English. University of Vermont.

West Virginia
MURDER, MANIA, AND MYSTERY (u). English; and LOVE,
SEX AND MARRIAGE (u). English; and SPECIAL TOPICS
(u). English. West Liberty State College.

Wisconsin
BESTSELLING BOOKS (u). English. University of Wisconsin, Superior.
WOMEN IN LITERATURE (u). English; and SPORTS IN LITERATURE
(u). English. University of Wisconsin, Stevens Point.

TV/Radio

Alabama
FOUNDATIONS OF BROADCASTING (u). Communications. Auburn
University.

Arizona
INTRODUCTION TO TELECOMMUNICATIONS (u). Speech/Theatre.
Northern Arizona University.

California
HISTORY AND PHILOSOPHY OF AMERICAN MASS
COMMUNICATION (u). Communications. California
State University, Fullerton.
POLITICAL SOCIALIZATION THROUGH FILMS AND TELEVISION
(u).   Political Science. California State University, North Ridge.
TELEVISION TODAY: A CRITICAL PERSPECTIVE (u). Art; and
FILM, TELEVISION, SOCIETY (u). Art. Immaculate Heart
College.
TV: A MODERN ART FORM (u). Radio/Television. Palomar College.
THEORY OF RADIO AND TELEVISION CRITICISM (u).
Communications. Pitzer College.
HISTORY OF BROADCASTING (u). Theatre Arts; and
PROBLEMS AND ISSUES IN BROADCAST MEDIA (u). Theatre Arts;
and FILM, TELEVISION, AND SOCIETY (u). Theatre Arts.
UCLA.
SURVEY OF AMERICAN MASS MEDIA (u). Journalism. California
State College at Los Angeles.
MASS MEDIA AND POPULAR CULTURE (u). Communication Arts; and
INTRODUCTION TO MASS MEDIA (u). Communication Arts; and

MASS MEDIA AND SOCIETY (u). Communication Arts. University of San Francisco.

Colorado
HISTORY OF RADIO BROADCASTING (u). Communication Arts. Regis College.
CONTEMPORARY MASS MEDIA (u). Journalism; and MASS MEDIA AND SOCIETY (u/g). Communication. University of Colorado.

Connecticut
TELEVISION (u). Sociology. Wesleyan University.

Delaware
COMPARATIVE AND INTERNATIONAL BROADCASTING (u/g). Communications. University of Delaware.

Florida
RADIO, TELEVISION AND SOCIETY (u). RTV; and INTERNATIONAL BROADCASTING (u). Radio/TV. University of Central Florida.
BROADCAST JOURNALISM (u). Radio/TV. University of North Florida.
BROADCASTING AND SOCIETY (u). Communications. Florida Atlantic University.

Idaho
INTRODUCTION TO RADIO-TV BROADCASTING (u). Radio/TV. University of Idaho.

Illinois
MEDIA STUDIES: RADIO-TV (u). Communications. DePaul University.
THE DOCUMENTARY IN FILM AND BROADCASTING (u). Theatre. Illinois State University.
BROADCASTING AND SOCIETY (u). Speech. Speech Communication; and HISTORY OF BROADCASTING (u/g). Speech Communication. Northern Illinois University.

Indiana
POPULAR CULTURE: TV (u). English. Indiana University/Purdue University of Indianapolis.
FOUNDATIONS OF BROADCASTING (u). Communication Arts. Indiana University, South Bend.
MYTHOLOGY OF TELEVISION (u). American Studies; and TELECOMMUNICATIONS (u). American Studies. Notre Dame University.

Iowa
TELEVISION AND SOCIETY (u/g). Broadcasting and Film. University of Iowa.

TELEVISION AND THE PUBLIC ETHIC (u/g). Speech/Theatre.
Luther College.
TV'S VISION (u). English. Northwestern College.
THE GREAT ESCAPE: RADIO, THE MOVIES, AND DEPRESSION
AMERICA (u). Iowa State University.

Kentucky
LIVE TV DRAMA (u). Telecommunications. Kentucky Wesleyan.
CHILDREN'S TELEVISION (u). Communications; and
BROADCASTING TODAY (u). Communications; and
FILM IN TELEVISION (u). Communications; and
ALTERNATIVE MODES OF BROADCASTING (u). Communi-
cations. Northern Kentucky University.

Louisiana
INTRODUCTION TO BROADCAST MEDIA (u). Speech; and
RADIO AND TV IN SOCIETY (u/g). Speech. Louisiana
State University.
SURVEY OF BROADCASTING (u). Speech; and
SENIOR SURVEY IN BROADCASTING (u). Speech; and
SEMINAR IN COMMERCIAL BROADCASTING (g). Speech.
University of Southwestern Louisiana.

Maryland
TV AND AMERICAN CULTURE (u). American Studies.
University of Maryland, Baltimore County.
INTRODUCTION TO RADIO AND TELEVISION (u). Radio/TV/Film;
and PUBLIC BROADCASTING (u). Radio/TV/Film; and
TELEVISION AND POLITICS (u). Radio/TV/Film; and
BROADCAST CRITICISM (u/g). Radio/TV/Film; and
SPECIAL SEMINARS IN BROADCASTING (g). Radio/TV/Film.
University of Maryland, College Park.

Michigan
TELECOMMUNICATION IN THE U.S. (u). Telecommunication; and
TELECOMMUNICATION PROCESS (u). Telecommunication; and
HISTORY AND ECONOMICS OF TELECOMMUNICATION—
CABLE COMMUNICATION (u). Telecommunication; and
INTERNATIONAL TELECOMMUNICATION (u/g). Tele-
communication; and TRENDS AND ISSUES IN TELECOMMUNICA—
TION (g). Telecommunication; and PUBLIC BROADCASTING (g).
Telecommunication; and EVALUATION AND CRITICISM
IN BROADCASTING AND FILM (g). Telecommunication; and
GLOBAL BROADCASTING (g). Telecommunication. Michigan
State University
SPECIAL TOPICS IN BROADCAST CONTENT (u/g). Speech and
Dramatic Arts; and MUSIC IN BROADCASTING (g).
Speech and Dramatic Arts. Central Michigan University.

Minnesota
HISTORY OF BROADCASTING (u). Speech; and
DOCUMENTARY IN FILM AND TELEVISION (u/g). Speech;
and SEMINAR IN COMMUNICATIONS MEDIA (u). Speech.
University of Minnesota, Duluth.

Missouri
MASS COMMUNICATION: RADIO (u).Radio/TV/Film; and
MASS COMMUNICATION: TELEVISION (u). RTVF. Stephens
College.

New Hampshire
TV: A CRITICAL APPROACH (u). Drama. Dartmouth College.

New Jersey
HISTORY OF TELEVISION (u). Fine Arts. Fairleigh Dickinson
University, Madison.
TELECOMMUNICATIONS SEMINAR (u). Communications; and
CONTEMPORARY TV ANALYSIS AND CRITICISM (u).
Communications. Fairleigh Dickinson University,
Teaneck.
TELEVISION AS AN ART FORM (u). Fine Arts. Montclair State
College.
DEVELOPMENT AND SIGNIFICANCE OF CABLE TV (u). Seton
Hall University.

New Mexico
PRINCIPLES OF BROADCAST NEWS (u). Journalism.
New Mexico State University.

New York
TELEVISION CRITICISM (u). Humanities; and
DEVELOPMENT OF NETWORK TELEVISION PROGRAMMING (u).
Humanities. Fordham University, College at
Lincoln Center.
HISTORY AND DEVELOPMENT OF RADIO AND TV IN AMERICAN
SOCIETY (u). Speech; and TV AND AMERICAN CULTURE
(u). English. SUNY at New Paltz.
INTRODUCTION TO BROADCAST MEDIA (u). Speech; and
SPECIAL PROBLEMS IN RADIO AND TELEVISION (u). Speech.
SUNY at Fredonia.
CONTEMPORARY ISSUES IN BROADCASTING (u). Journalism.
SUNY at Buffalo.

North Dakota
STUDY IN RADIO—TV CRITICISM (u). Speech; and STAR TREK
(u). English; and AMERICAN TV (u). English. University
of North Dakota.

Ohio
POPULAR CULTURE AND THE MEDIA (u). Popular Culture; and
   TELEVISION AS POPULAR CULTURE (u). Popular Culture;
   and ELECTRIC MEDIA (u). Popular Culture;
   and RADIO AND TELEVISION BROADCASTING (u).
Radio/TV/Film;
   and BROADCAST HISTORY (u). Radio/TV/Film; and
PROCESSES AND EFFECTS OF MASS COMMUNICATION (u).
   Radio/TV/FILM. Bowling Green State University.
ELEMENTS OF TELECOMMUNICATION (u). Communication; and
   BROADCASTING IN AMERICA (u). Communication;
   and INTERNATIONAL BROADCASTING (u). Communication;
   and ADVANCED STUDES IN TELEVISION AND RADIO (g).
   Communication. Ohio State University.
SURVEY OF RADIO/TV (u). Speech; and BROADCAST
   HISTORY (u). Speech; and SENIOR COLLOQUIM IN
   TELECOMMUNICATION (u). Speech; and BROADCAST
   DOCUMENTARY (u). Speech; and SPECIAL TOPICS
   IN TELECOMMUNICATION (u/g). Speech; and BROADCAST
   CRITICISM (g). Speech; and BROADCAST COMMUNICATION
   THEORY (g). Speech. Kent State University.

Oregon
INTRODUCTION TO BROADCASTING (u). Speech Communications;
   and BROADCAST PROGRAMMING (u). Speech Communications.
   Oregon State University.

Pennsylvania
OLD TIME RADIO (u). Albright College.
SURVEY OF RADIO—TV BROADCASTING HISTORY (u). Speech and
   Drama. Millersville State College.
HISTORY OF AMERICAN TELEVISION (u). Speech Communication.
   Pennsylvania State University, Abington.
THE MASS MEDIA AND SOCIETY (u). Journalism; and
   WOMEN, MINORITIES, AND THE MEDIA (u). Journalism;
   and CULTURAL ASPECTS OF THE MASS MEDIA (u). Journalism;
   and THE MASS MEDIA AND THE PUBLIC (u/g). Journalism;
   and THE HISTORY OF AMERICAN TELEVISION (u). Speech
   Communication; and THE DRAMATIC ARTS IN THE MASS MEDIA
   (u). Theatre Arts; and DOCUMENTARY IN FILM AND
   TELEVISION (u/g). Theatre Arts. Pennsylvania
   State University.

South Dakota
INTRODUCTION TO RADIO AND TELEVISION (u). Journalism/Mass
   Communications. South Dakota State University.

Tennessee
MASS MEDIA AND SOCIETY (u). Journalism; and
   MASS COMMUNICATIONS (u). Sociology. East Tennessee
   State University.

TRENDS IN BROADCAST COMMUNICATION (u). Journalism; and
RADIO, TV, AND FILM IN SOCIETY (u). Speech and Drama; and
HISTORY OF AMERICAN BROADCASTING (u). Speech and
Drama. Memphis State University.

Texas
HISTORY OF ELECTRONIC MEDIA (g). Radio/TV/Film. North
Texas State University.
INTRODUCTION TO BROADCASTING (u). Speech and Drama; and
RADIO—TV COMMERCIAL PRACTICES (u). Speech and Drama;
and COMPARATIVE BROADCAST SYSTEMS (u). Speech and Drama;
and BROADCASTING SEMINAR (u). Speech and Drama. East
Texas State University.

Virginia
TV: ETHICS FOR HIRE? (u). Religion; and TV AND FILM:
HOLLYWOOD AND THE VALUES OF COMMERCIAL ART
(u/g). English/Religion. University of Richmond.
MASS MEDIA (u). Journalism; and TELECOMMUNICATIONS
(u). Journalism. Washington and Lee University.

Washington
SURVEY OF BROADCASTING (u). Speech. Walla Walla College.

West Virginia
THE TELEVISION GENERATION (u). Freshman Studies. Bethany
College.
TELEVISION PROBLEMS AND CHILDREN (u). Education. University
of West Virginia.
SPECIAL TOPICS (u). Business. West Liberty State College.

Washington, D.C.
FILM AND SOCIETY: TELEVISION DOCUMENTARY (u/g).
Communications. American University.
COMMUNICATIVE EFFECTS OF BROADCAST PROGRAMMING (u).
Speech
and Drama. George Washington University.

Film

Alabama
INTRODUCTION TO FILM (u). Speech/Theatre. Auburn University,
Montgomery.

Arizona
HISTORY OF AMERICAN MOTION PICTURES (u/g). Drama; and
HISTORY OF WORLD MOTION PICTURES (u/g). Drama. University
of Arizona.

Arkansas
MOTION PICTURE APPRECIATION (u). Speech. Arkansas State
University.
SEMINARS ON FILM (u/g). Speech. University of Arkansas,
Fayetteville.

California
SPECIAL TOPICS IN FILM GENRE (u). Film; and THE HISTORY
OF FILM (u). Film; and A CRITIQUE OF MASS MEDIATED
CULTURE: CINEMA AND TELEVISION (u). Special Studies;
and NATIVE AMERICANS AND THE CINEMA (u). Special
Studies. University of California, Berkeley.
FILM GENRES (u). English. California State University, Fresno.
HISTORY AND AESTHETICS OF MOTION PICTURES (u).
Communications; and FILM DIRECTORS AND GENRES
(u). Communications; and THIRTIES AMERICA THROUGH FILMS
(u). American Studies; and THE DARK SIDE OF AMERICAN FILM
(u). American Studies; and ECONOMICS THROUGH CLASSIC
FILMS AND DOCUMENTARIES (u). Economics. California State
University—Fullerton.
HOLLYWOOD AND U.S. HISTORY TO 1900 (u). History; and
HOLLYWOOD AND U.S. HISTORY SINCE 1900 (u). History;
and POLITICAL SOCIALIZATION THROUGH FILMS AND
TELEVISION (u). Political Science. California State
University—Northridge.
MOVIES AND THE CRITICS (u). Art; and MOVIES TODAY (u).
Art; and FILM, TELEVISION, SOCIETY (u). Art;
and AMERICA IN FILM (u). Art; and THE IMAGE OF WOMEN
IN FILM (u). Art. Immaculate Heart College.
FILM SUBJECT (u). Cinema; and HUMANISM IN THE CINEMA
(u). Cinema. Palomar College.
HISTORY THROUGH FILM (u). History. San Diego State
University.
FILM HISTORY (u). Film; and FILM APPRECIATION (u).
Film; and FILM THEORY AND CRITICISM (u). Film; and
FILM AND SOCIETY (u). Film. San Francisco State
University.
ANTHROPOLOGY OF FILM (u). Anthropology; and HISTORY OF
FILM (u/g). Journalism; and TOPICS IN FILM STUDY
(u/g). Journalism; and MASS MEDIA IN SOCIETY (u/g).
Journalism; and DOCUMENTARY FILM (u/g). Journalism;
and COMMUNICATION MEDIA AND SOCIAL CHANGE (u/g).
Journalism. Stanford University.
THE GERMAN FILM IN CULTURAL CONTEXT (u). Germanic
Languages; and ITALIAN CINEMA (u). Italian;
and FILM AND SOCIAL CHANGE (u). Theatre Arts;
and FILM GENRES (u). Theatre Arts; and SEMINAR
IN SOCIAL REALISM IN FILM (g). Theatre Arts; and
FILM, TELEVISION, AND SOCIETY (g). Theatre Arts;
and SEMINAR IN FILM GENRE (g). Theatre Arts. UCLA.
HISTORY OF BROADCASTING AND FILM (u). Broadcasting;

and BROADCASTING AND FILM AS SHAPERS OF THE PUBLIC
MIND (u). Broadcasting. California State College
at Los Angeles.
POLITICS THROUGH FILM (u). Political Science. California Polytechnic
State University.
IMAGES OF WOMEN IN FILM (u). Sociology; and STYLES
OF JAPANESE FILM (u). Asian Studies; and
INTRODUCTION TO MOTION PICTURES (u). Dramatic Arts;
and FRENCH CINEMA (u). French; and WORLD CINEMA (u).
Italian; and HISTORY OF CINEMA (u). Film Studies;
and THE SOCIAL AND ARTISTIC IMPORTANCE OF THE
HOLLYWOOD STUDIO (u). Film Studies; and
DOCUMENTARY FILM (u). Film Studies; and CHARLIE
CHAPLIN, BUSTER KEATON AND THE COMEDY TRADITION
(u). Film Studies; and THE WESTERN SINCE 1950
(u). Film Studies; and AMERICAN FILM (u). Film
Studies; and THE AMERICAN LEFT IN HOLLYWOOD (u).
Film Studies; and HITCHCOCK AND HAWKS (u). Film
Studies; and HEROES, HEROINES AND SEX ROLES IN
HOLLYWOOD FILM (u). Film Studies; and THE MUSICAL
FILM (u). Film Studies; and READINGS IN FILM STUDIES
(u). Film Studies. University of California, Santa
Barbara. INTRODUCTION TO THE FILM (u). Communication
Arts. California State Polytechnic University.
THE HISTORY OF FILM (u). Drama. University of
California—Irvine.

Colorado
THEMES AND GENRES IN FILM (u). Communication Arts; and
FILM COMEDY (u). Communication Arts. Regis College.
FILM HISTORY I, II (u). Film Studies; and MAJOR FILM
MOVEMENTS (u). Film Studies; and MAJOR FILM DIRECTORS
(u). Film Studies. University of Colorado.

Connecticut
FILM STUDIES (u). English. University of New Haven.
COSTUME HISTORICAL EPIC MOVIES (u). Art; and THE
WESTERN FILM (u). Art; and THE DIRECTORIAL STYLE
(u). Art; and JAPANESE FILM (u). Art. Wesleyan
University.
MOVIES AS HISTORY (u). History; and POPULAR CULTURE:
MASS MEDIA AND THE HORROR CINEMA (u). Sociology;
and POLITICS: PROPAGANDA AND CINEMA (u). Political
Science. University of Connecticut.

Delaware
FILM AND AMERICAN SOCIETY 1929-1955 (u). English/History.
University of Delaware.

Florida
HISTORY OF MOTION PICTURE (u); and PRINCIPLES OF MOTION
PICTURE ART (u). University of Central Florida.

FILM AS LITERATURE (u). Language and Literature. University
of North Florida.
THE MOTION PICTURE (u). Communication; and DOCUMENTARY
FILM (u). Communication. Florida Atlantic University.

Georgia
INTRODUCTION TO FILM (u). English. Augusta College.
THE MOTION PICTURE (u). English and Speech. Berry College.
HISTORY OF THE MOTION PICTURE (u). Drama. Georgia State
University.

Hawaii
THE MOTION PICTURE IN AMERICAN CULTURE (u). American
Studies. University of Hawaii.

Idaho
HISTORY OF FILM (u). Film; and AMERICAN DOCUMENTARY FILM
(u). Film. University of Idaho.

Illinois
HISTORY AND TECHNIQUE OF THE FILM (u). English.
Augustana College.
COMEDY IN FILM AND FICTION (u). English; and GOTHIC
IN FILM AND FICTION (u). English; and THE WESTERN
IN FILM AND FICTION (u). English; and IMAGE OF WOMEN
IN AMERICAN FILM (u). History. Bradley University.
CONTEMPORARY CINEMA (u). Humanities; and MEDIA
STUDIES: FILM (u). Communications. DePaul University.
FILM GENRES (u). Fine Arts. Illinois Wesleyan University.
THE DOCUMENTARY IN FILM AND BROADCASTING (u). Theatre;
and HISTORY OF THE CINEMA (u). Theatre; and
INTRODUCTION TO FILM ART (u). Theatre. Illinois
State University.
TOPICS IN FILM (u). Communications. Mundelein College.
LITERATURE AND FILM (u). English; and COMMUNICATIVE
IMPACT OF FILM (u). Speech Communications; and HISTORY
OF FILM (u/g). Speech Communications. Northern Illinois
University.

Indiana
WOMEN AND AFRO-AMERICANS IN THE MOVIES (u). History.
Indiana State University, Terre Haute.
INTRODUCTION TO FILM (u). English; and THE FILM IN
SOCIETY (u). English; and POPULAR CULTURE: AMERICAN
SILENT FILM (u). English; and POPULAR CULTURE: EARLY
FILM (u). English; and POPULAR CULTURE: TALKING
PICTURES (u). English. Indiana University/Purdue
University at Indianapolis.
THE MOVIES (u). English; and FILM HISTORY TO 1938
(u/g). English; and FILM HISTORY SINCE 1938 (u/g).

English. Purdue/Calumet Campus.
AN INTRODUCTION TO FILM (u). Humanities; HISTORY OF
THE MOTION PICTURE (u). History. Indiana University
Southeast.
AMERICAN FILM CULTURE (u). English; and ENGLISH FILM
CULTURE (u). English; and HISTORY OF EUROPEAN AND
AMERICAN FILMS (u). Communications. Indiana University,
South Bend.
THE AMERICAN GENRE (u). Speech Drama; and THE IMAGE OF
MINORITIES IN THE AMERICAN FILM (u). Speech Drama;
and THE AMERICAN FILM (u). American Studies. University
of Notre Dame.

Iowa
FILM (u). Drake University.
TOPICS IN AMERICAN FILM (u). American Studies/English.
Grinnell College.
FILM (u). Speech and Theatre. Luther College.
SITTING IN THE DARK: A FOCUS ON FILM (u). English; and
MEN AND WOMEN IN THE MOVIES (u). English. Westmar
College.
FILM TOPICS (u). English; and STUDIES IN FILM:
AMERICAN GENRES (u). English; and DEVELOPMENT OF THE
MOTION PICTURE (u). Speech; and THE GREAT ESCAPE:
RADIO, THE MOVIES, AND DEPRESSION AMERICA (u).
University Studies. Iowa State University.
SEMINAR: AMERICAN FILM AND AMERICAN CULTURE (g).
American Studies; and WORLD WAR I IN FILM (g).
History; and SURVEY OF FILM (u). Broadcasting and
Film; and THE AMERICAN FILM (u/g). Broadcasting and
Film. University of Iowa.

Kansas
HISTORY OF FILM (u). Liberal Arts. Baker University.

Kentucky
THE FILM AND LITERATURE (u). English. Murray State
University.
FILM AND TELEVISION (u). Communication. Northern Kentucky
University.

Louisiana
INTRODUCTION TO FILM (u). Speech; and HISTORY OF FILM
(u/g). Speech. Louisiana State University.

Maine
THE FILM IN HISTORY (u). History. University of Southern
Maine.

Maryland
SOCIAL HISTORY OF AMERICAN MOTION PICTURES (g). History.
    Morgan State University.
FILM CLASSICS: ORIGINS TO 1945 (u). Film; and FILM
    CLASSICS: 1945 TO PRESENT (u). Film. University
    of Maryland, Baltimore County.
INTRODUCTION TO FILM (u). RTVF; and HISTORY OF THE FILM
    (u). RTVF; and FILM GENRES (u/g). RTVF; and DOCUMENTARY
    FILM (u/g). RTVF. University of Maryland, College Park.

Massachusetts
FILM APPRECIATION (u). English. Anna Maria College.
AMERICAN FILM (u). Mass Communication; and BLACK FILM
    (u). Mass Communication. Emerson College.
THE IMAGE OF BLACKS IN AMERICAN CINEMA (u/g).
    Afro-American Studies. Harvard University.
HISTORY OF THE MOTION PICTURE (u). Fine Arts. Merrimack
    College.
HISTORY AND FILM (u). History; and HISTORY OF FILM
    (u). Drama and Speech; and THE AMERICAN FILM (u).
    Drama and Speech; and THE DOCUMENTARY FILM (u). Drama
    and Speech. Northeastern University.
AMERICAN CULTURE AND THE FILM (u). History. University
    of Lowell.
WESTERN CIVILIZATION AND FILMS (u). History.
    Southeastern Massachusetts University.
INTRODUCTION TO FILM (u). Art. University of Massachusetts.

Michigan
HISTORY OF FILM: THE SILENT ERA (u). English; and
    AMERICA ON FILM (u). American Thought and Language;
    and CONTEMPORARY FILM AND SOCIETY (u). American
    Thought and Language; and HISTORY OF THE MOTION PICTURE
    (u). Telecommunications; and THE DOCUMENTARY FILM
    (u). Telecommunication; and EVALUATION AND CRITICISM
    IN BROADCASTING AND FILM (u). Telecommunication;
    and INTRODUCTION TO FILM (u). University College.
    Michigan State University.
HISTORY OF DOCUMENTARY FILM (u). Speech. Central Michigan
    University.

Minnesota
TOPICS IN FILM (u). History. University of Minnesota.
CINEMA AND SOCIETY (u). Speech; and DOCUMENTARY IN FILM
    AND TELEVISION (u). Speech. University of Minnesota,
    Duluth.

Missouri
INTRODUCTION TO FILM (u). English. Southeast Missouri State
    University.
MASS COMMUNICATIONS: FILM (u). Radio-TV-Film. Stephens College.

Montana
THE WESTERN FILM (u/g). English. University of Montana.

Nebraska
FILM: DOCUMENTARY (u). English; and HISTORY OF
  AMERICAN FILM (u). English; and AMERICAN FILM OF
  THE THIRTIES (u). English; and FILM GENRE: FILM NOIR
  (u). English. University of Nebraska.

New Hampshire
BLACK EXPERIENCE IN DRAMA AND FILM (u). Drama; and
  HISTORY OF FILM (u). Drama; and MOVIE—GOING (u).
  Drama. Dartmouth College.

New Jersey
THE FILM EXPERIENCE (u). English; and AMERICAN FILM (u).
  Fine Arts. Fairleigh Dickinson University, Madison.
HISTORY OF FILM (u), Communications; and FILM STUDIES:
  SCIENCE FICTION (u). Communications. Fairleigh
  Dickinson University, Teaneck.
FILM AND SOCIETY (u). English. Montclair State College.
FILM AND HISTORY (u). (u/g). American Studies. Seton
  Hall University.
COMEDY FILM (u). Art; and INTRODUCTION TO FILM (u).
  Art. St. Peter's College.

New Mexico
INTRODUCTION TO CINEMA (u). Journalism. New Mexico State
  University.

New York
AMERICAN FILM GENRES: WESTERN AND GANGSTER (u).
  Humanities. Fordham University, College at Lincoln
  Center.
HISTORY OF MOTION PICTURES (u). Art. Long Island
  University.
EARLY FILM ART (u). Communications Arts; and RELIGIOUS
  THEMES IN CONTEMPORARY CINEMA (u). Religious Studies.
  Molloy College.
HISTORY OF CINEMA (u). Communications. Queens College, CUNY.
CONTEMPORARY FILM (u). and FILM HISTORY AND CRITICISM
  (g). Rochester Institute of Technology.
FILM (u). English. Skidmore College.
POPULAR FILM (u/g). English. University of Rochester.
MOVIES AND MODERN AMERICAN CULTURE (u). History; and
  HISTORY OF CINEMA (u). English; and STUDIES IN CINEMA (u).
  English. SUNY, Buffalo.

North Dakota
THE WESTERN MYTH IN FILM (u). History. University of North Dakota.

Ohio
HISTORY THROUGH FILMS (u). History; and STUDIES IN
LITERATURE AND FILM (U). English; and THE ITALIAN
CINEMA (u). Romance Languages; and THE RUSSIAN FILM
(u). German/Russian; and THE GERMAN FILM (u). German
Russian; and EUROPEAN AND LATIN AMERICAN CINEMA (u).
Romance Languages; and FILM HISTORY AND CRITICISM (u).
Radio-TV-Film; and INTRODUCTION TO POPULAR FILM (u).
Popular Culture; and ADVANCED STUDIES IN POPULAR FILMS
(u). Popular Culture; and STUDIES IN THE HISTORY OF
AMERICAN POPULAR FILM (u). Popular Culture; and TOPICS
IN POPULAR FILM (g). Popular Culture. Bowling Green
State University.
RELIGION AND FILMS (u). Religion; and STUDIES IN FILM
(u). English; and AMERICAN FILMS AS HISTORY (u).
History. University of Dayton.
INTRODUCTION TO FILM AND DRAMA (u). English; and
SOCIOLOGY OF FILM (u). Sociology. Youngstown State
University.
HISTORY OF THE MOTION PICTURE (u). Motion Pictures;
and STUDIES IN FILM HISTORY (u). Motion Pictures;
and STUDIES IN FILM AUTHORSHIP (u). Motion Pictures; and
STUDIES IN FILM GENRES (u). Motion Pictures; and
SELECTED TOPICS IN FILM (u). Motion Pictures. Wright
State University.
SILENT CINEMA (u). Photography and Cinema; and CINEMA:
1948-PRESENT (u). Photography and Cinema. Ohio State University.

Oklahoma
FILM COMMUNICATION AND SOCIETY (g). Speech; and FILM
(u). English. University of Oklahoma.
INTRODUCTION TO FILM (u). English. Central State University.

Oregon
GENRE STUDIES IN FILM (u). English. Southern Oregon State
College.
HISTORY OF CINEMA (u). English. Willamette University.

Pennsylvania
THE FILM AS SOCIAL AND INTELLECTUAL HISTORY (u). History.
University of Pennsylvania.
CINEMA APPRECIATION (u). Mass Communication; and HISTORY
OF FILM (u). Mass Communication. Bloomsburg State
College.
HOLLYWOOD AND AMERICAN LIFE (u). American Studies. Franklin
and Marshall College.
INTRODUCTION TO FILM (u). General Programs. Haverford College.
HISTORY THROUGH THE FILMS OF GARY COOPER (u). History;
and HOLLYWOOD GOES TO WAR (u). History; and THE
BRITISH EMPIRE ON FILM (u). History. University of
Pennsylvania, Indiana.

FILM AND POPULAR CULTURE (u). Social Relations. Lehigh
   University.
ANTHROPOLOGY AND FILM (g). Radio/TV; and U.S.HISTORY
   THROUGH FILM (u). History. Temple University.
INTRODUCTION TO FILM (u). History; and HISTORY OF FILM
   (u). History; and FILM AND AMERICAN SOCIETY (u).
   History. Millersville State College.

South Carolina
THE FILM EXPERIENCE (u). English. University of South Carolina,
   Aiken.
THE FILM EXPERIENCE (u). English. University of South Carolina.
   FILM (u). English. Clemson University.

Tennessee
RADIO, TV FILM AND SOCIETY (u). Speech and Drama; and
   ORIGINS OF FILM (u). Speech and Drama; and
   CONTEMPORARY FILM (u). Speech and Drama; and
   POPULAR FILM (u). English. Memphis State University.

Texas
FILM APPRECIATION (u). Communication. Abilene Christian
   University.
FILM AUTHORSHIP (u/g). Communication; and FILM GENRE
   (u/g) Communication; and FILM HISTORY (u/g).
   Communication. Lamar University.
HISTORY OF THE MOTION PICTURE (u). Radio/TV/Film; and
   SEMINAR: FILM GENRES (g). Radio-TV-Film; and
   SEMINAR: SILENT FILM (g). Art. North Texas State
   University.
AMERICAN POPULAR FILM (u/g). Broadcasting-Film. Southern
   Methodist University.
MAJOR THEMES IN U.S. FILMS (u/g). Radio/TV/Film. Texas
   Christian University.
HISTORY OF THE MOVIES (u), Theatre/Cinema. Texas Southern
   University.
LITERATURE OF FILM (u). English. Trinity University.
FILM GENRE: THE WESTERN (u). Arts. Rice University.
HISTORY AND AESTHETICS OF FILM (u). English. East Texas
   State University.

Utah
INTRODUCTION TO AMERICAN FILM (u). English. University
   of Utah.
FILMS OF FRANK CAPRA AND JOHN FORD (u). Theatre and
   Cinematic Arts. Brigham Young University.

Vermont
DEVELOPMENT OF THE MOTION PICTURE (u). Communication; and
   SEMINAR IN FILM (u/g). Communication; and THE
   CONTEMPORARY CINEMA (u/g). Communication; and THE BLACK

MAN IN FILM (u/g). Communication. University of Vermont.

Virginia
FILM (u). English. George Mason University.
HOLLYWOOD AND THE VALUES OF COMMERCIAL ART (u/g).
English and Religion. University of Richmond.
INTRODUCTION TO THE MOTION PICTURE (u). Journalism; and
THE CONTEMPORARY MOTION PICTURE (u). Journalism.
Washington and Lee University.
HISTORY AND APPRECIATION OF THE MOTION PICTURE (u).
Theatre and Speech. College of William and Mary.

West Virginia
THE FILMS OF ALFRED HITCHCOCK (u). English; and THE
WESTERN (u). English; and AMERICAN FILM COMEDY (u).
English. Bethany College.

Wisconsin
FILM AND POPULAR CULTURE (u/g). Journalism. Marquette
University.
INTRODUCTION TO MODERN CINEMA (u). English. Milwaukee Area
Technical College.
INTRODUCTION TO FILM (u). English. University of Wisconsin,
Eau Claire.
HISTORY OF FILM (u). Communication; and FILM GENRES (u/g).
Communication; and WOMEN AND FILM (u/g). Communication.
University of Wisconsin, Superior.
HISTORY OF CINEMA (u). Mass Communications. University of
Wisconsin, Whitewater.

Washington, D.C.
AMERICAN FILM GENRES (u/g). Literature; and FILM AND
SOCIETY: THE DOCUMENTARY (u/g). Communications; and
HISTORY OF MOTION PICTURES I AND II (u/g). Communications.
The American University.
THE AMERICAN CINEMA (u). Speech and Drama. George Washington
University.

Music

Alabama
HISTORY OF JAZZ (u). Music. Auburn University.

Arizona
MUSIC IN WORLD CULTURES (u/g). Music. University of Arizona.

California
THE POP MUSIC INDUSTRY (u). Afro-American Studies; and
JAZZ: BLACK CLASSICAL MUSIC (u). Afro-American Studies;
and AFRO—AMERICAN MUSIC (u). Music. University of
California, Berkeley.
HISTORY OF JAZZ (u). Music; and HISTORY OF ROCK (u).
Music; and JAZZ: PAST, PRESENT, FUTURE (u). Anthropology.
California State University—Fullerton.
INTRODUCTION TO JAZZ (u). Music; and MUSIC IN
CONTEMPORARY SOCIETY (u). Music. California State
University, Northridge.
BLUES, RHYTHM AND BLUES, SOUL (u). Afro-American Studies.
San Diego State University.
DEVELOPMENT OF JAZZ (u). Music; and AMERICAN POPULAR
MUSIC (u). Music; and NEW ORLEANS JAZZ (u). Music.
UCLA.
MUSIC IN MOTION PICTURES (u). Music; and SURVEY OF
JAZZ (u). University of Southern California.
HISTORY OF JAZZ (u). Music. California State College,
Los Angeles.
HISTORY AND LITERATURE OF JAZZ (u). Music. California
Polytechnic State University.
ETHNOGRAPHY OF THE BLUES (u). Black Studies; and
HISTORY OF JAZZ (u). Black Studies; and HISTORY
OF SOUL MUSIC (u). Black Studies. University of
California, Santa Barbara.

Colorado
HISTORY OF POPULAR MUSIC AND JAZZ IN AMERICA (u). Music.
Western State College.
AFRO—AMERICAN MUSIC HISTORY (u). Black Studies; and
HISTORY OF JAZZ (u/g). Music. University of
Colorado.

Connecticut
POP MUSIC SINCE 1840 (u). Music; and AFRO—AMERICAN
MUSIC (u). Music. Central Connecticut State College.
POPULAR HYMNODY (u). Music; and ROCK 'N' ROLL
(u). Music/American Studies. Wesleyan University.

Delaware
AFRO—AMERICAN MUSIC (u). Black American Studies. University
of Delaware.

Florida
WHAT IS GOOD MUSIC AND WHY? (u). Music; and BLACK
MUSIC (u). Music. University of North Florida.
HISTORY AND APPRECIATION OF JAZZ (u). Music; and
HISTORY AND APPRECIATION OF ROCK (u). Music.
Florida Atlantic University.

Georgia
MUSIC: JAZZ (u). Music; and MUSIC: BLACK MUSIC (u).
Music. Emory University.

Hawaii
MUSIC IN MODERN AMERICA (u). American Studies. University
of Hawaii.

Idaho
AMERICAN MUSIC (u). Music. University of Idaho.

Illinois
AMERICAN JAZZ, POPULAR AND COMMERCIAL MUSIC (u). Music.
Augustana College.
BLACK MUSIC II (u). Music; and MUSIC OF 20TH CENTURY
AMERICA (u). Music. Illinois State University.

Indiana
HISTORY OF JAZZ (u). Music; and BLACK MUSIC IN AMERICA
(u). Music; and CONTEMPORARY JAZZ AND SOUL (u).
Music. Indiana University, South Bend.
INTRODUCTION TO JAZZ (u). Music. University of Notre Dame.

Iowa
POPULAR MUSIC IN AMERICA (u). Music. Grinnell College.

Louisiana
HISTORY AND DEVELOPMENT OF POPULAR MUSIC
PROGRAMMING IN AMERICA (u). Speech. University of Southwestern
Louisiana.

Maryland
THE AMERICAN MUSICAL THEATRE (u). Music. Goucher College.
AMERICAN POPULAR SONG (u). Music. University of Maryland,
Baltimore County.
JAZZ AND ITS INFLUENCE (g). Music. Western Maryland College.
JAZZ: THEN AND NOW (u/g). Music; and POPULAR MUSIC IN
AMERICA, 1945-PRESENT (u). American Studies. University
of Maryland, College Park.

Massachusetts
HISTORY OF AFRO—AMERICAN MUSIC (u/g) Afro-American
Studies. Harvard University.
HISTORY OF JAZZ (u). Music; and POPULAR MUSIC SINCE
1950 (u). Music. Emerson College.
HISTORY OF JAZZ (u). Fine Arts. Merrimack College.
JAZZ (u). Music; and AMERICAN MUSIC (u). Music;
and SEMINAR IN AMERICAN MUSIC (u). Music. University
of Massachusetts.

Michigan
THE MUSIC OF BLACK AMERICANS (u). Music; and HISTORY
  OF JAZZ (u). Music. Oakland University.
TOPICS IN AMERICAN CULTURE: JAZZ STYLES (u). American
  Culture. University of Michigan.
MUSIC AND BROADCASTING (g). Speech and Dramatic Arts; and
  SURVEY OF JAZZ STYLES (u). Music. Central Michigan
  University.

Minnesota
AMERICAN POPULAR MUSIC (u/g). Music. University of Minnesota.

Mississippi
HISTORY OF MUSIC IN AMERICA I, II (u/g). Music. William
  Carey College.

Missouri
POPULAR MUSIC IN AMERICA (u). Music. Southeast Missouri
  State University.

Nebraska
MUSIC AND THE CHURCH (u). Music. University of Nebraska.

New Hampshire
SEMINAR IN MUSIC OF JOHN COLTRANE (u). Music. Dartmouth
  College.

New Jersey
DEVELOPMENT OF JAZZ AND POP (u). Fine Arts. Fairleigh
  Dickinson University.
JAZZ, ROCK, AND CINEMA (u). Seton Hall University.

New York
MUSIC OF LATIN AMERICA (u). Music. Daemen College.
HISTORY OF JAZZ (u). Music; and UNDERSTANDING
  CONTEMPORARY POPULAR MUSIC (u). Music. Molloy
  College.
HISTORY OF JAZZ (u). Music. SUNY at New Paltz.
ROCK EXPERIENCE (u). English/Humanities. SUNY Technical
  College.
MAN IN WORLD MUSIC (u). Music. Colgate University.
MUSIC AND CULTURE: AMERICA (u). Humanities. School of
  Visual Arts.
AMERICAN POPULAR MUSIC IN THE 20TH CENTURY (u). Music;
  and JAZZ AND ROCK FOUNDATIONS (u). Music; and MODERN
  JAZZ MUSIC (u). Music; and URBAN BLUES AND ROCK (u).
  Music; and COUNTRY MUSIC U.S.A. (u). Music. SUNY,
  Buffalo.

North Carolina
INTRODUCTION TO JAZZ (u). Music. Duke University.

HISTORY OF THE AMERICAN MUSICAL THEATRE (u). Theatre.
North Carolina Wesleyan College.

Ohio
INTRODUCTION TO POPULAR MUSIC (u). Popular Culture; and
    CONCEPTS OF POPULAR MUSIC (u). Popular Culture;
    and POPULAR MUSIC AND SOCIETY (u). Sociology. Bowling
    Green State University.
AMERICA'S MUSIC (u). Music; and HISTORY OF JAZZ (u).
    Music; and MUSIC IN AMERICAN CULTURE (g). Music;
    and MUSIC OF EARLY CHRISTIAN CHURCH (g). Music.
    Kent State University.
POPULAR CONCERT MUSIC (u). Music; and AMERICAN
    MUSIC (u/g). Music. Miami University.
HISTORY OF JAZZ (u). Black Studies; and SURVEY OF THE MUSIC
    INDUSTRY (u/g). Music. Ohio State University.

Oregon
HISTORY OF JAZZ (u). Music; and AMERICAN MUSICAL
    THEATRE (u). Honors; and MUSIC CULTURES OF THE WORLD
    (u). Music. Oregon State University.

Pennsylvania
MUSIC AND WORDS (u). General Programs/Music/English.
    Haverford College.
POPULAR MUSIC (u). Social Relations. Lehigh University.
HISTORY OF JAZZ (u). Music. Muhlenberg College.
EVOLUTION OF JAZZ (u). Music. Pennsylvania State University.

South Carolina
AMERICAN POPULAR CULTURE: COUNTRY MUSIC (u). History.
    University of South Carolina.
COUNTRY MUSIC EXPERIENCE (u). History. University of South
    Carolina, Lancaster.

South Dakota
AMERICAN MUSIC AND SOCIETY (u). Music. South Dakota State
    University.

Tennessee
SURVEY OF POPULAR MUSIC (u). Music. Middle Tennessee
    University.
JAZZ APPRECIATION (u). Music; and ELVIS (u). University
    College. Memphis State University.

Texas
JAZZ AND ROCK MUSIC (u). Music. University of Texas, San
    Antonio.

Vermont
JAZZ LITERATURE (u). Music. University of Vermont.

Washington
MUSIC OF BLACK AMERICANS (u). Black Studies. Washington State
    University.
COUNTRY MUSIC (u). The Evergreen State College.

Wisconsin
PHONOGRAPH RECORD AND POPULAR CULTURE (u).
Speech/Broadcasting;
    and SEMINAR IN AMERICAN MUSIC (u). Fine Arts; and
HISTORY OF JAZZ (u). Fine Arts. Marquette University.
POPULAR MUSIC IN AMERICA (u). Music. University of Wisconsin,
    Stevens Point.
MUSIC AND AMERICAN CULTURE (u). American Studies/Music.
    University of Wisconsin, Whitewater.

Washington, D.C.
EVOLUTION OF JAZZ AND ROCK (u). Music. The American University.
HISTORY OF JAZZ (u). Music. George Washington University.

Sports

Arizona
HISTORY OF SPORT (u). Physical Education. University of Arizona.

California
SPORTS AND AMERICAN CULTURE (u). American Studies. California
    State University, Fullerton.
SPORT, CULTURE AND SOCIETY (u). Physical Education. California
    State University, Northridge.
SPORTS CULTURE (u/g). Journalism; and SEMINAR: SOCIOLOGY
    OF CONTEMPORARY SPORT (g). Physical Education and
    Recreation. Stanford University.

Colorado
SPORTS HUMANITIES (u). Physical Education and Recreation.
    University of Colorado.

Connecticut
SOUTH—PAW PITCHING (u). American Studies; and THE NATURE
    OF SPORT (u). Physical Education. Wesleyan University.
HISTORY OF SPORT (u). History; and SOCIOLOGY OF SPORT
    (u). Sociology. University of Connecticut.

Delaware
SOCIOLOGY OF SPORT (g). Physical Education; and WOMEN
    IN SPORTS (u). Physical Education. University of Delaware.

Hawaii
SPORTS IN LITERATURE (u). Arts and Sciences. University
    of Hawaii.

Illinois
SOCIOLOGY OF SPORT (u). Sociology. DePaul University.
COMPARATIVE HISTORY OF SPORT AND PHYSICAL EDUCATION
    (u/g). Health, Physical Education, Recreation, and Dance.
    Illinois State University.

Indiana
HISTORY OF SPORTS IN THE U.S. (u). History. Indiana University
    Southeast.
SOCIOLOGY OF SPORT (u). Sociology. University of Notre Dame.

Iowa
SPORT AND SOCIETY (u). University Studies. Iowa State University.

Kansas
SPORTS IN AMERICA (u). American Studies. Wichita State
    University.

Kentucky
SPORT IN MODERN AMERICA (u). HPE; and SOCIOLOGY OF SPORT
    (u). Sociology. Northern Kentucky University.

Maine
HISTORY OF SPORT IN THE U.S. (u). History. University
    of Southern Maine.

Maryland
SPORT IN AMERICAN SOCIETY (g). Physical Education. Morgan
    State University.
SOCIOLOGY OF SPORT (u). Sociology/Anthropology. Goucher
    College.
SPORTS AND AMERICAN CULTURE (u). American Studies. University
    of Maryland, Baltimore County.
SOCIOLOGY OF SPORT (g). Physical Education. Western Maryland
    College.
SPORT AND AMERICAN SOCIETY (u). Physical Education, Recreation
    and Health; and SPORT AND THE AMERICAN WOMAN (u).
    Physical Education, and Health; and SOCIOLOGY OF SPORT
    IN CONTEMPORARY PERSPECTIVE (g). Physical Education,
    Recreation and Health; and HISTORY OF SPORT IN WESTERN
    CULTURE (g). Physical Education, Recreation, and Health.
    University of Maryland, College Park.

Massachusetts
HISTORY OF SPORT IN AMERICA (u). History. Northeastern
    University.
THE LITERATURE OF SPORTS (u). English. University of Lowell.

Michigan
SPORTS AND SOCIETY (u). Health, Physical Education, and
  Recreation; and HISTORY OF SPORT IN AMERICA (u). History.
  Michigan State University.
SOCIOLOGY OF SPORT (u). Sociology; and HISTORY OF PHYSICAL
  EDUCATION AND SPORTS (u). Central Michigan University.

Minnesota
SPORT AND SOCIETY (u). Physical Education. St. Olaf College.
HISTORY OF PROFESSIONAL SPORTS (u). History. University
  of Minnesota, Morris.
SPORT AND THE AMERICAN SOCIETY (u). Physical Education;
  and THE WORLD OF SPORT (u). Physical Education. University
  of Minnesota, Duluth.

Mississippi
PHILOSOPHY OF SPORTS (u). Philosophy. University of Mississippi.

New Jersey
SPORTS IN AMERICAN LIFE (u). American Studies. Rider College.
SOCIOLOGY OF SPORT (u). Sociology. Seton Hall University.

New York
SOCIOLOGY OF SPORT (u). Sociology. SUNY at Fredonia.

North Carolina
THE SOCIOLOGY OF SPORT (u). Sociology. Duke University.
HISTORY OF SPORT (u). History. Western Carolina University.

Ohio
SOCIOLOGY OF SPORTS (u/g). Sociology. Bowling Green
  State University.
FRESHMAN SEMINAR: SPORTS AND SOCIETY (u). Findlay College.
SOCIAL FORCES IN CONTEMPORARY SPORT (u). Health, Physical
  Education, and Recreation; and SPORT AND SOCIETY (g).
  Health, Physical Education, and Recreation. Kent State
  University.
SPORT FOR THE SPECTATOR (u). Physical Education; and
  PERSPECTIVES OF SPORT (u). Physical Education; and
  SPORT IN CONTEMPORARY AMERICA (u). Physical Education;
  and INTERNATIONAL SPORT (g). Physical Education; and
  SEMINAR: THE ROLE OF SPORTS IN SOCIETY (g). Physical
  Education. Ohio State University.

Oklahoma
SPORTS IN LITERATURE (u). English. University of Oklahoma.
SOCIOLOGY OF SPORTS (u). Sociology. Central State University.

Oregon
SPORT AND SOCIETY (u). Physical Education; and WOMEN
   AND SPORT (g). Physical Education. Oregon State University.
SPORT AND AMERICAN LIFE (u). Sociology. Willamette
   University.

Pennsylvania
BASEBALL AND AMERICAN CULTURE (u). Sociology; and
   SOCIOLOGY OF LEISURE AND SPORT (u). Sociology. Albright
   College.
SPORTS AND PLAY (u). Social Relations. Lehigh University.
HISTORY OF SPORT IN AMERICAN SOCIETY (u/g). Physical
   ducation. Pennsylvania State University.
HISTORY OF SPORT IN AMERICAN SOCIETY (u/g). Physical
   Education. Pennsylvania State University, Abington.
SOCIOLOGY OF SPORT AND LEISURE (u). Sociology. Temple
   University

Texas
AMERICAN SPORT FICTION (u). English. Texas Christian University.
SPORTS AND U.S. SOCIETY (u). School of Arts and Humanities.
   University of Texas, Dallas.

Vermont
SOCIOLOGY OF SPORT (u). Sociology. University of Vermont.

Washington
The Black American in Athletics (u). Black Studies. Washington
   State University.

West Virginia
SPORTS: SERVICE OR SERVITUDE (u). Freshman Studies. Bethany
   College.

Wisconsin
SPORTS AND SOCIETY (u). Physical Education. University
   of Wisconsin, Whitewater.

Ethnic Studies

Arizona
MINORITY RELATIONS AND URBAN SOCIETY (u). Sociology/Black
   Studies; and THE CHICANO IN AMERICAN SOCIETY (u).
   Sociology/Mexican-American Studies; and MEXICAN—AMERICAN
   CULTURE (u/g). Anthropology/American Indian Studies; and
   CONTEMPORARY INDIAN AMERICA (u). Anthropology, American
   Indian Studies; and MINORITY BROADCASTING (u/g).
   Radio/TV; and MODERN JAPANESE SOCIETY (u/g). Oriental
   Studies. University of Arizona.

California
MASS COMMUNICATION IN THE AFRICAN—AMERICAN
COMMUNITY (u). Pan-African Studies; and PAN—AFRICAN GAMES
AND DANCES (u). Pan-African Studies. California State University,
Northridge.
BLACK LIFE AND CULTURE IN THE U.S. (u). Afro-American Studies;
and SELECTED ISSUES IN BLACK LIFE AND CULTURE (u).
Afro-American Studies; and THE BLACK FAMILY IN AMERICAN
SOCIETY (u). Afro-American Studies; and AFRO—AMERICAN
MUSIC (u). Music; and NATIVE AMERICANS AND THE CINEMA
(u). Special Studies. University of California,
Berkeley.
MINORITY GROUP POLITICS (u). Political Science; and
BLACK PEOPLE'S THEATRE IN AMERICA (u). Theatre Arts.
UCLA
THE PSYCHOLOGY OF THE AFRO—AMERICAN (u). Afro-American
and African Studies; and CONTEMPORARY CHICANO ISSUES
(u). Chicano Studies. Palomar College.
ASIAN AMERICANS AND MASS MEDIA (u). American Studies; and
TEATRO CHICANO (u). American Studies. University of
Southern California.
AMERICAN MINORITIES (u). Sociology; and ETHNIC GROUPS
IN AMERICAN HISTORY (u). History. California Polytechnic
State University.
ANALYSIS OF THE RACIST EXPERIENCE (u). Black Studies; and
HISTORY OF AFRO—AMERICA (u). History; and
CONTEMPORARY ASIAN—AMERICAN (u). Asian-American Studies;
and BLACK DRAMA (u). Dramatic Art; and RELIGION IN
BLACK AMERICA (u). Black Studies; and THE MEXICAN
CULTURAL HERITAGE OF THE CHICANO (u). Chicano Studies;
and THE EVOLVING CHICANA (WOMAN) (u). Chicano Studies.
University of California, Santa Barbara.
CHICANO CULTURE (u). Social Sciences; and
SPECIAL TOPICS IN ETHNIC STUDIES (u). Social Sciences.
University of California, Irvine.

Colorado
RACE AND MINORITY PROBLEMS (u). Sociology; and
BLACK WOMAN IN AMERICAN SOCIETY (u). Black Studies;
and AFRO-AMERICAN MUSIC HISTORY (u). Black Studies;
and CULTURE, RACISM AND ALIENATION (u). Black
Studies/Psychology; and THE CONTEMPORARY MEXICAN
AMERICAN (u). Chicano Studies/Sociology; and ASIAN
AMERICAN ETHNIC AMERICAN (u). Sociology; and
CHICANOS AND THE MASS MEDIA (u), Chicano Studies; and
BLACK POLITICS (u). Political Science. University of
Colorado.

Connecticut
ETHNICITY AND POPULAR ENTERTAINMENT IN AMERICA (u).
American Studies/Music; and RELIGIOUS BIOGRAPHIES AND
AUTOBIOGRAPHIES OF AFRO—AMERICANS. (u). Afro-American
Studies/Religion; and FOLK MUSIC AND FOLKLORE OF
EURO—AMERICANS (u). American Studies/Music. Wesleyan
University.

Delaware
SOCIOLOGY OF THE BLACK COMMUNITY (u). Sociology; and
AFRO—AMERICAN PEOPLE AND ISSUES (u). Black American
Studies; and HISTORY OF BLACK AMERICA (u). Black American
Studies; and AFRO—AMERICAN MUSIC (u). Black American
Studies; and THEMES IN BLACK AMERICAN STUDIES (u). Black
American Studies; and BLACK COMMUNITY STUDIES (g). Black
American Studies. University of Delaware.

Florida
ETHNIC LITERATURE IN AMERICA (u). Literature. University
of Central Florida.
AFRO—AMERICAN ART (u). Art History; and BLACK MUSIC (u).
Music; and HUMAN CONFLICT IN BLACK AND WHITE (u).
Psychology. University of North Florida.

Georgia
THE AMERICAN BLACK EXPERIENCE (u). Afro-American Studies.
Mercer University.

Idaho
COMMUNICATION OF MINORITIES (u). Speech. University of Idaho.

Illinois
ETHNIC LITERATURE (u). Humanities. DePaul University.
BLACK MUSIC II (u). Music; and MINORITY RELATIONS (u).
Sociology. Illinois State University.
SOCIO—CULTURAL FACTORS IN CONTEMPORARY BLACK LIFE
(u). Sociology; and ETHNIC POLITICS IN THE U.S. (u). Government.
Southern Illinois University.

Indiana
WOMEN AND AFRO—AMERICANS IN THE MOVIES (u). History.
Indiana State University, Terre Haute.
CHICANOS IN THE U.S. (u). Anthropology. University of
Notre Dame.
BLACK MUSIC IN AMERICA (u). Music. Indiana University—
South Bend.

Iowa
IMAGES OF THE AMERICAN INDIAN (u). Science and
  Humanities; and STUDIES IN AMERICAN INDIAN LITERATURE
  (u). English; and CONTEMPORARY AFRO—AMERICAN LITERATURE
  (u). English. Iowa State University.
CONTEMPORARY BLACK EXPERIENCE (u). Afro-American
  Studies; and THE BLACK WOMAN IN AMERICA (u/g).
  Afro-American Studies. University of Iowa.

Kentucky
MINORITY LITERATURES (u). English. Murray State University;
  and BLACK AMERICAN LITERATURE (u). English. University of
  Kentucky.
AFRO-AMERICAN HISTORY (u). History. Northern Kentucky
  University.

Louisiana
HISTORY OF BLACKS IN AMERICA (u). History; and NEGRO IN
  AMERICA (u). History. Louisiana State University.
AFRO—AMERICAN HISTORY (u). History; and MINORITY GROUPS
  (u). Sociology. University of Southern Louisiana.

Maryland
ETHNIC EXPERIENCE IN AMERICA (u). History; and
  COMPARATIVE CULTURE AND THE BLACK EXPERIENCE (u).
  English; and MINORITIES (u). Sociology. Morgan State
  University.
AFRO—AMERICAN HISTORY (u). English; and ETHNIC
  LIBERATION MOVEMENTS (u). Sociology; and THE CULTURAL
  HERITAGE OF   THE UKRANIAN AMERICAN (u). IDS. Western
  Maryland College.
BLACKS IN AMERICAN LIFE 1865-PRESENT (u/g). History;
  and AFRO—AMERICAN HISTORY (u). History; and
  AFRO-AMERICAN FOLKLORE AND CULTURE (u/g). English;
  and SOCIAL AND CULTURAL EFFECTS OF COLONIZATION
  AND RACISM (u). Afro-American Studies. University of
  Maryland.

Massachusetts
THE BLACK FAMILY IN AMERICA (u/g). Afro-American Studies;
  and HISTORY OF AFRO—AMERICAN MUSIC (u/g). Afro-American
  Studies; and THE IMAGE OF BLACKS IN AMERICAN CINEMA
  (u/g). Afro-American Studies. Harvard University.
BLACKS AND THE VISUAL MEDIA (u). Afro-American Studies.
  Northeastern University.

Michigan
LATINO TODAY (u). Latin-American Studies; and RACE
  AND ETHNICITY (u). American Arts, Culture and Society;

and AFRO—AMERICAN LITERATURE (g). American Arts, Culture, and Society. Grand Valley State College.
THE MUSIC OF BLACK AMERICANS (u). Music. Oakland University.
CONTEMPORARY SOCIAL ISSUES III: ETHNICITY AND AMERICAN CITIES (u). Sociology. University of Michigan.
CONTEMPORARY SPANISH AMERICAN CULTURE AND SOCIETY (u). Romance and Classical Languages; and AMERICAN MINORITIES (u). American Thought and Language; and THE BLACK MAN IN THE U.S. (u). History; and CONTEMPORARY PROBLEMS OF THE AMERICAN INDIANS (u). Racial and Ethnic Studies; and MINORITIES AND WOMEN IN THE WORLD OF WORK (u). Racial and Ethnic Studies; and MINORITIES IN AMERICAN CITIES (u). Urban Development. Michigan State University.

Minnesota
AMERICAN INDIANS IN THE 20TH CENTURY (u). American Indian Studies. University of Minnesota, Duluth.
TOPICS IN LATIN—AMERICAN SOCIETY AND POLITY (u). History. University of Minnesota, Morris.

Nebraska
INDIANS OF CONTEMPORARY NORTH AMERICA (u). Anthropology; and MINORITY GROUPS (u). Sociology. University of Nebraska.

New Hampshire
BLACK EXPERIENCE IN DRAMA AND FILM (u). Drama. Dartmouth College.

New Jersey
ETHNIC AND CULTURAL ASPECTS OF PHYSICAL ACTIVITY (u). Physical Education. Montclair State College.
BLACK AMERICAN LITERATURE (u). English; and MULTI—ETHNIC LITERATURE IN AMERICA (u). English; and AMERICAN ETHNIC GROUPS: ITALIAN, JEWISH, AND IRISH AMERICANS (u). American Studies. Rider College.

New Mexico
AFRO—AMERICAN HISTORY I AND II (u). History. New Mexico State University.

New York
ETHNIC AMERICAN VOICES (v). English. Daemen College.
COMMUNICATIONS AND THE BLACK COMMUNITY (u). Black Studies. SUNY at New Paltz.
SEMINAR IN AFRO—AMERICAN CULTURES AND SOCIETIES (u/g).

Social Relations; and POWER, RACISM, AND PRIVILEGE (u).
Social Relations; and AFRO—AMERICAN EXPERIENCE (u).
University Studies. Colgate University.
AMERICAN MINORITY LITERATURE (u/g). English. Herbert H.
Lehman, CUNY.
THE BLACK PERFORMER (u). Humanities. School of Visual Arts.
THE IMAGE OF BLACKS IN AMERICAN LITERATURE (u). English;
and BLACK EXPERIENCE IN AMERICA (u). Africano Studies;
and BLACK URBAN AMERICA (u). Africano Studies;
and TOPICS IN THE HISTORY OF BLACK AMERICANS (u).
History. Vassar College.
FOLKLORE OF AMERICAN ETHNIC GROUPS (u). English; and
MINORITY GROUPS (u). Sociology. SUNY, Fredonia.
TOPICS IN AFRO—AMERICAN STUDIES (u). Black Studies.
SUNY, Buffalo.

North Carolina
BLACK CULTS AND SECTS IN AMERICA (u). Afro-American
Studies/Religion; and THE BLACK IN THE CITY (u).
Afro-American Studies/Sociology. Duke University

Ohio
THE BLACK IN AMERICAN LITERATURE (u). English; and
FAMILY LIFE OF THE AMERICAN NEGRO (u). Home Economics;
and POPULAR CULTURE AND MINORITIES (u). Popular
Culture; and RACISM AND AMERICAN CULTURE (u). Popular
Culture, Bowling Green State University.
U.S. MINORITY GROUPS (u). English; and RACE RELATIONS
(u). Sociology; and RESEARCH SEMINAR IN BLACK STUDIES
(u). Sociology; and MYTH OF THE BLACK MAN'S PAST
(u). Pan-American Studies; and RACISM AND POVERTY
(u). English. Kent State University.
THE HISTORY OF BLACK AMERICA (u). History; and
HISTORY OF BLACK RELIGION IN AMERICA (u). Religion.
Miami University.
BLACK ROLE MODELS: RACISM AND SEXISM (g). Black Studies.
Ohio State University.
THE AFRO-AMERICAN IN U.S. HISTORY (u). History. Wright State
University.

Oklahoma
LITERATURE OF MINORITIES AND ETHNIC GROUPS (u/g).
Oklahoma State University.

Pennsylvania
RACE RELATIONS (u/g). Sociology. Pennsylvania State
University.

South Dakota
MINORITY LITERATURE (u). English. Black Hills State College.

Tennessee
HISTORY OF THE AMERICAN INDIAN (u). History; and
AMERICAN NEGRO HISTORY (u). History; and
    SOCIAL AND ETHNIC MINORITIES (u). Sociology/Anthropology.
    Memphis State University.

Texas
BLACK AMERICAN CULTURE (u/g). English/History. Abilene
    Christian University.
THE BLACK COMMUNITY (u). University Courses. North Texas
    State University.
AFRO-AMERICANS IN THE U.S. (u). Urban Studies. Trinity
    University.
THE NEGRO IN AMERICAN LIFE (u). History. East Texas State
    University.
THE BLACK PREACHER (u/g). Speech Communications. Texas
    Southern University.

Utah
AMERICAN ETHNIC LITERATURE (u). English. Brigham Young
    University.

Vermont
THE BLACK MAN IN FILM (u/g). Communication; and
    MINORITY GROUPS (u). Sociology. University of Vermont.

Virginia
RACE AND ETHNIC RELATIONS (u). Sociology. Washington and
    Lee University.

Washington
MUSIC OF BLACK AMERICANS (u). Black Studies; and
    AFRO—AMERICAN HISTORY (u). Black Studies; and
    BLACK AMERICAN IN ATHLETICS (u). Black Studies; and
    SOCIOLOGY OF CHICANOS (u). Sociology. Washington State
    University.

West Virginia
MINORITIES AND EDUCATION (u). Education. West Liberty State
    College.

Wisconsin
ETHNIC MUSIC (u/g). University of Wisconsin, Superior.

Washington, D.C.
RACE AND MINORITY GROUPS (u). Sociology. George
    Washington University.

History and Popular Culture

Arizona
HISTORY OF WOMEN IN AMERICA (u). History. University
of Arizona.

Arkansas
THE HISTORY OF AMERICAN POPULAR CULTURE (u). History.
University of Arkansas.

California
HOLLYWOOD AND U.S. HISTORY TO 1900 (u). History; and
HOLLYWOOD AND U.S. HISTORY SINCE 1900 (u). History.
California State University, Northridge.
HISTORY THROUGH FILM (u). History. San Diego State
University.
SOCIAL HISTORY OF AMERICAN WOMEN (u). History. UCLA.
HISTORY OF SCIENCE AND TECHNOLOGY (u). History; and
ETHNIC GROUPS IN AMERICAN HISTORY (u). History; and
WOMEN IN HISTORY (u/g). History. California Polytechnic
State University.
AMERICAN POPULAR CULTURAL HISTORY (u). History; and
HISTORY OF AFRO—AMERICA (u). History. University of
California, Santa Barbara.

Colorado
POPULAR CULTURE IN AMERICA (u). History. Western State
College.
HISTORY OF WOMEN IN THE UNITED STATES (u). History.
University of Colorado.

Connecticut
RELIGION IN 19TH CENTURY AMERICA (u). Religion; and
19TH CENTURY ENGLAND AND POPULAR CULTURE (u). English
and History. Wesleyan University.
HISTORY OF SPORT (u). History. University of Connecticut.

Delaware
AMERICAN DREAM (u). History; and HISTORY OF BLACK
AMERICA (u). Black American Studies; and HISTORY
OF BLACK THEATRE (u). Black American Studies. University
of Delaware.

Florida
THE TEXTURE OF AMERICAN HISTORY (u). American History; and
YOUR HISTORY AND MINE (u). History; and WOMEN'S ROLE:
PAST AND PRESENT (u). History. University of North
Florida.

Georgia
HISTORY OF POPULAR CULTURE IN AMERICA (u). History; and
  STUDIES IN AMERICAN POPULAR CULTURE: 1870-1920 (g).
  GILA. Emory University.

Indiana
HISTORY OF THE MOTION PICTURE (u). History; and
  HISTORY OF SPORTS IN THE U.S. (u). History. Indiana
  University Southeast.

Iowa
SOCIAL AND CULTURAL HISTORY OF THE UNITED STATES (u).
  History; and THE GREAT ESCAPE: RADIO, THE MOVIES AND
  DEPRESSION AMERICA (u). University Studies. Iowa
  State University.
HISTORY OF MASS COMMUNICATION IN THE U.S. (u/g). Journalism.
  University of Iowa.

Kentucky
AFRO—AMERICAN HISTORY (u). History; and HISTORY OF MASS
  COMMUNICATION (u). Communication. Northern Kentucky
  University.

Louisiana
HISTORY OF BLACKS IN AMERICA (u). History; and HISTORY
  OF FILM (u). Speech; and HISTORY OF AMERICAN
  JOURNALISM (u). Journalism; and THE FIFTIES (u).
  English. Louisiana State University.
AFRO-AMERICAN HISTORY (u). History; and HISTORY AND
  DEVELOPMENT OF POPULAR MUSIC PROGRAMMING IN
  AMERICA (u). Speech. University of Southwestern
  Louisiana.

Maine
THE FILM AND HISTORY (u). History; and THE NOVEL AND
  HISTORY (u/g). History; and HISTORY OF SPORT IN THE
  U.S. (u). History; and MODERN WAR AND ITS IMAGES
  (u/g). History. University of Southern Maine.

Maryland
HISTORY AND PHILOSOPHY OF RECREATION (g). Health,
  Physical Education and Recreation; and HEALTH AND
  SOCIETY IN EARLY AMERICA (g). History; and HISTORY
  OF POPULAR CULTURE IN THE U.S. (g). History; and
  SOCIAL HISTORY OF AMERICAN MOTION PICTURE (g). History;
  and WOMEN IN AMERICAN HISTORY (g). History. Morgan State
  University.
AMERICAN SOCIAL HISTORY (u). History. U.S. Naval Academy.

AFRO-AMERICAN HISTORY (g). History. Western Maryland
College.
HISTORY AND INTRODUCTION TO RECREATION (u/g). Physical
Education, Recreation and Health; and HISTORY OF
SPORT IN WESTERN CULTURE (g). Physical Education,
Recreation and Health.
AFRO—AMERICAN HISTORY (u). History; and BLACKS IN
AMERICAN LIFE: 1865—Present (u/g). History; and
HISTORY OF RELATIONS BETWEEN MEN AND WOMEN IN
WESTERN CIVILIZATION (u). History; and SOCIETY
IN AMERICA: HISTORICAL TOPICS (g). History; and
A CULTURAL AND SOCIAL HISTORY OF THE AMERICAN
WORKER (u/g). History.
HISTORY OF THE FILM (u/g). Radio/TV/Film; and
HISTORY OF MASS COMMUNICATION (u). Journalism.
University of Maryland, College Park.

Massachusetts
BIOGRAPHY AS HISTORY (u). History. Merrimack College.
HISTORY AND FILM (u). History; and HISTORY OF
SPORTS IN AMERICA (u). History. Northeastern University.
HISTORY OF POPULAR CULTURE (u). History. University of
Lowell.
WESTERN CIVILIZATION IN FILMS (u). History. Southeastern
Mass. University.

Michigan
HISTORY OF THE FILM (u). Cinema; and MODERN AMERICAN
CULTURE (u). History; and AMERICAN SPORT HISTORY (u).
History; and THOSE WERE THE DAYS (u). New Charter
College. Oakland University.
HISTORY AND PHILOSOPHY OF DANCE IN THE 20TH CENTURY
(u). American Culture. University of Michigan.
HISTORY OF THE CULT (u). History. Northern Michigan
University.
HISTORY OF SPORT IN AMERICA (u). Michigan State University.

Minnesota
AMERICAN HISTORY: FILM, POPULAR CULTURE 1890—1960 (u).
History. University of Minnesota.
AMERICAN FRONTIER HERITAGE (u). Humanities. University of
Minnesota, Duluth.

New Mexico
HISTORY AND ETHICS OF THE MASS MEDIA (u). Journalism.
AFRO—AMERICAN HISTORY I & II (u). History. New Mexico
State University.

New York
AMERICAN HISTORY: POPULAR CULTURE (u). History. Long
Island University.
HISTORY OF POPULAR CULTURE IN AMERICA (u). History.
Rochester Institute of Technology.
HISTORY OF THE FUTURE (u). History. SUNY, Binghamton.
RECENT SOCIAL AND CULTURAL HISTORY OF THE AMERICAN
PEOPLE (u). History; and HISTORY AND DEVELOPMENT
OF RADIO AND TV IN AMERICAN SOCIETY (u). Speech.
SUNY, New Paltz.
POPULAR CULTURE IN 17TH CENTURY EUROPE (u). History.
Baruch College.
THEME FROM WESTERN CIVILIZATION: WOMEN AND SEX (u).
History. SUNY, Fredonia.
AMERICAN POPULAR CULTURE HISTORY 1900—1945 (u).
History; and MOVIES AND MODERN AMERICAN SOCIETY
HISTORY (u). History; and 20TH CENTURY AMERICAN POPULAR
CULTURE HISTORY (u). History. SUNY, Buffalo.

North Carolina
AMERICAN CULTURAL HISTORY: OUR NATIONAL GAME (u).
History. North Carolina Wesleyan College.

Ohio
HISTORY OF POPULAR CULTURE (u). Popular Culture. Bowling
Green State University.
AMERICAN FILMS AS HISTORY (u). History. University of
Dayton.
HISTORY OF AMERICAN JOURNALISM (u). Journalism. Kent State
University.
HISTORY AND POPULAR CULTURE (u). History; and
HISTORY OF BLACK AMERICA (u). History; and
HISTORY OF BLACK RELIGION IN AMERICA (u).Religion.
Miami University.
THE AFRO AMERICAN IN UNITED STATES HISTORY (u). History.
Wright State University.

Oregon
AMERICAN HISTORY THROUGH NOVELS (u). History. Southern
Oregon State College.

Pennsylvania
AMERICAN STUDIES IN 1930s (u). English/General Program;
Haverford College.
THE FILM AS SOCIAL AND INTELLECTUAL HISTORY (u).
History. University of Pennsylvania.
HISTORY OF POPULAR CULTURE IN AMERICA (u). History.
Cabrini College.

UNITED STATES HISTORY THROUGH FILM (u). History;
and POPULAR CULTURE 20TH CENTURY AMERICA (u). History.
Temple University.
TECHNOLOGY AND SOCIETY IN AMERICAN HISTORY (u). History;
and HISTORY OF SPORT IN AMERICAN SOCIETY (u/g).
Physical Education; and HISTORY OF AMERICAN TELEVISION
(u). Speech Communication. Pennsylvania State
University.

South Carolina
AMERICAN POPULAR CULTURE SINCE 1890 (u). History.
University of South Carolina.
AMERICAN POPULAR CULTURE SINCE 1890 (u). History. University
of South Carolina, Lancaster.

Tennessee
HISTORY OF THE AMERICAN INDIAN (u). History; and
AMERICAN NEGRO HISTORY (u). History. Memphis State
University.

Texas
POPULAR CULTURE AND AMERICAN HISTORY (u). History. Austin
College.
AMERICAN SOCIETY AND CULTURE 1900—PRESENT (u). History;
and AMERICAN POLITICS AND HISTORY FROM FDR TO JIMMY
CARTER (u). History. Southern Methodist University.
MAIN CURRENTS AND PRE—INDUSTRIAL CULTURE (u). American
Studies; and MAIN CURRENTS AND INDUSTRIAL AMERICAN
CULTURE (u). American Studies. University of Texas,
San Antonio.

Virginia
AMERICAN BETWEEN THE WARS 1920s TO 1930s (u). American
Studies. Lynchburg College.

West Virginia
SPECIAL TOPICS (u). History. West Liberty State College.

Wisconsin
POPULAR CULTURE SINCE 1800 (u). History. University of
Wisconsin, Eau Claire.
THE AMERICAN MORMON (u). History. University of Wisconsin,
Stevens Point.

Washington, D.C.
HISTORY OF WOMEN IN AMERICA (u). Humanities; and
DANCE HISTORY (u). Human Kinetics and Leisure Studies.
George Washington University.

Mass Media

Alabama
SURVEY OF MASS COMMUNICATION (u). Communication; and
MEDIA LAW AND ETHICS (u). Communication. Auburn
University.

Alaska
THE MODERN MEDIA: MAN SPEAKS TO MAN (u). Humanities.
University of Alaska.

Arizona
NEWS IN MASS COMMUNICATIONS (u). Journalism; and
THE PRESS AND SOCIETY (u/g). Journalism; and
INTERNATIONAL COMMUNICATIONS (u/g). Journalism; and
READINGS IN MASS COMMUNICATION (u/g). Journalism;
and SEMINAR IN THE MEDIA (g). Journalism. University
of Arizona.
INTRODUCTION TO MASS COMMUNICATIONS (u). Journalism; and
MASS COMMUNICATIONS LAW AND ETHICS (u). Journalism
Northern Arizona University.

California
INTRODUCTION TO MEDIA (u). English. California College
of Arts and Crafts.
HISTORY AND PHILOSOPHY OF AMERICAN MASS
COMMUNICATION (u). Communications; and
COMMUNICATION AND POPULAR CULTURE (u).
Communications. California State
University—Fullerton.
MASS COMMUNICATION AND POPULAR CULTURE (u). Journalism;
and MASS COMMUNICATION IN THE AFRO—AMERICAN
COMMUNITY (u). Pan-African Studies; and
MASS COMMUNICATION AND SOCIAL INFLUENCE (u).
Sociology. California State University, Northridge.
MASS MEDIA AND MODERNIZATION (u). History/Latin
American Studies. San Diego State University.
MASS COMMUNICATION AND SOCIETY (u/g). Communication;
and MASS MEDIA IN SOCIETY (u/g). Journalism; and
COMMUNICATION MEDIA AND SOCIAL CHANGE (u). Journalism.
Stanford University.
ANALYSIS OF THE PUBLIC ARTS (u/g). Broadcast
Communication Arts; and MARXIST APPROACHES TO THE
PUBLIC ARTS (u/g); and CODES AND SYMBOLS IN THE PUBLIC
ARTS I & II (g). Broadcast Communication Arts;
and JOURNAISM AND MASS MEDIA (u). Journalism;
and TODAY'S MEDIA (u/g). Journalism; and MASS
MEDIA OF COMMUNICATION (u/g). English. San Francisco
State University.

MASS COMMUNICATIONS (u). Sociology; and
  HISTORY OF BROADCASTING (u). Theatre Arts; and
  PROBLEMS AND ISSUES IN BROADCAST MEDIA (u). Theatre
  Arts. UCLA.
THE MASS MEDIA AND SOCIETY (u). Journalism; and
PROPAGANDA AND THE MASS MEDIA (u). Journalism; and
  PUBLIC OPINION, PROPAGANDA, AND THE MASS MEDIA (g).
  Journalism; and MEDIA AND SOCIETY (u). Special Studies;
  and A CRITIQUE OF MASS MEDIATED CULTURE: CINEMA AND
  TELEVISION (u). Special Studies. University of
  California, Berkeley.
ASIAN AMERICANS AND MASS MEDIA (u). American Studies;
  and MASS MEDIA AND POLITICS (u). Political Science.
  University of Southern California.
MASS COMMUNICATIONS (u). Sociology; and SURVEY OF
  AMERICAN MASS MEDIA (u). Journalism. California State
  College, Los Angeles.
MASS MEDIA AND POPULAR CULTURE (u). Communication Arts;
  and INTRODUCTION TO MASS MEDIA (u). Communication
  Arts; and MASS MEDIA AND SOCIETY (u). Communication
  Arts. University of San Francisco.
MASS COMMUNICATIONS AND HUMAN BEHAVIOR (u). Speech; and
  THEORIES OF MASS COMMUNICATION (g). Speech; and
  SOCIOLOGY OF MASS COMMUNICATIONS (u). Sociology.
  University of California, Santa Barbara.
INTRODUCTION TO MASS COMMUNICATIONS (u). Communications
  Arts; and HISTORY OF MASS COMMUNICATION (u).
  Communications Arts. California State Polytechnic
  University.
PARTICIPATION IN MASS MEDIA (u). Social Sciences. University
  of California, Irvine.

Colorado
MASS MEDIA AND SOCIETY (u). Speech. Western State
  College.
THEORIES OF MASS COMMUNICATION (g). Journalism; and
  MASS COMMUNICATION AND THE ARTS (g). Journalism;
  and CONTEMPORARY MASS MEDIA (u). Journalism; and
  MASS MEDIA AND SOCIETY (u/g). Communication.
CHICANOS IN THE MASS MEDIA (u). Chicano Studies. University
  of Colorado.

Connecticut
GOVERNMENT AND THE NEWS MEDIA (u). Government. Wesleyan
  University.

CHILDREN'S LITERATURE AND THE MEDIA (u). English. University
  of Connecticut.

Delaware
INTRODUCTION TO MASS COMMUNICATION (u). Communication;
   and SEMINAR IN MASS COMMUNICATION (g). Communication;
   and SOCIOLOGY OF MASS COMMUNICATIION (u). Sociology.
   University of Delaware.

Florida
MEDIA AND POPULAR LITERATURE (g). English; and MASS
   MEDIA AND POPULAR CULTURE (u). Mass Media Communications;
   and MASS MEDIA AND POLITICS (u). Political Science.
   University of Central Florida.
MASS MEDIA AND SOCIETY IN AMERICA. mmc; and
   VENTURES AND ADVENTURES IN THE MASS MEDIA. University
   of North Florida.
MODERN MEDIA (u). Art. Florida Atlantic University.

Georgia
INTRODUCTION TO MASS MEDIA (u). Language and Literature.
   Wesleyan College.
INTRODUCTION TO MASS COMMUNICATIONS (u).
   Speech/Journalism. West George College.
MASS MEDIA AND SOCIETY (u). Sociology. Mercer University.

Idaho
MASS COMMUNICATION IN A FREE SOCIETY (u). Communication;
   and STUDENT MEDIA EXPERIENCE (u). Communication;
   and ADVERTISING AND THE MEDIA (u). Communication;
   and COMMUNICATIOINS AND ATTITUDE CHANGE (u).
   Communication; and HISTORY OF MASS COMMUNICATION
   (u). Communication; and MASS COMMUNICATION AND PUBLIC
   OPINION (u). Communication. University of Idaho.

Illinois
MEDIA AND SOCIETY (u). Communication. DePaul University.
SEMINAR IN MASS COMMUNICATION (g). Speech Communication.
   Illinois State University.
MASS MEDIA AND SOCIETY (u). Communications. Mundelein College.
MASS COMMUNICATIONS (u). Speech Communication; and
   MASS MEDIA IN MODERN SOCIETY (u). Journalism. Northern
   Illinois University.
HISTORY OF MASS COMMUNICATION (u). Journalism. Southern
   Illinois University.
Indiana
INTRODUCTION TO MASS COMMUNICATION (u). Communication
   Arts; and THE MEDIA AS SOCIAL INSTITUTIONS (u).
   Communication Arts. Indiana University at South Bend.
MASS COMMUNICATION (u). Speech Drama; and
   THE MASS MEDIA (u). American Studies; and
   TELECOMMUNICATIONS (u). American Studies. University
   of Notre Dame.

Iowa
PERSUASION, PROPAGANDA, AND THE MASS MEDIA (u).
  Speech Theatre. Luther College.
WORKSHOP IN VERBAL AND VISUAL LANGUAGES OF THE MEDIA
  (u). English. Iowa State University.
MASS MEDIA AND MASS SOCIETY (u). Communication Studies;
  and MEDIA AND CONSUMERS (u). Journalism; and
  POPULAR CULTURE AND MASS COMMUNICATION (u/g).
  Journalism; and HISTORY OF MASS COMMUNICATION IN THE U.S.
  (u/g). Journalism; and MASS COMMUNICATIONS IN MODERN
  SOCIETY: CONTEMPORARY ISSUES (u/g). Journalism;
  and MASS COMMUNICATION AND CULTURAL THEORY (u/g).
  Journalism; and AMERICAN BROADCASTING (u). Broadcasting
  and Film; and SOCIAL IMPACT OF MASS COMMUNICATION (g).
  Broadcasting and Film; and SEMINAR: MASS COMMUNICATION
  RESEARCH (g). Broadcasting and Film. University of
  Iowa.

Kansas
INTRODUCTION TO MASS COMMUNICATIONS (u). Mass
  Communications; and HISTORY OF MASS COMMUNICATIONS
  (u). Mass Communications. Baker University.

Kentucky
MASS MEDIA AND SOCIETY (u). Radio/Television.
  Murray State University.
MASS MEDIA AND MASS CULTURE (u). Communication; and
  SOCIAL ASPECTS OF MASS COMMUNICATION (u).
  Sociology. University of Kentucky.
CONTEMPORARY MASS MEDIA (u). Communications; and
  MEDIA AND POLITICAL COMPAIGNING (u). Communications;
  and HISTORY OF MASS COMMUNICATION (u). Communications;
  and MASS COMMUNICATION AND MODERN SOCIETY (u).
  Communications. Northern Kentucky University.

Louisiana
INTRODUCTION TO MASS MEDIA (u). Journalism; and
  THE LAW OF THE MASS MEDIA (u/g). Journalism; and
  INTERNATIONAL MASS COMMUNICATIONS (u). Journalism;
  and MASS COMMUNICATION AND SOCIETY (g). Journalism;
  and MASS COMMUNICATION THEORY (g). Journalism. Louisiana
  State University.
CONTEMPORARY TRENDS IN COMMUNICATION (u). Speech; and
  MASS MEDIA AND POPULAR CULTURE (u). Speech; and
  THEORY AND RESEARCH IN MASS COMMUNICATION (g). Speech;
  and COMMUNICATIONS AND CULTURE (u). English. University
  of Southwestern Louisiana.

Maryland
WIT, HUMOR AND SATIRE IN MASS COMMUNICATIONS (u).
  Communications; and TEARS, TERROR, SPIRIT AND HEROICS
  (u). Communications. Goucher College.
STUDIES IN MASS COMMUNICATION (g). English; and
  LIMITS OF PERSUASION (u/g). English. Western
  Maryland College.
LAW OF MASS COMMUNICATIONS (u). Journalism; and
  INTRODUCTION TO MASS COMMUNICATIONS (u). Journalism;
  and HISTORY OF MASS COMMUNICATIONS (u). Journalism;
  and HISTORY OF MASS COMMUNICATIONS (u/g). Journalism;
  and GOVERNMENT AND MASS COMMUNICATIONS (u/g).
  Journalism; and COMPARATIVE MASS COMMUNICATIONS (u/g).
  Journalism; and PUBLIC CULTURE AND MASS COMMUNICATIONS (u)
  Journalism; and MASS MEDIA AND SOCIETY (g). Journalism;
  and MASS COMMUNICATION IN 20TH CENTURY SOCIETY (u).
  Radio/TV/Film. University of Maryland, College Park.

Massachusetts
MASS MEDIA IN SOCIETY (u). English. Westfield State
  College.
THE MASS AND THE MEDIA (u). Drama and Speech; and
  MASS COMMUNICATION AND PUBLIC OPINION (u). Sociology;
  and POLITICS AND THE MASS MEDIA (u). Political
  Science; and BLACKS AND THE VISUAL MEDIA (u).
  Afro-American Studies. Northeastern University.

Michigan
FRESHMAN ENGLISH III: THE MASS MEDIA (u). Humanities;
  and INTRODUCTION TO COMMUNICATIONS MEDIA (u).
  Humanities. Michigan Technological University.
FORMS AND EFFECTS OF MASS COMMUNICATION (u). Sociology.
  Oakland University.
SOCIAL ROLE OF THE MASS MEDIA (u). Journalism; and
  MASS MEDIA SEMINAR (u). Journalism; and
  COMMUNICATION AND CONTEMPORARY CULTURE (u). Speech;
  and MASS MEDIA (u). Humanities. Western Michigan
  University.
THE EFFECTS OF MASS COMMUNICATION (u). Communication;
  and MASS COMMUNICATION THEORY AND RESEARCH (g).
  Communication; and SEMINAR IN MASS COMMUNICATION
  (g). Journalism; and PROSEMINAR IN MASS MEDIA AND
  AUDIENCE (g). Journalism; and GOVERNMENT AND
  COMMUNICATION (g). Journalism; and PRESS AND POLITICAL
  MASS COMMUNICATION (g). Journalism. Michigan State
  University.
SURVEY OF MASS MEDIA (u). Speech and Dramatic Arts.
  Central Michigan University.

Minnesota
MASS MEDIA (u). Speech. St. Olaf College.
CONTEMPORARY MASS COMMUNICATION (u). Journalism. College
of St. Thomas.
INTRODUCTION TO MASS MEDIA (u). Speech. University of
Minnesota—Morris.
INTRODUCTION TO MASS COMMUNICATIONS (u). Journalism;
and MASS COMMUNICATION AND SOCIETY (u). Speech;
and SEMINAR IN THE COMMUNICATION MEDIA (u/g). Speech.
University of Minnesota, Duluth.
MASS MEDIA IN A DYNAMIC SOCIETY (u/g). Mass Communications;
and OPINION AND COMMUNICATION: SOCIAL FACTORS (u/g).
Sociology. University of Minnesota.

Missouri
MASS COMMUNICATIONS (u). Radio-TV-Film. Stephens College.

Nebraska
INTRODUCTION TO MASS COMMUNICATIONS (u). Journalism;
and HISTORY OF JOURNALISM (u). Journalism. Kearny
State College.
LITERATURE AND MASS MEDIA (u). English; and
INTRODUCTION TO MASS MEDIA (u). Journalism; and
MASS MEDIA AND SOCIETY (u). Journalism; and
MASS MEDIA AND HISTORY (u). History; and
MASS MEDIA LAW (u). Journalism; and
INTERNATIONAL COMMUNICATIONS (u). Journalism;
and MASS COMMUNICATION THEORY (u). Journalism;
and CONTEMPORARY MASS COMMUNICATION: THE MESSAGE
(u). Journalism; and ISSUES IN MASS COMMUNICATION
(u). Journalism; and MASS MEDIA AND GOVERNMENT (u).
Journalism; and MASS COMMUNICATION (u). Society.
University of Nebraska.

New Jersey
MEDIA CRITICISM (u). English; and POPULAR CULTURE
AND THE MEDIA (u). Communications; and THEORIES OF
MASS COMMUNICATION (u). Mass Communications; and
MYTH, MEDIA, AND SYMBOL (u). Communications.
Fairleigh Dickinson University—Teaneck.
MEDIA HISTORY: PERSONALITIES AND TRENDS (u).
Communications. Rider College.

New Mexico
INTRODUCTION TO MASS COMMUNICATIONS (u). Journalism;
and HISTORY AND ETHICS OF THE MASS MEDIA (u).
Journalism; and INTRODUCTION TO ADVERTISING AND THE
MEDIA (u). Journalism; and LEGAL RESPONSIBILITIES
AND THE MASS MEDIA (u). Journalism; and SENIOR SEMINAR
IN MASS COMMUNICATIONS (u). Journalism; and

INTERNATIONAL COMMUNICATIONS (u). Journalism; and LAW OF
MASS COMMUNICATIONS (u). New Mexico State University.
New York
ARTIFACTS OF MASS CULTURE (u). Communications; and
MEDIA, ENTERTAINMENT AND SOCIAL CONSCIOUSNESS (g).
Communications. Fordham University.
SOCIOLOGY OF MASS COMMUNICATIONS (u). Sociology; and
AESTHETIC ISSUES IN THE MEDIA (u). Humanities; and
ETHICAL ISSUES IN THE MEDIA (u). Humanities; and
MEDIA AND POLITICS (u). Social Science. Fordham
University, College at Lincoln Center.
COMMUNICATION IN THE 20TH CENTURY (u). Media Arts.
Long Island University.
MASS MEDIA AND SOCIAL CHANGE (u). Communications; and
MASS COMMUNICATION AND SOCIETY (u). Sociology.
Molloy College.
MASS MEDIA AND SOCIAL CHANGE (u). Communications; and
MEDIA ANALYSIS: CRITICISM (u). Communications. Queens
College.
POPULAR CULTURE AND SOCIETY (u). General Studies. SUNY
at Binghamton.
WORDS AND IMAGES: MOVING IMAGES (u). English; and
TOPICS IN MASS CULTURE (g). English; and
COMMUNICATION AND MEDIA (u). Speech; and
MASS MEDIA AND POPULAR CULTURE (u). Sociology; and
PUBLIC OPINION AND PROPAGANDA (u). Sociology; and
INTRO TO MASS COMMUNICATIONS (u). Journalism; and
HISTORY OF MASS COMMUNICATIONS (u). Journalism. SUNY
at Buffalo.
COMMUNICATIONS AND THE BLACK COMMUNITY (u). Black
Studies. SUNY at New Paltz.
STUDIES IN CULTURE AND COMMUNICATION (u). Social Relations.
Colgate University.
THE CONTEMPORARY PRESS (u). English. Vassar College.
COMMUNICATION THEORY (u); and PRESS AND POLITICS
(u). Political Science. SUNY at Fredonia.

North Carolina
SOCIOLOGY OF MASS COMMUNICATION (u). Sociology.
Duke University.

Ohio
MASS MEDIA AND PUBLIC POLICY (u). Political Science;
and POPULAR CULTURE AND MASS MEDIA (u). Popular
Culture; and INTRODUCTION TO MASS COMMUNICATIONS
(u). Journalism; and PROCESSES AND EFFECTS
OF MASS COMMUNICATIONS (u). Radio/TV/Film. Bowling
Green State University.
SURVEY OF AMERICAN MASS COMMUNICATION (u).
Speech/Radio/TV. Youngstown State University.

TECHNIQUES OF MEDIA UTILIZATION (u). Speech; and
  MASS MEDIA AND SOCIETY (u). Journalism; and
  PUBLIC OPINION AND MASS COMMUNICATION (u). Sociology;
  and THEORY OF MASS COMMUNICATION (u). Journalism;
  and LEGAL PROBLEMS OF MASS COMMUNICATION (u).
  Journalism; and ETHICS OF MASS COMMUNICATION (u).
  Journalism; and READINGS IN MASS COMMUNICATION
  (u). Journalism. Kent State University.
INTRO TO MASS COMMUNICATION (u). Communication and
  Theatre; and MASS MEDIA AUDIENCE ANALYSIS (u).
  Communications and Theatre; and MASS MEDIA AND
  GOVERNMENT (u/g). Communication and Theatre;
  and MASS COMMUNICATION RESEARCH METHODS (g).
  Communication and Theatre; and MASS COMMUNICATION
  THEORY (g). Communication and Theatre; and TOPICS
  IN MASS COMMUNICATION (g). Communication and Theatre;
  and MASS MEDIA AND POLITICS (u). Political Science.
  Miami University.
MASS MEDIA (u). Communication. Wright State University.
SOCIAL IMPACT OF MASS MEDIA (u). Denison University.
INTRODUCTION TO MASS COMMUNICATIONS (u). Journalism;
  and DEVELOPMENT OF MASS MEDIA IN AMERICA (u/g).
  Journalism; and MASS MEDIA, SOCIETY AND BASIC ISSUES
  (u/g). Journalism; and SOCIOLOGICAL ASPECTS
  OF MASS COMMUNICATION (g). Sociology. Ohio State
  University.

Oklahoma
LEGAL PROBLEMS OF COMMUNICATION MEDIA (g). Law; and
  MASS MEDIA AND PUBLIC OPINION (u/g). Journalism;
  and MASS MEDIA PERSPECTIVES (u/g). Journalism;
  and MASS MEDIA ECONOMICS (g). Journalism.
  University of Oklahoma.
INTRO TO MASS COMMUNICATIONS (u). Journalism; and
  CONSUMER HEALTH AND MASS MEDIA (u). Health, Physical
  Educaton and Recreation. Central State University.

Oregon
CURRENT CULTURE (u). English. Southern Oregon State
  College.

Pennsylvania
MASS MEDIA AND SOCIETY (u). Annenberg School of Communications;
  and INTRO TO THE SOCIOLOGY OF MASS COMMUNICATION
  (u). Annenberg School of Communication; and
  MASS MEDIA CRITICISM (u/g). Annenberg School of
  Communication. University of Pennsylvania.
MASS COMMUNICATION AND THE POPULAR ARTS (u). Mass
  Communication. Bloomsburg State College.

ROLE OF MASS MEDIA IN CONTEMPORARY SOCIETY (u). English and Communications. Cabrini College.

MASS MEDIA AND POPULAR CULTURE (u). English. Gannon College.

JOURNALISM AND POPULAR CULTURE (u). Journalism; and COMMUNICATION AND POPULAR CULTURE (u). Speech. Temple University.

POPULAR CULTURE AND THE MEDIA OF MASS COMMUNICA— TION (u). Communications. Millersville State College.

INTRO TO MASS COMMUNICATION (u). Language, Literature and Communication. Misericordia College.

MASS MEDIA AND SOCIETY (u). Journalism; and MASS MEDIA IN HISTORY (u/g). Journalism; and CULTURAL ASPECTS OF MASS MEDIA (u). Journalism; and THE DRAMATIC ARTS IN THE MASS MEDIA (u). Theatre. Pennsylvania State University, Abington.

THE MASS MEDIA AND SOCIETY (u). Journalism; and WOMEN, MINORITIES AND THE MEDIA (u). Journalism; and CULTURAL ASPECTS OF THE MASS MEDIA (u/g). Journalism; and THE MASS MEDIA AND THE PUBLIC (u/g). Journalism; and THE DRAMATIC ARTS IN THE MASS MEDIA (u). Theatre Arts. Pennsylvania State University.

South Carolina

MASS MEDIA AND SOCIETY (u). Journalism. University of South Carolina

South Dakota

INTRO TO MASS COMMUNICATION (u). Mass Communication; and MASS COMMUNICATION (u). Journalism; and MASS MEDIA AND SOCIETY (g). Journalism; and SEMINAR IN MASS COMMUNICATION (g). Journalism. South Dakota State University.

Tennessee

MASS MEDIA AND SOCIETY (u). Journalism; and SEMINAR IN MASS COMMUNICATIONS (u). Journalism; and MASS COMMUNICATIONS (u). Sociology. East Tennessee State University.

SURVEY OF MASS COMMUNICATION (u). Journalism. Memphis State University.

Texas

CULTURAL COMMUNICATION (u/g). Communications. Abilene Christian University.

MASS MEDIA AND SOCIETY (u/g). Communications. Lamar University.

PERSPECTIVES ON MEDIA, TELEVISION AND FILM (u).

Radio/TV/Film; and PERSUASION AND MASS COMMUNICATION
(u/g). Radio/TV/Film; and THEORIES OF MASS COMMUNICATION
(g). Radio/TV/Film; and INTERNATIONAL MASS COMMUNI—
CATION (g). Radio/TV/Film; and MASS MEDIA AND AMERICAN
POLITICS (u). Political Science; and SOCIOLOGY OF MASS
COMMUNICATION (u/g). North Texas State University.
RADIO, TV AND FILM (u). Broadcast Film. Southern
  Methodist University.
CONTEMPORARY FRANCE AS REFLECTED IN THE PRESS (u).
  Modern Language. Texas Christian University.
MASS MEDIA AND POPULAR CULTURE (g). Communication.
  Texas Eastern University.
COMMUNICATION AND URBAN LIFE (u). Journalism,
  Broadcasting, Film and Urban Studies. Trinity
  University.
INTRO TO MASS COMMUNICATION (u). Journalism. East Texas
  State University.

Utah
INTRO TO MASS COMMUNICATION (u). Communications. University
  of Utah.
INTRO TO MASS COMMUNICATIONS (u). Communications.
  Brigham Young University.

Vermont
SURVEY OF MASS COMMUNICATION (u). Communication; and
  INTERNATIONAL MASS COMMUNICATIONS (u). Communication.
  University of Vermont.

Virginia
MASS MEDIA (u). American Studies. Lynchberg College.
  AESTHETICS IN MASS COMMUNICATIONS (u). Hampton
  Institute.
THE MASS MEDIA (u). Journalism. Washington and Lee
  University.

Washington
MASS COMMUNICATIONS AND SOCIETY (u). Communications;
  and SOCIOLOGY OF MASS COMMUNICATIONS (u). Sociology;
  and HISTORY OF MASS COMMUNICATIONS (u). Communications.
  Washington State University.
MASS MEDIA (u). Journalism. Walla Walla College.

West Virginia
INTRO TO MASS MEDIA (u). Speech Communications; and
  EFFECTS OF MEDIATED COMMUNICATION (u). Speech
  Communications; and MEDIA AND COMMUNICATION AND
  EDUCATION (g). Speech Communication; and
  RESEARCH AND THEORY IN MASS COMMUNICATIONS (g).
  Speech Communications. University of West Virginia.

Wisconsin
MASS MEDIA (u). Communications. Beloit College.
COPING WITH MASS MEDIA (u). Speech (Broadcasting).
  Marquette University.
POPULAR ARTS (u/g). Communication. University of Wisconsin,
  Stevens Point.
RADIO/TV/FILM IN SOCIETY (u). University of Wisconsin,
  Whitewater.

Washington, D.C.
WOMEN AND THE POPULAR MEDIA (u). American Studies.
  American University.
PUBLIC OPINION AND MASS COMMUNICATION (u). Sociology;
  and INTRO TO MASS COMMUNICATION (u). Journalism;
  and INTERNATIONAL COMMUNICATION (u/g). Psychology.
  George Washington University.

Popular Arts

California
HISTORY OF MUSICAL COMEDY (u). Drama. University of Southern
  California.
ANALYSIS OF PUBLIC ARTS (u/g). Broadcast Communication Arts;
  and CODES AND SYMBOLISM IN PUBLIC ARTS (u). Broadcast
  Communication Arts; and AESTHETICS OF BROADCAST
COMMUNICATION ARTS (u/g). Broadcast Communication Arts;
and SEMINAR IN PUBLIC ARTS (g). Broadcast Communication Arts;
and ARTS, POPULAR CULTURE AND SOCIETY (u/g). Social
Science; and HUMOR AND SOCIETY (u/g). Social Science. San
Francisco State University.
SOCIOLOGY OF THE THEATRE (u). Sociology. UCLA.
HUMOR AS COMMUNICATION (u/g). Communication. Stanford
  University.
POPULAR ARTS IN AMERICA (u). English. University of the
  Pacific.
BLACK DRAMA (u). Dramatic Art. University of California—Santa
Barbara.
MUSICAL THEATRE IN THE U.S. (u). Theatre; and
  SEMINAR IN POPULAR THEATRE AND ENTERTAINMENT (g).and
  PUPPETRY (u). Art. California State University—Northridge.

Colorado
MASS COMMUNICATION AND ARTS (g). Journalism. University
  of Colorado.

Delaware
COMEDY AND SOCIETY (u). Theatre. University of Delaware.

Florida
CONTEMPORARY ART (u). Art History; and KITSCH:
  BEAUTY IN ART (u). Art History; and AFRO—AMERICAN
  ART (u). Art History. University of North Florida.

Georgia
ART OF UTILITARIAN OBJECTS (u). Art History. Emory
  University.
AMERICAN MUSICAL THEATRE (u). Wesleyan College.

Illinois
CRITICISM IN THE PUBLIC ARTS (u). TV-Radio; and
  SONG AND POETRY (u). English/Music. Southern Illinois
  University.

Indiana
MUSICAL THEATRE (u). Commercial Arts. Indiana University,
  South Bend.
AMERICAN MUSICAL THEATRE (u). Purdue Calumet College.

Iowa
VISUAL ARTS AND AMERICAN CULTURE (u/g). American Studies;
  and COMMUNICATION, CULTURE AND THE POPULAR ARTS (g).
  Speech and Dramatic Art. University of Iowa.

Kansas
THE WESTERN (IN POPULAR ARTS) (u). American Studies.
  Wichita State University.

Maryland
WIT, HUMOR AND SOCIETY IN MASS COMMUNICATIONS (u).
  Goucher College.

Massachusetts
ART IN AMERICA (u). History. Merrimack College.
CULTURE, SOCIAL STRUCTURE AND THE POPULAR ARTS IN THE
  CARIBBEAN (u/g). Sociology. Harvard University.

Michigan
THE POPULAR ARTS (u). Western Michigan University.
MUSICAL THEATRE (u). Speech and Drama. Central Michigan
  University.

Missouri
COURSES IN THEATRE HISTORY (u). Theatre. Stephens
  College.

Montana
WAYS OF SEEING (u). Humanities. University of Montana.

New Hampshire
THE BLACK EXPERIENCE IN DRAMA AND FILM (u). Drama.
Dartmouth College.

New Jersey
SOCIAL BASES OF THE ARTS (u). Sociology; and
ETHNIC AND CULTURAL ASPECTS OF PHYSICAL ACTIVITY (u).
P.E.; and PHOTOGRAPHY AS CONTEMPORARY ART (u).
Fine Arts. Montclair State College.
AMERICAN IDENTITY IN THE ARTS (u). American Studies. Rider
College.
HISTORY OF COMMERCIAL ART (u). Fine Arts. Fairleigh
Dickinson University.

New York
THE BLACK PERFORMER (u). Humanities. School of Visual Arts.
HISTORY OF MUSICAL COMEDY (u). Communication Arts;
and BROADWAY TODAY (u). English. Molloy College.
ARTIFACTS OF MASS CULTURE (u). Communications. Fordham
University.
MUSIC, LITERATURE AND THE VISUAL ARTS IN AMERICA (u).
Sociology. SUNY at Binghamton.
WORDS AND IMAGES: PRINT (u). English. SUNY at New Paltz.

North Carolina
FORMS OF POPULAR ART (u). English; and HISTORY OF
THE AMERICAN MUSICAL THEATRE (u). Theatre; and
THE POPULAR ARTS IN AMERICA (u). Convocations. North
Carolina Wesleyan Collge.

Ohio
HISTORY OF MUSICAL THEATRE (u). Theatre. Bowling Green
State University.
CONTEMPORARY THEATRE (g). Speech; and REVIEWING THE
ARTS (u). Journalism. Kent State University.
AMERICAN THEATRE (u/g). Theatre and Communications.
Miami University.

Pennsylvania
MASS COMMUNICATION AND THE POPULAR ARTS (u). Mass
Communications. Bloomsburg State College.
RELIGION IN THE ARTS (u). Religion. Temple University.
THE POPULAR ARTS (u). Art; and THE DRAMATIC ARTS
AND THE MASS MEDIA (u). Theatre. Pennsylvania State
University, Abington.
THE SKYSCRAPER (u/g). Art History; and THE DRAMATIC
ARTS IN THE MASS MEDIA (u). Theatre Arts. Pennsylvania
State University.

Texas
THE POPULAR ARTS (u). Humanities. University of Texas,
San Antonio.

Virginia
POPULAR ART (u). American Studies. Lynchburg Collge.
AMERICAN MUSICAL THEATRE (u). Theatre Arts. University
of Richmond.

Washington
INTRODUCTION TO ART: POPULAR CULTURE (u). Fine Arts;
and CLOTHES AND CULTURE (u). Washington State
University.

Wisconsin
HISTORY OF THE MUSICAL IN AMERICA (u). Speech. Marquette
University.
POPULAR ARTS (u/g). Communication; and WAR AND THE
ARTS (u). Peace Studies; and AMERICAN PERSONALITY
AND THE CREATIVE ARTS (u). University of Wisconsin,
Stevens Point.

Washington, D.C.
THE POPULAR ARTS IN AMERICA (u). American Studies. The
American University.
MUSICAL THEATRE (u). Speech and Drama; and THE HISTORY
OF FURNITURE (u). Art; and DANCE HISTORY (u). Leisure
Studies. George Washington University.

Religion

Alabama
RELIGION AND POPULAR CULTURE (u). Religion. Auburn
University.

California
ISLAM: POPULAR RELIGION AND MODERN DEVELOPMENTS (u).
Religious Studies.
MAGIC, RELIGION AND WITCHCRAFT (u). Anthropology; and
RELIGION AND BLACK AMERICA (u). Black Studies; and
RELIGION IN AMERICA TODAY (u). Religious Studies.
University of California, Santa Barbara.

Connecticut
RELIGION AND THE MEANINGS OF AMERICA (u). Religion;
and RELIGIOUS BIOGRAPHIES (u). Religion; and
POPULAR HYMNODY (u). Music; and RELIGION AND AMERICAN
CULTURE (u). Religion; and RELIGION IN 19TH CENTURY
AMERICA (u). Religion. Wesleyan University.

228 Popular Culture Studies in America

Florida
EASTERN CULTS AND WESTERN MATERIALISM (u). Sociology;
and THE NEW RELIGIONS (u). Sociology.

Illinois
THE CHRISTIAN FAITH IN THE MODERN WORLD (u). Religion.
Augustana College.

Maryland
RELIGION, MYTH, MAGIC (u). Sociology. Goucher College.

Massachusetts
THE OCCULT AS RELIGION (u). Philosophy.

Michigan
RELIGION IN AMERICA (u). American Arts, Culture, and
Society. Grand Valley College.
RELIGION IN AMERICAN CULTURE (u). Religious Studies.
Michigan State University.
RELIGION AND SEXUALITY (u). Religion; and WITCHCRAFT,
MAGIC AND OCCULT PHENOMENA (u). Religion. Michigan
State University.

New Hampshire
RELIGION AND SOCIETY IN AMERICA (u). Religion. Dartmouth
College.

New Jersey
RELIGION IN AMERICA (u). American Studies. Rider College.

New York
RELIGIOUS THEMES IN CONTEMPORARY AMERICA (u). Molloy
College.
RELIGION AND EARLY POPULAR RELIGION IN NEW YORK (u).
History. University of Rochester.

North Carolina
BLACK CULTS AND SECTS IN AMERICA (u). Afro-American
Studies/Religion; and MODERN AMERICAN RELIGIOUS CULTS
(u). Religion. Duke University.

Ohio
CULTISM IN AMERICA (u). Popular Culture. Bowling Green
State University.
RELIGION IN FILMS (u). Religion. University of Dayton.
POPULAR RELIGIOUS EXPRESSIONS (u). Religion. Wright
State University.
CURRENT ISSUES IN RELIGION (u). Religion. Miami University.

Pennsylvania
RELIGION IN THE ARTS (u). Religion. Temple University.

Tennessee
RELIGIOUS JOURNALISM (u). Journalism. Memphis State
  University.

Vermont
RELIGIOUS DEVIANCE, MAGIC AND THE OCCULT (u). Sociology;
  and RELIGION AND SECULAR CULTURE (u). Religion;
  and CHURCH, CULT AND TOTEM: THE SOCIAL FORMS OF
  RELIGIOUS LIFE (u). Religion; and MYTH, SYMBOL AND
  RITUAL (u). and RELIGION IN AMERICA (v). Religion; and
  STUDIES IN CULTURAL LORE (u). Religion. University
  of Vermont.

Virginia
RELIGION AND SCIENCE FICTION (u). Philosophy/Religion.
  George Mason University.
AMERICAN SECTS AND CULTS (u). Religion. College of William
  and Mary.

Wisconsin
SEXUAL IMAGES AND MYTHS IN RELIGION (u). Religious Studies.
  University of Wisconsin, Stevens Point.

Washington, D.C.
EASTERN RELIGIOUS MOVEMENTS IN THE MODERN WEST (u).
Religion.
  George Washington University.

Technology and Society

Alabama
TECHNOLOGY, SOCIETY AND THE ENVIRONMENT (u/g). History.
  Auburn University, Montgomery.

Arizona
TECHNOLOGY AND CULTURE (u). Industrial Education; and
  MAN AND HIS ELECTRONIC WORLD (u). Industrial Education.
  Northern Arizona University.

California
SCIENCE AND TECHNOLOGY IN AMERICAN CULTURE (u).
American Studies. San Diego State University.
IMPACT OF TECHNOLOGY ON SOCIETY (u). Engineering. California
  State College, Los Angeles.

HISTORY OF SCIENCE AND TECHNOLOGY (u). History. California
Polytechnic State University.
ENVIRONMENT, TECHNOLOGY AND CULTURE (u). Social Sciences.
California State Polytechnic University.
CHEMISTRY: ENVIRONMENT AND TECHNOLOGY (u). Chemistry.
Palomar College.

Colorado
TECHNOLOGY AND MODERNIZATION (u/g). Sociology. University
of Colorado.

Connecticut
TECHNOLOGY IN MODERN SOCIETY (u). Engineering. University
of New Haven.

Florida
ENGINEERING AND TECHNOLOGY IN HISTORY (u). Engineering;
and COMPUTERS, CYBERNETICS AND SOCIETY (u). Engineering;
and TECHNOLOGY AND SOCIAL CHANGE (u). Engineering.
University of Central Florida.
TECHNOLOGY AND SOCIETY (u). History; and MAN AND THE
COMPUTER (u). Mathematics; and NUCLEAR ENERGY:
BOON OR BANE (u). Natural Sciences. University
of North Florida.

Georgia
MAN AND TECHNOLOGY (u). English. Southern Technical Institute.

Idaho
TECHNOLOGY AND HUMAN VALUES (u). Interdisciplinary Programs.
University of Idaho.

Illinois
MAN AND TECHNOLOGY (u). Interdisciplinary Studies. Illinois
Wesleyan University.
MAN AND TECHNOLOGY (u/g). Industrial Technology.
Illinois State University.

Iowa
TECHNOCRATIC VIEWS OF SOCIETY (u). History. Grinnell College.

Massachusetts
THE IMPACT OF SCIENCE ON SOCIETY (u). Merrimack College.
TECHNOLOGY AND TRANSFORMATION OF THE WORLD (u).
History/Electrical Engineering. Northeastern
University.
ENERGY ALTERNATIVES (u). Physics; and SCIENCE,
TECHNOLOGY AND SOCIETY (u). Physics. Southeastern
Massachusetts University.

Michigan
SOCIETY AND TECHNOLOGY (u). General Motors Institute.
SCIENCE, TECHNOLOGY AND HUMAN VALUES (u). Natural Science;
and TECHNOLOGY AND SOCIETY (u). Natural Science;
and TECHNOLOGY ASSESSMENT (u). Natural Science;
and COMPUTERS IN SOCIETY (u). Computer Science.
Michigan State University.

Minnesota
MODERN TECHNOLOGY AND SOCIETY (u). Sociology. College
of St. Thomas.

New Jersey
TECHNOLOGY AND SCIENCE IN AMERICA (u). American Studies.
Rider College.

New Mexico
TECHNOLOGY ASSESSMENTS (u). Honors Program. New Mexico
State University.

New York
SOCIETY AND TECHNOLOGY (u). General Studies. SUNY,
Binghamton.
SCIENCE, TECHNOLOGY AND SOCIETY (u). Social Science. SUNY
Technical College.
TECHNOLOGY AND MAN. New York Institute of Technology.
HUMANITIES AND TECHNOLOGY (u). English/Engineering.
SUNY, Fredonia.
TECHNOLOGY, SOCIETY AND SELF (u). Sociology. SUNY, Buffalo.

North Carolina
TECHNOLOGY AND SOCIETY (u). History. North Carolina
Wesleyan College.

North Dakota
TECHNOLOGY AND ENVIRONMENT (u). Environmental Studies;
and TECHNOLOGY AND SOCIETY (u). Engineering. North
Dakota State University.

Ohio
HISTORY OF TECHNOLOGY (u). Technology. Kent State University.
TECHNOLOGY AND SOCIETY (u). Sociology. Wright State
University.
MAN, TECHNOLOGY AND SOCIETY (u). Sociology. Youngstown
State University.

Pennsylvania
TECHNOLOGY AND SOCIETY IN AMERICA (u). History. Pennsylvania
State University, Abington.

TECHNOLOGY AND SOCIETY IN AMERICAN HISTORY (u). History;
and PHYSICS, COMMUNICATIONS, NOISE AND SOCIETY (u).
Physics; and WILDERNESS, TECHNOLOGY AND SOCIETY (u).
Science, Technology and Society. Pennsylvania State
University.

South Dakota
COMPUTERS AND SOCIETY (u). Computer Science. South Dakota
State University

Texas
THE INTERACTION OF SCIENCE AND MAN IN OUR SOCIETY (u).
Chemistry/Physics. East Texas State University.

Utah
TECHNOLOGY AND HUMAN VALUES (u). Humanities Arts and
Social Sciences. Utah State University.

Vermont
TECHNOLOGY AND SOCIETY (u). Technology.University of
Vermont.

Washington
COMPUTERS AND SOCIETY (u). Computer Science. Washington
State University.

Washington, D.C.
COMPUTERS AND SOCIETY (u). Experimental Humanities. George
Washington University.

Introduction to Popular Culture

Arkansas
POPULAR CULTURE IN CONTEMPORARY AMERICA (u).
Humanities. University of Arkansas.

California
POPULAR CULTURE: THE MODERN VISUAL HERITAGE
(u). California Institute of the Arts.
SOCIOLOGY OF POPULAR CULTURE (u). Sociology. California
State University, Fresno.
A SURVEY OF POPULAR CULTURE AND ITS PLACE IN
CONTEMPORARY SOCIETY (u). California State
University, Northridge.
POPULAR CULTURE: MIRROR OF AMERICAN LIFE (u).
Sociology. Palomar College.
ARTS, POPULAR CULTURE AND SOCIETY (u/g). Social
Science; and POPULAR CULTURE AND SOCIETY (u).
Sociology. University of the Pacific.

AMERICAN POPULAR CULTURE (u). American Studies.
California State College, Los Angeles.
INTRODUCTION TO POPULAR CULTURE (u). Humanities.
Harvey Mudd College.
FOLKLORE AND POPULAR CULTURE (u). Social Sciences.
University of California, Irvine.

Colorado
POPULAR CULTURE IN AMERICA (u). History. Western State
College.
SOCIOLOGY OF POPULAR CULTURE AND POPULAR TASTE
(u). Sociology. University of Colorado.

Florida
STUDIES IN POPULAR CULTURE (u). Language and Literature.
University of North Florida.

Georgia
STUDIES IN AMERICAN POPULAR CULTURE (g). Graduate
Institute of the Liberal Arts. Emory University.
POPULAR CULTURE AND THE TEACHING OF ENGLISH (u).
Graduate and Professional Education. Mercer University.
AMERICAN POPULAR CULTURE (u). American Studies.
Wesleyan College.

Hawaii
POPULAR CULTURE (u). American Studies. University of
Hawaii.

Illinois
POPULAR CULTURE (u). Information Science; and
INTRODUCTION TO HUMANITIES. Malcolm X College.
STUDIES IN POPULAR CULTURE (u). Communications.
Mundelein College.

Indiana
POPULAR CULTURE (u). Humanities. Indiana State
University, Terre Haute.
POPULAR CULTURE STUDIES (g). English. Purdue
Calumet University.

Iowa
POPULAR CULTURE (u). English. Westmar College.
SELECTED TOPICS IN POPULAR CULTURE (u). Iowa
State University.
ISSUES IN AMERICAN CULTURE (u). American Studies;
and POPULAR CULTURE (u/g). American Studies;
and THEORY OF POPULAR CULTURE (u/g). Journalism;
and SOCIOLOGY OF POPULAR CULTURE (u/g). Sociology.
University of Iowa.

Kansas
POPULAR CULTURE (u). Sociology. Baker University.
AMERICAN POPULAR CULTURE (u). History/American Studies.
  Wichita State University.

Maryland
HISTORY OF U.S. POPULAR CULTURE (g). History;
  and SEMINAR IN POPULAR CULTURE (g). Popular Culture.
  Morgan State University.
AMERICAN SOCIAL HISTORY (u). History. U.S. Naval
  Academy.
INTRODUCTION TO POPULAR CULTURE (u). American Studies.
  University of Maryland, Baltimore County.
POPULAR CULTURE IN AMERICA (u/g). American Studies;
  and POPULAR CULTURE IN AMERICA II (u/g). American
  Studies; and POPULAR CULTURE IN AMERICA (g). American
  Studies. University of Maryland, College Park.

Massachusetts
POPULAR CULTURE (u). American Studies. Merrimack College.
POPULAR CULTURE (u). English. University of Lowell

Michigan.
THE POPULAR ARTS (u). Humanities. Western Michigan University.
POPULAR CULTURE (u). English. Northern Michigan University.
INTRODUCTION TO POPULAR CULTURE (u). English. Michigan
  State University.
POPULAR CULTURE IN AMERICA (u). English. Central
  Michigan University

Minnesota
INTRODUCTION TO POPULAR CULTURE (u). St. Olaf College.
SOCIOLOGY OF POPULAR CULTURE (u/g). University of Minnesota.

Missouri
POPULAR CULTURE IN 20TH CENTURY AMERICA (u). American
  Studies. Stephens College.

Montana
POPULAR CULTURE AND THE IMPACT OF MASS MEDIA ON
  SOCIETY (u). Humanities and Social Science. Montana
  College of Mineral Science and Technology.

New Jersey
SOCIOLOGY OF POPULAR CULTURE (u). Sociology. Rider
  College.
URBAN POPULAR CULTURE (u). Urban Studies. St. Peters
  College.

New York
POPULAR CULTURE (u). Sociology. Fordham University.
AMERICAN SOCIAL HISTORY: POPULAR CULTURE (u). History.
  Long Island University.
MYTH AND AMERICAN POPULAR CULTURE (u). English. Queens
  College, CUNY.
HISTORY OF POPULAR CULTURE IN AMERICA (u). Rochester
  Institute of Technology.
SOCIOLOGY OF POPULAR CULTURE (u). Skidmore College.
POPULAR CULTURE (u). New York Institute of Technology.
POPULAR CULTURE (u). General Studies. SUNY, Binghamton.
POPULAR CULTURE (u). New York Institute of Technology.
INTRODUCTION TO POPULAR CULTURE (u). English. SUNY,
  Fredonia.
SEMINAR IN AMERICAN POPULAR CULTURE (u). History. SUNY,
  Buffalo.

North Dakota
U.S. POPULAR CULTURE (u). History. University of North
  Dakota.

Ohio
INTRODUCTION TO POPULAR CULTURE (u). Popular Culture.
  Bowling Green State University.
POPULAR CULTURE (u). English. Franklin University.
SOCIOLOGY OF EVERYDAY LIFE (g). Sociology. Ohio
  State University.

Oklahoma
INTRODUCTION TO POPULAR CULTURE (u). English.
  Oklahoma State University.

Oregon
AMERICAN POPULAR CULTURE (u). Sociology. Willamette University.

Pennsylvania
INTRODUCTION TO AMERICAN POPULAR CULTURE (u). American
  Civilization. University of Pennsylvania.
POPULAR CULTURE IN AMERICA (u). History. Bloomsburg State
  College.
HISTORY OF POPULAR CULTURE IN AMERICA (u). History.
  Cabrini College.
POPULAR CULTUR IN 20TH CENTURY AMERICA (u). History.
  Temple University.
POPULAR CULTURE AND THE MEDIA OF MASS
  COMMUNICATION (u). Communications. Millersville
  State College.
INTRODUCTION TO POPULAR CULTURE (u). American Studies.
  Pennsylvania State University, Abington.

South Carolina
AMERICAN POPULAR CULTURE SINCE 1890 (u). History.
  University of South Carolina.
INTRODUCTION TO POPULAR CULTURE (u). English.
  Clemson University.

Tennessee
SEMINAR IN POPULAR CULTURE (u). English. Middle
  Tennesse University.

Texas
MODERN AMERICAN POPULAR CULTURE (u). History. Austin
  College.
POPULAR CULTURE (u). Sociology. Rice University.

Utah
POPULAR CULTURE IN AMERICA (u). History. Brigham Young
  University.

Virginia
POPULAR CULTURE (u). American Studies. Lynchburg College.

West Virginia
POPULAR CULTURE (u). English. University of West Virginia.
MASS SOCIETY AND POPULAR CULTURE (u). Sociology.
  West Virginia Wesleyan College.
POPULAR CULTURE (u). History. West Liberty State
  College.

Wisconsin
POPULAR CULTURE SINCE 1800 (u/g). History. University
  of Wisconsin, Eau Claire.
AMERICAN POPULAR CULTURE (u). American Studies/History.
  University of Wisconsin, Whitewater.

Washington, D.C.
CONTEMPORARY POPULAR CULTURE IN AMERICA (u). American
  Studies. Galaudet College.

Recreation and Leisure
California
LEISURE AND RECREATION IN SOCIETY (u). Leisure and Recreation
  Studies. California State College, Los Angeles.

Colorado
TRENDS IN AMERICAN RECREATION (u). Physical Education.
  University of Colorado.

Connecticut
BREAD AND CIRCUSES (u). English/American Studies;
  and ETHNICITY AND POPULAR ENTERTAINMENT IN AMERICA
  1870-1970 (u). American Studies. Wesleyan University.

Florida
RECREATION FOR LEISURE (u/g). Physical Education.
  University of North Florida.

Idaho
MAN AND LEISURE (u). Recreation. University of Idaho.

Louisiana
INTRODUCTION TO RECREATION (u). Landscape Architecture.
  Louisiana State University.

Maryland
HISTORY AND INTRODUCTION TO RECREATION (u). Recreation;
  and MODERN TRENDS IN RECREATION (g). Recreation.
  University of Maryland, College Park.

Michigan
LEISURE AND RECREATION RESOURCES (u). Park and Recreation
  Resources; and DIMENSIONS OF RECREATION AND LEISURE
  (g). Park and Recreation Resources. Michigan State University.
LEISURE, SPORT AND RECREATION (u). History. Central
  Michigan University.

Mississippi
LEISURE AND POPULAR CULTURE (u). Sociology. University
  of Mississippi.

North Carolina
SOCIOLOGY OF RECREATION (u). Sociology. University of
  North Carolina, Wilmington.

Ohio
INTRODUCTION TO OUTDOOR RECREATION (u). Recreation and
  Dance; and POPULAR ENTERTAINMENTS (u/g). Popular
  Culture. Bowling Green State University.
HISTORY OF RECREATION (u). Health, Physical Education
  and Recreation; and SOCIOLOGY OF LEISURE (u). Sociology.
  Kent State University.
WORK AND LEISURE IN MASS SOCIETY (u/g). Sociology.
  Ohio State University.

Oklahoma
CONTEMPORARY TRENDS IN LEISURE (u). Health, Physical
  Education and Recreation. University of Oklahoma.

Pennsylvania
SOCIOLOGY OF LEISURE (u). Sociology. Albright College.
LEISURE AND THE INDIVIDUAL (u). Recreation.
   Temple University.
MAN AND LEISURE (u). Recreation and Parks. Pennsylvania
   State University.

South Carolina
GEOGRAPHY OF RECREATION AND SPORT. Geography. University
   of South Carolina.

South Dakota
INTRODUCTION TO PUBLIC RECREATION (u). Health, Physical
   Education and Recreation. South Dakota State
   University.

Tennessee
INTRODUCTION TO RECREATION (u). Health, Physical Education
   and Recreation. Memphis State University.

Texas
SOCIOLOGY OF LEISURE (u). Sociology. Rice University.

Vermont
SOCIOLOGY OF LEISURE (u). Sociology. University of Vermont.

Washington
RECREATION IN AMERICA (u). Physical Education. Washington
   State University.
RECREATION, LEISURE AND SOCIETY (u). Health, Physical
   and Recreational Education. Walla Walla College.

Women's Studies

Arizona
WOMEN IN LITERATURE (u/g). English; and HISTORY OF
   WOMEN IN AMERICA (u). History; and WOMEN IN
   CONTEMPORARY SOCIETY (u). Womens Studies. University of
   Arizona.
WOMEN IN CONTEMPORARY SOCIETY (u). Sociology. Northern
   Arizona University.

California
IMAGE OF WOMEN IN FILM (u). Art. Immaculate Heart
   College.
SOCIOLOGICAL PERSPECTIVE ON WOMEN (u). Sociology.
   Palomar College.

SOCIAL HISTORY OF AMERICAN WOMEN (u). History;
and WOMEN IN ITALY (u). Italian. UCLA
WOMEN IN HISTORY (u/g). History. California
Polytechnic State University.
IMAGES OF WOMEN IN FILM (u). Sociology; and WOMEN IN
AMERICAN SOCIETY (u). Sociology. University of
California, Santa Barbara.
MODERN AMERICAN WOMEN: CONFLICT AND CREATION (u).
Special Studies; and WOMEN, WORK AND SOCIETY (u).
Special Studies. University of California, Berkeley.

Colorado
HISTORY OF WOMEN IN THE U.S. (u). History; and
THE BLACK WOMAN IN AMERICAN SOCIETY (u). Black
Studies. University of Colorado.

Delaware
SOCIOLOGY OF SEX ROLES (u). Women's Studies; and
WOMEN IN SPORTS (u). Physical Education. University
of Delaware.

Florida
WOMAN'S ROLE, PAST AND PRESENT (u). History; and
UNDERSTANDING WOMEN (u). Psychology. University
of North Florida.

Illinois
IMAGE OF WOMEN IN AMERICAN FILM (u). History.
Bradley University.
WOMEN TODAY (u). Interdisciplinary Studies. Illinois
State University.
WOMEN IN CONTEMPORARY AMERICA (u). Interdisciplinary
Studies. Northern Illinois University.

Indiana
WOMEN AND AFRO—AMERICANS IN THE MOVIES (u). History.
Indiana State University, Terre Haute.
WOMEN'S ROLE (u). Women's Cultural Studies. Indiana
University, South Bend.

Iowa
THE BLACK WOMAN IN AMERICA (u/g). Afro-American Studies;
and WOMEN IN SOCIETY (u). Sociology. University
of Iowa.

Maryland
WOMEN IN AMERICA (u/g). History. Western Maryland
College.
HISTORY OF RELATIONS BETWEEN MEN AND WOMEN IN
WESTERN CIVILIZATION (u). History; and

WOMEN IN EUROPE AND AMERICA (u). History; and
SEX ROLES (u). Sociology. University of Maryland,
College Park.

Massachusetts
WOMEN IN LITERATURE (u). English. Emerson College.

Michigan
WOMEN AND AMERICAN FAMILIES (u). Women's Studies.
University of Michigan.
WOMEN IN AMERICA (u). American Thought and Language;
and WOMEN IN INDUSTRIAL SOCIETY (u). History;
and MINORITIES AND WOMEN IN THE WORLD OF WORK (u).
Racial and Ethnic Studies; and SELECTED TOPICS
IN THE PSYCHOLOGY OF WOMEN (u). Psychology of Women.
Michigan State University.

New Jersey
WOMEN IN THE POLITICAL SYSTEM (u). Political Science.
Seton Hall University.

New York
WOMEN IN FILM (u). English. Baruch College.
WOMEN IN CROSS CULTURAL PERSPECTIVE (u). Social Relations.
Colgate University.
WOMEN IN POLITICS AND LAW (u). Political Science; and
WOMEN AND VICTORIAN LITERATURE (u). English. Vassar
College.
WOMEN AND SEX (u). History; and WOMEN AND WORK (u).
History; and IMAGES OF WOMEN (u). Women's Studies.
SUNY, Fredonia.

North Dakota
WOMEN AND LITERATURE (u). English. University of North
Dakota.

Ohio
IMAGES OF WOMEN AND POPULAR CULTURE (u). Popular Culture.
Bowling Green State University.
WOMEN IN LITERATURE (u). English. Youngstown State
University.
WOMEN IN POLITICS (u). Political Science. Miami University.
WOMEN'S PLACE IN THE SEVENTIES (u). Sociology. Wright
State University.

Oklahoma
TOPICS IN WOMEN'S STUDIES. University of Oklahoma.

Oregon
WOMEN AND SPORT (g). Physical Education. Oregon State
University.

Pennsylvania
WOMEN, MINORITIES, AND THE MEDIA (u). Journalism.
Pennsylvania State University.

Texas
ROLE OF WOMEN IN SOCIETY (u). University Studies.
North Texas State University.

Vermont
WOMEN AND SOCIETY (u). Sociology; and WOMEN IN
LITERATURE (u). English. University of Vermont.

Washington
SOCIOLOGICAL PERSPECTIVES ON WOMEN (u). Sociology.
Washington State University.

Wisconsin
WOMEN IN CROSS CULTURAL PERSPECTIVES (u). Anthropology.
University of Wisconsin, Eau Claire.
WOMEN IN LITERATURE (u). English. University of Wisconsin,
Stevens Point.
WOMEN AND FILM (u). Communication. University of
Wisconsin, Superior.
WOMEN AND AMERICAN CULTURE (u). Arts and Humanities.
University of Wisconsin, Whitewater.

Washington, D.C.
WOMEN AND THE POPULAR MEDIA (u). American Studies.
The American University.
WOMEN, SEX ROLES, AND SOCIALIZATION (u). Sociology;
and HISTORY OF WOMEN IN AMERICA (u). History;
and WOMEN AND WESTERN RELIGION (u). Religion;
and WOMEN AND THE AMERICAN WORK FORCE (u). Women's
Studies. George Washington University.

Other—Popular Culture Course Types

Alabama
PUBLIC OPINION AND PROPAGANDA (u). Sociology. Auburn
University.

Arizona
COLLECTIVE BEHAVIOR AND SOCIAL MOVEMENTS (u). Sociology;
and SOCIOLOGY OF THE MALE AND FEMALE ROLES (u/g).
Women's Studies/Sociology; and STUDIES IN MODERN
MATERIAL CULTURE (u). Anthropology; and
HISTORY OF COSTUME (u). Home Economics; and

MODERN JAPANESE SOCIETY (u/g) Oriental Studies.
University of Arizona.
RECENT TRENDS (u). Humanities. Northern Arizona
University.

California
SOCIOLOGY OF POPULAR CULTURE (u). Sociology. California
State University, Fresno.
THE HERO IN AMERICAN POPULAR CULTURE (u). American
Studies; and HISTORY OF THE OCCULT AND PSEUDO—
SCIENCES (u). History. California State University—
Fullerton.
POLITICAL SOCIALIZATION THROUGH FILMS AND TELEVISION
(u). Political Science. California State University, Northridge.
DYNAMICS OF COMMUNICATION (u). English; and
CONTEMPORARY SOCIAL ISSUES (u). English; and
SOCIOLOGY OF AGING (u). Sociology; and
MAN, SCIENCE AND ENVIRONMENT (u). Chemistry/Biology.
Palomar College.
AMERICAN POPULAR HUMOR (u). American Studies; and
POPULAR CULTURE IN LATIN AMERICA (u). History. San
Diego State University.
HUMOR AND SOCIETY (u/g). Social Science. San Francisco
State University.
COMMUNICATION AND CHILDREN (u/g). Communication.
Stanford University.
COMMUNICATION AND POLITICS (u). Political Science.
University of California, Berkeley.
MINORITY GROUP POLITICS (u). Political Science; and
SEMINAR ON THEATRE AND SOCIAL ORDER (u). Theatre
Arts. UCLA.
SEX, POWER AND POLITICS (u). Political Science; and
URBAN AND RURAL BEHAVIOR (u). Sociology. University
of Southern California.
POPULAR CULTURE AND POLITICAL CONSCIOUSNESS (u).
Humanities; and FUTURE STUDIES (u). Humanities;
and BUSINESS AND SOCIETY (g). Business. California
Polytechnic State University.
PUBLIC OPINION (u). Political Science; and
UNIVERSITY AND SOCIETY (u). Sociology; and
SOCIOLOGY OF NEWS (u). Sociology; and
SOCIOLOGY OF MASS COMMUNICATIONS (u). Sociology.
University of California, Santa Barbara.
COLLECTIVE BEHAVIOR AND SOCIAL MOVEMENTS (u).
Behavioral Sciences; and AMERICAN DREAMS, MYTHS,
AND REALITIES (u). Social Sciences. California
State Polytechnic University.

Colorado
SOCIOLOGY OF ADOLESCENCE (u). Sociology; and
  PUBLIC OPINION AND POPULAR CULTURE (u). Sociology;
  and SOCIOLOGY OF THE FUTURE (u/g). Sociology;
  and HERITAGE OF AMERICAN IDEAS (u). Social Sciences;
  and FRANCE TODAY (u). French; and
  ITALY AND THE ITALIANS (u). Italian/Sociology;
  and GERMANY AND GERMANS (u). Germanic Languages
  and Literature; and INTRODUCTION TO RUSSIAN
  CULTURE (u). Russian. University of Colorado.

Connecticut
THE EARLY CONNECTICUT HOUSE: 1690-1840 (u). American
  Studies; and THE GOVERNMENT AND THE NEWS MEDIA (u).
  Government; and THE AUTOMOBILE (u). Physics.
  Wesleyan University.

Delaware
CONTEMPORARY FRANCE (u). French; and MAN AS AN
  AGENT OF ENVIRONMENTAL CHANGE (g). Geography;
  and COLLECTIVE BEHAVIOR (u). Sociology; and
  SOCIOLOGY OF SEX ROLES (u). Women's Studies.
  University of Delaware.

Florida
EFFECTS OF ADVERTISING ON SOCIETY (g). Mass Media
  and Communications; and PHYSICS OF SCIENCE
  FICTION (u). Physics; and MASS MEDIA AND
  POLITICS (u). Political Science. University
  of Central Florida.
AMERICAN STUDIES (u). Language and Literature; and
  THE AMERICAN CITY (u). History; and SCIENCE AND
  PSEUDO-SCIENCE (u). Natural Sciences; and
  SCIENCE AND SOCIETY (u). Natural Science;
  and SEXUALITY, MARRIAGE AND ALTERNATIVES (u).
  Sociology; and SOCIAL MOVEMENTS AND SOCIAL
  CHANGE (u). Sociology; and HUMAN CONFLICT IN
  BLACK AND WHITE (u). Psychology; and
  ALTERED STATES OF CONSCIOUSNESS (u). Psychology;
  and RADICAL ECONOMICS (u). Economics. University
  of North Florida.

Georgia
VIOLENCE IN AMERICA (u). History. Georgia Southwestern
  College.
SOCIOLOGY OF DEATH AND DYING (u). Sociology. Georgia State
  University.

Hawaii
THE AMERICAN CITY (u). American Studies; and
AMERICAN VALUES (u/g). American Studies; and
MEN AND WOMEN IN AMERICAN THOUGHT (u/g). American
Studies; and CULTURE AND ARTS: SURVEY (u/g).
American Studies; and AS OTHERS SEE US (u). American
Studies. University of Hawaii.

Idaho
ADVERTISING IN THE MEDIA (u). Communication; and
COMMUNICATION AND ATTITUDE CHANGE (u). Communication.
University of Idaho.

Illinois
TOPICS IN AMERICAN STUDIES (u). English; and
NEWSPAPERS AND MAGAZINES (u). Communication.
DePaul University.
AMERICAN HEROES (u). English. Bradley University.
SPECIAL TOPICS (u). Interdisciplinary Studies. Illinois
Wesleyan University.
MALENESS AND MASCULINITY (u). History. Illinois
State University.
PERSUASIVE CAMPAIGNS (u). Speech Communication; and
COMMUNICATIVE IMPACT OF FILM (u). Speech Communication;
and PHYSICS IN SOCIETY (u). Physics. Northern
Illinois University.
WITCHCRAFT, MAGIC AND THE OCCULT (u). History; and
CONTRIBUTIONS OF JOURNALISM TO LITERATURE (u).
Journalism; and SCIENCE AND SCIENCE FICTION (u).
English/Physics; and AMERICAN POLITICAL BEHAVIOR (u).
Government. Southern Illinois University.

Indiana
POLITICS OF NEWS (u). Political Science. Indiana
University/Purdue University at Indianapolis.
CHANGING SEX ROLES (u). Sociology; and AMERICAN
FAMILY (u). American Studies. University of
Notre Dame.
POPULAR CULTURE STUDIES (g). English. Purdue
Calumet College.
TOPICS IN FOREIGN CULTURE STUDIES (u). Foreign Languages;
and SOCIOLOGY OF WORK (u). Sociology. Indiana
University, South Bend.

Iowa
THE 1950'S: WERE THEY HAPPY DAYS (u). History; and
CALIFORNIA PARADISE/CALIFORNIA BABYLON (u). American
Studies. Grennell College.
BELIEF AND RITUAL (u). Sociology. Westmar College.
PROPAGANDA SERVICE AND ANALYSIS (u). English; and

CROSS CULTURE EXPLORATIONS: INTRODUCTION TO
THIRD WORLD CULTURES (u). Humanities. Iowa
State University.

Kansas
THE AMERICAN HERO (u). American Studies; and
CRIME IN AMERICA (u). American Studies; and
THE 1950s IN AMERICA (u). American Studies. Wichita
State University.

Kentucky
CULTURE AND PERSONALITY (u/g). Sociology/Anthropology.
University of Kentucky.
SOCIOLOGY OF PORNOGRAPHY AND OBSCENITY (u). Sociology;
and COLLECTIVE BEHAVIOR (u). Sociology; and
MEDIA AND POLITICAL CAMPAIGNING (u). Communication;
and ADVERTISING (u). Communication. Northern Kentucky
University.

Louisiana
THE FIFTIES (u). English; and COLLECTIVE BEHAVIOR
(u). Sociology; and SOCIAL TRENDS AND SOCIAL PROBLEMS
(u/g). Sociology; and SEX ROLES IN CONTEMPORARY SOCIETY
(u/g). Sociology; and PUBLIC OPINION AND POLITICAL
PARTICIPATION (u/g). Political Science; and
CLOTHING AND HUMAN BEHAVIOR (u). Home Economics.
Louisiana State University.

Maine
MAN'S SEARCH FOR IDENTITY (u). Arts and;
Humanities/Environmental Studies; and HOW MAN
COMMUNICATES (u). Arts and Humanities/Environmental
Studies; and MAN AND SOCIETY (u). Arts and
Humanities/Environmental Studies. Unity College.

Maryland
SEMINAR IN POPULAR CULTURE (g). Popular Culture; and
POPLULAR CULTURE THESIS (g). Popular Culture. Morgan
State University.
SOCIOLOGY OF MEDICINE (u). Sociology. Goucher College.
THE 1950s (u). American Studies. University of Maryland,
Baltimore County.
LIMITS OF PERSUASION (u/g). English; and
LIBERATION MOVEMENTS (u). Sociology; and
THE WORLD OF THE AMERICAN WORKER (u). History; and
CULTURE OF NEW ORLEANS (u). American Studies. Western
Maryland College.
SEX ROLES (u). Sociology; and COLLECTIVE
BEHAVIOR (u/g). Sociology; and CULTURAL AND
SOCIAL HISTORY OF THE AMERICAN WORKER (u/g).

History; and SPECIAL TOPICS (u). American Studies;
and AMERICAN HUMOR (u/g). American Studies; and
INQUIRIES INTO THE FUTURE OF THE COMMUNITY (u).
Human and Community Resources. University of
Maryland, College Park.

Massachusetts

WORKING: SOCIOLOGY OF OCCUPATIONS (u). Sociology;
and THE AMERICAN SCHOOL (u). Education. Merrimack
College.
SEX ROLES AND POLITICS (u). Political Science; and
CONSUMER EDUCATION (u). Education. Southeastern
Massachusetts University.
BIOLOGY AND SOCIETY (u). Biology. Westfield State
College.

Michigan
URBAN AMERICA (g).. American Arts, Culture and Society;
and THE AGRARIAN EXPERIENCE (g). American Arts,
Culture and Society; and COWBOY CULTURE (g). American
Arts, Culture and Society. Grand Valley State
College.
INDIVIDUAL AND SOCIETY IN MODERN AMERICA (u).
History/Sociology. Kalamazoo College.
INTERCULTURAL COMMUNICATIONS (u). Humanities; and
PEOPLES AND CULTURES OF THE WORLD (u). Social
Sciences. Michigan Technological University
MODERN AMERICAN CULTURE (u). History; and
THOSE WERE THE DAYS (u). New Charter College;
and TOOLING TOWARD 2001 (u). New Charter College.
Oakland University.
THE AMERICAN FAMILY (u). Sociology; and LITERARY
APPROACHES TO CULTURE: HOLLYWOOD AND AMERICAN
CULTURE (u). American Culture; and HISTORY
AND PHILOSOPHY OF DANCE IN THE AMERICAN
CULTURE (u). American Culture. University of
Michigan.
STUDIES IN POPULAR CULTURE (u). English; and
INTRODUCTION TO ADVERTISING (u). Advertising;
and CONSUMER BEHAVIOR (u). Advertising; and
AMERICAN EXPERIENCE (u). American Thought and Language;
and AMERICAN HUMOR (u). American Thought and Language;
and HISTORY OF COSTUME: WESTERN DRESS (u). Human
Environment and Design; and CLOTHING AND HUMAN BEHAVIOR
(g). Human Environment and Design; and REFUGEES, DISPLACED
PERSONS, HOSTAGES, EXILES (u). Interdisciplinary
Studies; and SCIENCE AND PSEUDO—SCIENCE (u). Natural
Science. Michigan State University

PUBLIC OPINION (u). Sociology; and GROWING UP IN
AMERICA (u). History. Central Michigan University.

Minnesota
AMERICAN PUBLIC ADDRESS (u). Speech. St. Olaf College.
THE SIXTIES (u). English/History; and
UNCONVENTIONAL LIFESTYLES (u). Sociology. College
of St. Thomas.
PUBLIC OPINION AND COMMUNICATIONS: SOCIAL FACTORS
(u/g). Sociology. University of Minnesota.

Mississippi
SOCIOLOGY OF PSYCHIC PHENOMENA (u). Sociology. University
of Mississippi.

Missouri
PROBLEMS IN ENGLISH: POPULAR CULTURE (g). English.
Southeast Missouri State University.
HISTORY OF COSTUME (u). Fashion. Stephens College.

Montana
THE FAMILY IN PERSPECTIVE (u). Humanities; and
VISUAL ANALYSIS OF ADVERTISING TECHNIQUES (u).
Humanities. University of Montana.

Nebraska
HUMAN SEXUALITY AND SOCIETY (u). Sociology; and
SEXISM IN THE ENGLISH LANGUAGE (u). English; and
HUMAN SEXUALITY AND SOCIETY (u). Anthropology; and
HISTORY OF COSTUME (u). Home Economics; and
MUSIC AND THE CHURCH (u). Music. University of
Nebraska.

New Jersey
NEW TRENDS IN JOURNALISM AND MEDIA (u). English.
Fairleigh Dickinson University.
GROWING UP AMERICAN (u). American Studies; and
AMERICA AND THE FUTURE (u). American Studies; and
RADICALISM IN 20TH CENTURY AMERICA (u). American
Studies; and SPECIAL SEMINARS IN AMERICAN STUDIES
(u). American Studies; and AMERICAN PHOTOGRAPHY (u).
American Studies. Rider College.
URBAN POPULAR CULTURE (u). Urban Studies. St. Peter's
College.

New Mexico
CONTEMPORARY GERMAN CULTURE (u). German; and
CONTEMPORARY AUSTRIAN AND SWISS CULTURE (u). German;
and CLOTHING AND HUMAN BEHAVIOR (u). Home Economics;
and THE INDIVIDUAL, WORK, AND SOCIETY (u). Honors

Program; and INTRODUCTION TO ADVERTISING IN THE MEDIA
(u). Journalism; and INTERNATIONAL ADVERTISING
(u). Journalism; and PUBLIC OPINION (u). Journalism;
and SOCIOLOGY OF THE FUTURE (u). Sociology;
and THE MEXICAN COMIC BOOK (u). Foreign Languages.
New Mexico State University.

New York
TOPICS IN INTERNATIONAL STUDIES (u). Interdisciplinary;
   and INSTITUTIONS OF CULTURE (u). Humanities.
   Daemen College.
POPULAR CULTURE AND THE SOCIAL SYSTEM (u).
   Communications. Fordham University.
AMERICAN MATERIAL CULTURE (u). American Studies. Skidmore
   College.
POPULAR CULTURE AND SOCIETY (u). General Studies; and
   SCIENCE FICTION AND SOCIAL FACT (u). General Studies.
   SUNY, Binghamton.
WORDS AND IMAGES: PRINT (u). English; and
   TOPICS IN MASS CULTURE (g). English; and
   PUBLIC OPINION AND PROPAGANDA (u). Sociology; and
   DAILY LIFE IN FRANCE (u). French. SUNY, New
   Paltz.
AMERICAN SOCIETY (u). Sociology. SUNY Technical College.
THE IDEA OF PROGRESS IN AMERICA (u). English;
   and POWER, RACISM AND PRIVILEGE (u). Social Relations;
   and VALUES AND INSTITUTIONS IN A CHANGING WORLD (u).
   University Studies. Colgate University.
ON WHEELS: AMERICAN AUTOMOBILE CULTURE (u).
   Language, Literature and Communication. Rensselaer
   Polytechnic University.
SOCIAL INSTITUTIONS (u). Humanities. School of Visual Arts.
THE HOLOCAUST AND THE DIMENSION OF EVIL (u). Sociology;
   and SOCIOLOGY OF SEX WORLDS (u). Sociology; and
   THE POLITICS OF THE FUTURE (u). Political Science;
   and IMAGES OF THE AMERICAN WEST: EL DORADO TO
   MARLBORO COUNTRY. (u). American Culture. Vassar
   College.
SEX, VIOLENCE AND RACISM (u). English/Special Studies;
   and LOVE AND DEATH IN MODERN AMERICA (u). English;
   and MEDIA LITERATURE AND TEACHING OF ENGLISH (u).
   English; and POPULAR CULTURE IN ENGLISH CURRICULUM (g).
   English; and PRESS AND POLITICS (u). Political Science;
   and COLLECTIVE BEHAVIOR (u). Sociology. SUNY,
   Fredonia.
COSTUME THROUGH THE AGES (u). Consumer Studies. SUNY,
   Buffalo.

North Carolina
HOLLYWOOD'S AMERICA (u). History; and AMERICAN
   ARCHITECTURE (u). Humanities. North Carolina
   Wesleyan College.
SEX ROLES IN SOCIETY (u). Sociology. University
   of North Carolina, Wilmington.

North Dakota
STAR TREK (u). English. University of North Dakota.

Ohio
ADVERTISING (u). Marketing; and SPACESHIP EARTH
   (u). Educational Foundations and Inquiry; and
   THE AMERICAN CITY (u). Geography; and
   CULTURAL GEOGRAPHY (u). Geography; and
   CONTEMPORARY GERMAN LIFE (u). German; and
   INTERPRETATIONS OF AMERICAN CULTURE (u). American
   Studies; and MASS MEDIA AND PUBLIC POLICY (u).
   Political Science; and SENIOR SEMINAR (u). Popular
   Culture; and TOPICS IN POPULAR CULTURE (u).
   Popular Culture; and PROBLEMS IN POPULAR CULTURE
   (u/g). Popular Culture; and TEACHING POPULAR
   CULTURE (g). Popular Culture; and THEORIES
   AND METHODS IN POPULAR CULTURE (g). Popular
   Culture; and SEMINAR IN POPULAR CULTURE (g).
   Popular Culture; and AMERICAN SOCIETY (u). Sociology.
   Bowling Green State University.
FRESHMAN SEMINAR (u). Findlay College.
PHYSICS OF SCIENCE FICTION (u). Physics. Youngstown
   State University.
CONTEMPORARY AMERICAN LANDSCAPES (u). Geography. Ohio
   Wesleyan University.
FIELD STUDY IN ARCHITECTURE (u). Chemistry; and
   THE INDIVIDUAL IN SOCIETY (u). Experimental Programs;
   and CONSUMER CHEMISTRY (u). Chemistry; and
   THE INDIVIDUAL IN SOCIETY (u). Experimental Programs;
   and VALUES FOR SURVIVAL (u). Experimental Programs;
   and HISTORY OF COSTUME (u). Home Economics; and
   CHANGING WORLDS OF MEN AND WOMEN (u). Home Economics;
   and CONSUMER AND TODAY'S SOCIETY (u). Home Economics;
   and GREAT CONTEMPORARY ISSUES IN JOURNALISM (u).
   Journalism; and ADVERTISING SEMINAR (u). Journalism;
   and CONSUMER/BUYER BEHAVIOR (u). Marketing;
   and CONTEMPORARY POLITICAL AFFAIRS (u). Political
   Science; and PUBLIC OPINION AND MASS COMMUNICATION
   (u). Sociology; and SOCIOLOGY OF WORK (u). Sociology;
   and CONSUMER FAMILY IN TODAY'S SOCIETY (g).
   Home Economics; and SOCIAL ROLE OF THE PRESS (g).
   Journalism; and MUSIC OF EARLY CHRISTIAN CHURCH (g).
   Music. Kent State University.

THE HOUSE (u). Architecture; and POLITICS,
  CULTURE AND SOCIETY (u). Political Science;
  and MASS MEDIA AND POLITICS (u). Political Science.
  Miami University.
CONSUMER BEHAVIOR (u). Marketing; and COLLECTIVE
  BEHAVIOR (u). Sociology. Wright State University.

Oklahoma
SOCIOLOGY OF DEATH (u/g). Sociology. Oklahoma State University.
ADVERTISING AND CONSUMER BEHAVIOR (g). Journalism; and
  MASS MEDIA AND PUBLIC OPINION (u/g). Journalism.
  University of Oklahoma.
CONSUMER HEALTH AND MASS MEDIA (u). Health, Physical
  Education and Recreation. Central State University.

Oregon
AMERICAN CAR CULTURE (u). History; and CURRENT CULTURE
  (u). English. Southern Oregon State College.
THE AMERICAN WEST (u). Sociology. Willamette University

Pennsylvania
ADVERTISING AND CONTEMPORARY SOCIETY (u/g). Journalism;
  and PHYSICS, COMMUNICATIONS, NOISE AND SOCIETY (u).
  Physics; and CONTEMPORARY MAN AND SOCIETY (u).
  Social Science. Pennsylvania State University.
HARLEM RENAISSANCE (u). English. Lincoln University.
JOURNALISM IN POPULAR CULTURE (u). Journalism; and
  COMMUNICATION AND POPULAR CULTURE (u). Speech;
  and CULTURE AND SOCIETY (g). Psychology. Temple
  University
POPULAR CULTURE AND THE MEDIA OF MASS COMMUNICA—
  TION FOR THE MIDDLE AND SECONDARY SCHOOL (u). Communi-
  cations; and ASPECTS OF CONTEMPORARY SPAIN (u/g). Spanish;
  and ASPECTS OF CONTEMPORARY LATIN AMERICA (u/g).
  Spanish. Millersville state College.
THE AMERICAN SCENE (u). Geography; and POPULAR
  MATERIAL CULTURE (u). American Studies. Pennsylvania
  State University, Abington.

South Carolina
SOUTHERN STUDIES (u). History. University of South
  Carolina, Aiken.

South Dakota
SOCIETY AND SEXUALITY (u). Social Science; and
  SOCIAL CHANGE (u). Social Change. Black Hills State
  College.

MYTHOLOGY AND LITERATURE (u). English; and
GEOGRAPHY OF THE FUTURE (u). Geography; and
PRINCIPLES OF ADVERTISING (u). Journalism; and
PUBLIC OPINION AND PROPAGANDA (g). Journalism.
South Dakota State University.

Tennessee

SURVEY OF ADVERTISING (u). Journalism; and
THE MAGAZINE (u). Journalism; and
SOCIOLOGY OF SEX ROLES (u). Sociology. Memphis State
University.

Texas
PUBLIC OPINION AND PROPAGANDA (g). Journalism; and
MASS MEDIA AND AMERICAN POLITICS (u). Political Science;
and PUBLIC OPINION AND PARTICIPATION (u/g); Political
Science; and CONTEMPORARY MORAL ISSUES (u). Philosophy.
North Texas State University.
CONTEMPORARY FRANCE AS REFLECTED IN THE PRESS (u).
Modern Languages. Texas Christian University.
THE BLACK PREACHER (u/g). Speech Communication. Texas
Southern University.
TOPICS IN THE AMERICAN WEST (u). History and Border Studies;
and CULTURE IN AMERICAN LITERATURE (u). American
Studies/English; and COMMUNICATING IN URBAN LIFE
(u). Journalism-Broadcasting-Film/Urban Studies;
and DEATH AND DYING (u). Sociology. Trinity University.
INDEPENDENT STUDIES IN AMERICAN CULTURE (u). American
Studies; and MAIN CURRENTS IN PRE-INDUSTRIAL CULTURE
(u). American Studies; and MAIN CURRENTS IN INDUSTRIAL
AMERICAN CULTURE (u). American Studies; and
SPECIAL STUDIES (u). American Studies. University of Texas,
San Antonio.
AMERICAN MANNERS AND MORALS (u). Religion. Rice University.
HOUSING IN THE UNITED STATES (g). Home Economics; and
SHAPING THE FUTURE (u). History. East Texas
State University.

Utah
LIBERAL EDUCATION SERIES (u). Liberal Education. University
of Utah.
KINSHIP, MARRIAGE AND THE FAMILY (u). Anthropology.
Brigham Young University.

Vermont
COLLEGE CULTURE (u). Anthropology; and
HISTORY OF COSTUME (u). Home Economics; and
ALIENATION IN MODERN SOCIETY (u). Sociology;
and DRUGS AND SOCIETY (u). Sociology. University
of Vermont.

Virginia
LITERARY APPROACH TO POPULAR CULTURE (u). English; and
   RELIGION AND SCIENCE FICTION (u). Philosophy/Religion.
   George Mason University.
AMERICAN HERO (u). American Studies. Lynchburg College.
   POLITICAL BEHAVIOR (u). Politics. Washington and
   Lee University.
CHANGING SEX ROLES IN CONTEMPORARY SOCIETY (u).
   Sociology; and FUTURE SOCIETY (u). Sociology. College of William
   and Mary.

Washington
CLOTHES AND CULTURE (u). Clothing, Interior Design, and Textiles;
   and COLLECTIVE BEHAVIOR AND SOCIAL MOVEMENTS. (u).
   Sociology. Washington State University.
PUBLIC OPINION AND PROPAGANDA (u). Journalism.
   Walla Walla College.
CHATAUQUA (u). Social Science; and ENVIRONMENTS,
   PERCEPTION AND DESIGN (u). Social Science; and
   INVENTION AND DISCOVERY (u). Social Science. The
   Evergreen State College.

West Virginia
CONS, FRAUDS, HYPES AND THE NATURE OF MAN (u). Freshman
   Studies. Bethany College.
MEDIA IN COMMUNICATION AND EDUCATION (g). Speech
   Communication. University of West Virginia.

Wisconsin
AMERICAN LIFE (u/g). Interdisciplinary Studies; and
   FUTURES (u). Peace Studies. University of Wisconsin,
   Superior.
PERSPECTIVES ON AMERICA (u). Arts and Humanities. University
   of Wisconsin, Whitewater.

Washington, D.C.
HISTORY OF FURNITURE (u). Art; and TRAVEL AND TOURISM
   (u). Human Kinetics and Leisure Studies; and
   PUBLIC OPINION AND POLITICAL SOCIALIZATION (u).
   Political Science; and SOCIAL MOVEMENTS (u). Sociology;
   and PUBLIC OPINION AND MASS COMMUNICATION (u).
   Sociology. George Washington University.

Appendix B

List of Contributors and Schools Surveyed

This appendix lists the schools surveyed and the contributors who supplied the information. The number behind the state name denotes the number of courses surveyed in that state. The number in parentheses behind the listing of each school indicates the number of courses in a particular school.

Alabama (15).
Patrick D. Morrow
English
Auburn University (4)
Auburn, Al. 36830

M.K. Marks
History and Political Science
Alabama A & M University (0)
Normal, AL 35762

Lloyd N. Denninger
English
University of South Alabama (2)
Montgomery, AL 36688

Lynda W. Brown
English
Auburn Univ. at Montgomery (8)
Montgomery 36117

Alaska (1)
University of Alaska (1)
Fairbanks 99701

Arizona (33)
Melvin E. Hecht
Geography
University of Arizona (21)
Tucson 85721

Glenn M. Reed
English/American Studies
Northern Arizona University (12)
Flagstaff 86011

Arkansas (7)
Dr. Fontane
English
Arkansas State University (2)
State University 72767

John W. Crawford
English
Henderson State University (2)
Arkadelphia 71923

Frank Scheide
Speech and Dramatic Art
University of Arkansas (3)
Fayetteville 72701

California (214)

Ms. Sydney Carson
English/Film & TV
CA College of Arts & Crafts (1)
Oakland 94618

Martin Van Buren & Norman Klein
Critical Studies
CA Institute of the Arts (2)
Fresno 93740

Joel Best
Sociology
CA State Univ.—Fresno (1)
Valencia 91355

Robert G. Porfirio
American Studies
California State Univ. (16)
Fullerton 92634

Heinrich Richard Falk
Theatre
California State University (15)
Northridge 91330

Velma Bourgeau Richmond
English
Holy Names College (0)
Oakland 95619

Leonore N. Dowling
Art
Immaculate Heart College (7)
Los Angeles 90027

Jim Becker
Communication
Pacific College (0)
Fresno 93702

Dana Hawkes
Telecommunications
Palomar College (15)
San Marcos 92069

Linda Malm
Communication
Pitzer College (1)
Claremont 91711

Paul Vanderwood
History/American Studies
San Diego State University (12)
San Diego 92115

Stanford University (11)
Stanford 94305

Arthur Asa Berger
Broadcast Communication Arts
San Francisco State University (17)
San Francisco 94132

Betty Rosenberg
Senior Lecturer Emeritus
Univ. of California, Los Angeles (28)
Los Angeles 90024

David N. Lyon
American Studies
University of the Pacific (2)
Stockton 95211

Joseph Simms
American Studies
University of Southern California (9)
Los Angeles 90007

Norman L. Friedman
Sociology and American Studies
CA State College, Los Angeles (8)
Los Angeles 90032

Edward Whetmore
Communication Arts
University of San Francisco (3)
San Francisco 94117

David Sanders
Humanities and Social Sciences
Harvey Mudd College (2)
Claremont 91711

University of California (19)
Berkeley 94720

Donald Lazere
English
CA Polytechnic State University (10)
San Luis Obispo 93433

Roderick Nash
History
Univ. of California, Santa Barbara (21)
Santa Barbara 93106

Richard S. Hyslop
Social Sciences
CA State Polytechnic University (8)
Pomona 91768

Darrell Hamamoto
Comparative Culture
University of California, Irvine (6)
Irvine 92712

Colorado (44)

Marcelle Rabbin
Romance Languages
Colorado College (0)
Colorado Springs 80903

John Griess
Communication Arts
Regis College (3)
Denver 80221

John Senatore
English and Philosophy
Univ. of Southern Colorado (2)
Pueblo 81001

Richard Wolniewicz
Economics, Geography & Management
USAF Academy (1)
Colorado Springs 80840

Zelda Jeanne Rouillard
English
Western State College (5)
Gunnison 81230

Russell E. Shain
Journalism
University of Colorado (33)
Boulder 80309

Connecticut (33)
Hughson Mooney
History
Central Connecticut State College (6)
New Britain 06050

Paul Stacy
English
University of Hartford (1)
West Hartford 06117

Douglas Robillard
English
University of New Haven (0)
West Haven 06516

Richard Ohwann
English
Wesleyan University (21)
Middletown 06457

Robert A. McDonald
Dramatic Arts
University of Connecticut (7)
Storrs 06268

Delaware (23)
Thomas Pauly
English
University of Delaware (23)
Newark 19711

Florida (67)
Sister Dorothy Jehle
English
Barry College (0)
Miami 33161

Richard Crepeau
History
Univ. of Central Florida (15)
Orlando 32816

Gary Littarman
Language and Literature
University of North Florida (43)
Jacksonville 32216

William Coyle
English
Florida Atlantic University (9)
Boca Raton 33431

Georgia (26)
Marya M. Dubose
English
Augusta College (2)
Augusta 30904

J.P. Telotte
English and Speech
Berry College (1)
Mt. Berry 30149

Thomas E. Williams
History
Emory University (6)
Atlanta 30322

May C. Brown
English
Georgia Institute of Technology (3)
Atlanta 30332

Steve Gurr
Social Sciences
Georgia Southwestern College (1)
Americus 31709

Derek Whordley
Graduate & Professional Education
Mercer University (3)
Atlanta 30341

Amos St. Germain
English & History
Southern Technical Insititute (2)
Marietta 30060

Earl F. Bargainnier
Language and Literature
Wesleyan College (3)
Macon 31201

Lisa B. McNerney
Fine Arts
West Georgia College (1)
Carrollton 30117

Eugene Hellahan
English
Georgia State University
Atlanta 30303

Adrienne Bond
English
Mercer University (1)
Macon 31201

Robert L. Caine
Social Science
Columbus College (0)
Columbus 31907

Hawaii (9)
Sarah Sanderson King
Communication
University of Hawaii, Manoa (9)
Honolulu 96822

Idaho (13)
University of Idaho (13)

Illinois (66)
R. Tweet

Marty Knepper
English
Augustana College (5)
Rock Island 61201

Edgar L. Chapman
English and Foreign Languages
Bradley University (6)
Peoria 61625

Elmer Pry
English
DePaul University (9)
Chicago 60614

Arnold E. Davidson
English
Elmhurst College (0)
Elmhurst 60126

Richard Harrison
Humanities
Eureka College (1)
Eureka 61530

Barbara Bowman
English
Illinois Wesleyan University (4)
Bloomington 61701

Robert J. Brake
Information Sciences
Illinois State University (11)
Normal 61761

Gerald Forsher
Humanities
Malcolm X College (1)
Chicago 60612

Mary Alma Sullivan
Communication
Mundelein College (4)
Chicago 60660

Robert T. Self
English
Northern Illinois University (11)
DeKalb 60115

Robert Lauer, Sociology
Jules Zanger, English
Southern Illinois University (13)
Edwardsville 62026

Edwin A. Hollatz
Speech Communication
Wheaton College (0)
Wheaton 60187

Indiana (43)
Jane S. Bakerman
English
Indiana State University (5)
Terre Haute 47809

Kathleen G. Klein
English
Indiana University/Purdue Univ. (1)
Indianapolis 46202

John C. Carlisle
English
Purdue Calumet (5)
Hammond 46323

John E. Findling
History
Indiana University Southeast (6)
New Albany 47150

Notre Dame University (13)
Notre Dame 46556

Larry Clipper
English
Indiana University (13)
South Bend 46615

Iowa (58)
G. Eckley
English
Drake University (3)
Des Moines 50311

Liahna Babener
American Studies and English
Grinnell College (8)
Grinnell 50112

Catherine Ann Collins
Speech and Theatre
Harland Nelson,
English
Luther College (4)
Decorah 52101

Roy M. Anker
Language and Literature
Northwestern College (1)
Orange City 54041

Patrick E. White
English
Westmar College (4)
LeMars 51031

Donald Dunlop
English
Iowa State University (15)
Ames 50011

University of Iowa (24)
Iowa City 52242

Kansas (11)
Thomas Ward
Sociology
Baker University (5)
Baldwin City 66006

Gregory S. Sojka
American Studies
Wichita State University (6)
Wichita 67228

Kentucky (33)
Gary R. Drum
Telecommunications
Kentucky Wesleyan College (1)
Owensboro 42301

Delbert E. Wylder
English
Murray State University (10)
Murray 42071

Jane E. Johnson
Registrar
Pikeville College (0)
Pikeville 41501

N. Van Tubergan
Communications
University of Kentucky (8)
Lexington 40506

Thomas Zaniello
Literature
Northern Kentucky Univ. (18)
Highland Heights 41076

Louisiana (36)
Fraser Snowden
Philosophy
Northwestern State University (1)
Natchitoches 71457

Jane Faile
English
Louisiana State University (24)
Baton Rouge 70803

John W. Fiero
English
Univ. of Southwestern Louisiana (11)
Lafayette 70504

Maine (6)
Katherine Donithorne
Anthropology
Unity College (3)
Unity 04888

Eugene Schleh
History
University of Southern Maine (3)
Gorham 04038

Maryland (93)
Suzanne Greene
History
Morgan State University (13)
Baltimore 21210

Brownlee Sands Corin
Performing Arts
Goucher College (7)
Towson 21204

Philip W. Warken
History
U.S. Naval Academy (1)
Annapolis 21402

Karen M. Stoddard
American Studies
Univ. of Maryland, Baltimore County (7)
Baltimore 21228

Robert Fallaw
History
Washington College (0)
Chestertown 21620

Keith Richwine
English
Western Maryland College (16)
Westminster 21157

Lawrence Mintz
American Studies
University of Maryland (49)
College Park 20742

Massachusetts (64)
Louise N. Soldoni
English
Anna Maria College (1)
Paxton 01612

Lawrence H. Fuchs
American Studies
Brandeis University (2)
Waltham 02194

Harvard University (4)
Cambridge 02138

Charlotte Lindoreau
English
Emerson College (8)
Boston 02116

Stanley A. Clark
Sociology
Gordon College (0)
Wenham 01984

John P. Fleming
English (American Studies)
Merrimack College (11)
North Andover 01845

George Winston
English and Humanities
Nichols College (0)
Dudley 01570

Gerald Herman, History
Jerry Griswold, English
Northeastern University (16)
Boston 01970

Gerard O'Connor
English
University of Lowell (6)
Lowell 01854

Marie L. Ahearn
English
Southeastern Massachusetts Univ. (9)
North Darthmouth 02747

Nicholas E. Tawa
Music
Univ. of Massachusetts, Boston (4)
Boston 02125

Bette B. Roberts
English
Westfield State College (3)
Westfield 01085

J. Rosenmeirer
English
Tufts College (0)
Medford 02155

Michigan (128)
Ronald C. Massanari
Religious Studies
Alma College (0)
Alma 48801

Gary Lend
History
Andrews University (0)
Berrien Springs 49102

David S. Bertolotti
Humanities and Social Science
General Motors Institute (1)
Flint 48502

Mary A. Seeger, Assistant Dean
College of Arts and Sciences
Grand Valley State College (11)
Allendale 49401

David Strauss
History
Kalamazoo College (2)
Kalamazoo 49003

Charles W. Nelson
Humanities
Michigan Technological Univ. (5)
Houghton 49931

Ann Marie Roberts
Nazareth College (0)
Nazareth 49074

A.D. Shumsky
Communications Division
Northwestern Michigan College (1)
Traverse City 49684

Maurice F. Brown
Mark E. Workman, English
Oakland University (14)
Rochester 48063

John R. Knott
English
University of Michigan (11)
Ann Arbor 48105

Lew Carlson
Humanities
Western Michigan University (3)
Kalamazoo 49008

Donald Palumbo
English
Northern Michigan University (2)
Marquette 49855

Sarah Rutcowska
Acting Dean of Studies
St. Mary's College (0)
Orchard Lake 48033

Larry N. Landrum
English
Michigan State University (60)
East Lansing 48824

Francis Molson
English
Central Michigan Univ. (18)
Mt. Pleasant 48858

Minnesota (44)
Roy W. Meyer
English
Mankato State University (8)
Mankato 56001

Erling T. Jorstad
History and American Studies
St. Olaf College (6)
Northfield 55057

Luann Kitchel
English
College of St. Thomas (8)
St. Paul 55105

University of Minnesota
Duluth (11)
Duluth 55812

Harold E. Hinds, Jr.
History
Univ. of Minnesota—Morris (3)
Morris 56267

Gary Alan Fine
Sociology
Darryl Hattenhauer
American Studies
University of Minnesota (8)
Minneapolis 55455

James E. Johnson
History
Bethel College
St. Paul 55113

Mississippi(5)

Frank M. Laurence
English
Mississippi Univ. for Women (0)
Columbus 39701

Larry W. DeBord
Sociology and Anthropology
Univ. of Mississippi (3)
University 38677

James C. Downey
Music
William Carey College (2)
Hattiesburg 39401

Missouri (20)

Rosemary K. Curb
Language and Literature
Missouri Southern State College (2)
Joplin 64801

Charles Hearn
English
Southwest Missouri State Univ. (5)
Cape Girardeau 63701

Alan R. Havig
History-Social Sciences
Stephens College (11)
Columbia 65201

Jeanne F. Bedell
Humanities
Univ. of Missouri, Rolla (2)
Rolla 65401

Montana (6)

Robert Ziegler
Humanities and Social Sciences
Montana College of Mineral Science
and Technology (1)
Butte 59701

Michael W. McClintock
English
University of Montana (5)
Missoula 59812

Nebraska (38)

Pierce Hazel
English
Kearney State College (3)
Kearney 68847

John Robinson
English
University of Nebraska (35)
Lincoln 68508

New Hampshire (8)

Dartmouth College (8)
Hanover 03755

New Jersey (55)

Walter Cummina
English
Fairleigh Dickinson Univ., Madison (10)
Madison 07940

Paul Levinson
Communications, Speech and Theatre
Fairleigh Dickinson Univ., Teaneck (10)
Teaneck 07666

Gerald Lee Ratliff
Speech/Theatre
Montclair State College (6)
Upper Montclair 07043

R.J. Butsch, Sociology
Albright G. Zimmerman, Amer. Studies
Rider College (15)
Lawrenceville 08648

Edward Shapiro
American Studies
Seton Hall University (6)
South Orange 07079

Thomas Mansheim, Urban Studies
William Thomaier, Fine Arts
St. Peter's College (6)
Jersey City 07306

Katherine M. Restaino, Dean
St. Peter's College, (0)
Englewood Cliffs 07632

Rhoda C. Freeman
Upsala College
East Orange 07019

New Mexico (20)

Charles Tatum
Foreign Languages
New Mexico State Univ. (20)
Las Cruces 88003

New York (167)
Robert A. Morace
English
Daemen College (5)
Amherst 14226

Herbert A. Wisbey Jr.
History
Elmira College (0)
Elmira 14901

Albert Kreiling
Communications
Fordham University, Bronx (4)
Bronx 10458

Margaret Lamb
Humanities Division
Fordhom Univ. College, Lincoln Center (9)
New York 10023

Joseph W. Slade
Media Arts
Long Island University (4)
Brooklyn 11201

Margaret Knapp
Media Arts
Molloy College (9)
Rockville Centre 11570

Frances M. Broderick
Communication Arts
College of Mt. St. Vincent (10)
Riverdale 10471

Harold Schechter
English
Queens College, CUNY (5)
Flushing 11367

Salvatore Mondeiro
History
Rochester Institute of Tech. (5)
Rochester 14623

Mary C. Lynn, American Studies
William S. Fox, Sociology
Skidmore College
Saratoga Springs 12866

Thomas P. Prioetti
Communication/Journalism
St. John Fisher College (0)
Rochester 14618

David G. Nielsen
General Studies & Professional Educa.
SUNY, Binghamton (8)
Binghamton 13901

Irving J. Weiss
English
SUNY, New Paltz (17)
New Paltz 12562

Barrett Potter
Social Science
SUNY Technical College (4)
Alfred 14802

George Grella
English
University of Rochester (3)
Rochester 14627

Marie Jean Lederman
English
Baruch College, CUNY (11)
New York 10022

D. Sewell
Social Relations
Colgate University (9)
Hamilton 13346

A. O'Brien
Media/Arts
New York Institute of Tech. (8)
Old Westbury 11568

Peter L. Stromberg
English
U.S. Military Academy (0)
West Point 10996

Charles L. Sanford
Language, Literature & Comm.
Rensselaer Polytechnic Institute (2)
Troy 12181

Ellen Feldman
Film
School of Fine Arts (5)
New York 10010

Clyde Griffen
History and American Culture
Vassar College (13)
Poughkeepsie 12601

Ronald J. Ambrosetti
English
SUC, Fredonia (20)
Fredonia 14063

Milton Plesur
History
SUNY, Buffalo (18)
Buffalo 14261

North Carolina (19)
David A. Jones
History
North Carolina Wesleyan College (4)
Rocky Mount 27801

Duke University (6)
Durham 27708

Julia Kirk Blackwelder
History
Univ. of North Carolina, Charlotte (0)
Charlotte 28223

Harold Farwell
English
Western Carolina University (2)
Cullowhee 28723

R. Von Tresckow Napp
Social Sciences
Winston-Salem State University (0)
Winston-Salem 27102

Steven Carter
English
Univ. of North Carolina, Wilmington (7)
Wilmington 28401

North Dakota (8)
Neil J. McCutehan
Speech
University of North Dakota (6)
Grand Forks 58201

North Dakota State University (2)
Fargo 58102

Ohio (164)
Michelle Kuebbeler
Popular Culture
Bowling Green State University (37)
Bowling Green 43403

Sharon Bannister
History
Findlay College (1)
Findlay 45840

Timothy E. Scheurer
Humanities
Franklin University (1)
Columbus 43215

Paul A. Rochford
Art
Hiram College (0)
Hiram 44234

Thomas Duan
English
Miami University, Hamilton (1)
Hamilton 45011

Leroy V. Eid
History
University of Dayton (5)
Dayton 54569

Ohio State University (22)
Columbus 43210

M.A. Budge, English
Sid Roberts, History
Youngstown State University (8)
Youngstown 44555

David H. Hickcox
Geography/Geology
Ohio Wesleyan University (2)
Delaware 43015

Kent State University (54)
Kent 44244

Richard D. Erlich
English
Miami University (18)
Oxford 45056

James M. Hughes
English
Wright State University (14)
Dayton 45435

Oklahoma (27)
Michael K. Schoenecke
English
Oklahoma State University (5)
Stillwater, 74074

Joan Worley
English
University of Oklahoma (12)
Norman 73069

Jerry G. Nye
Language Arts
Southwestern State University (2)
Weatherford 73096

Clifton Warren
Creative Studies
Central State University (8)
Edmond 73035

Oregon (15)
Michael Oriard
English
Oregon State University (8)
Corvallis 97331

Don L. Reynolds, Jr.
English
Southern Oregon State College (4)
Ashland 97520

Walter Gerson
Sociology
Willamette University (3)
Salem 97301

Pennsylvania (93)
Janice Radway
American Civilization
University of Pennsylvania (7)
Philadelphia 19109

D. Voigt
Sociology/Anthropology
Albright College (2)
Reading 19607

Paul A. Knights
History
Allegheny College (0)
Meadville 16335

C.T. Walters
Art
Bloomsburg State College (4)
Bloomsburg 17815

Jerome Zurek
English/Communications
Cabrini College (5)
Radnor 19087

John Andrews
American Studies
Franklin and Marshall College (1)
Lancaster 17604

Dennis K. Renner
English
Gannon College (2)
Haverford 19041

Neil Lehman
History
Indiana Univ. of Pennsylvania (9)
Indiana 15701

Edward J. Gallagher
Lehigh University (4)
Bethlehem 18015

Pennsylvania State University (18)
University Park 16802

Richard E. Hawes
English
Lincoln University (1)
Lincoln University 19352

Ralph S. Graber
English
Muhlenberg College (2)
Allentown 18104

Stephen G. Bolger
English/American Studies
Rosemont College (0)
Rosemont 19010

M.A. Conroy
English
Seton Hall College (0)
Greensburg, 15601

Sister M. Henrietta
Humanities
Gwynedd-Mercy College (0)
Gwynedd Valley 19437

J. Hayes
Journalism
Temple University (9)
Philadelphia 19101

Ellen M. Casey
English
University of Scranton (1)
Scranton 18510

John Bryant
English
Widner College (1)
Chester 19013

John F. O'Connell
English
Millersville State College (8)
Millersville 17551

Walter C.J. Andersen
Language, Literature and Comm.
College Misericordia (2)
Dallas 18612

James F. Smith
English/American Studies
Pennsylvania State U., Abington (13)
Abington 19001

South Carolina (17)
Louis Gallo
English
Columbia College (4)
Columbia 29203

B. Lee Cooper
History
Newberry College (0)
Newberry

Tom Mack
English
University of South Carolina (3)
Aiken 29801

John Scott Wilson
History
University of South Carolina (5)
Columbia 29208

Peter Neil Barry
Academic Affairs
University of South Carolina (2)
Lancaster 29720

Eva Mills
English
Winthrop College (0)
Rock Hill 29733

Charles H. Lippy, History
Roger B. Rollin, English
Clemson University (3)
Clemson 29631

South Dakota (8)
Dan Peterson
Social Science
Black Hills State College (6)
Spearfish 57783

J.W. Yarbrough
English
South Dakota State University (2)
Brookings 57006

Tennessee (31)
Paul F. Blankenship
Religion and Philosophy
Lambuth College (0)
Jackson 38301

Charles K. Wolfe
English
Middle Tennessee University (6)
Murfreesboro 37132

Larry R. Bowers
Human Resources
Morristown College (0)
Morristown 37814

Donald Menchise
English
Tennessee State University (1)
Nashville 37203

Jeffrey Folks
English
Tennessee Wesleyan College (2)
Athens 37303

Allen Rushing
History
East Tennessee State University (4)
Johnson City 37601

Nona Bolin
Philosophy
Memphis State University (18)
Memphis 38156

Stuart Stumpf
History
Tennessee Technical University (0)
Cookeville 38501

Texas (80)
David B. Merrell
English
Abilene Christian University (4)
Abilene 79601

Light T. Cummins
History
Austin College (3)
Sherman 75090

Harvey Solganick
Communications
Dallas Eastfield College (4)
Mesquite 75150

Lane Roth
Communication
Lamar University (3)
Beaumont 77707

F. Leslie Smith, Radio/TV/Film
John F. Miller, Philosophy
North Texas State University (18)
Denton 76203

Ken Burke
Broadcasting/Film
Southern Methodist University (4)
Dallas 75275

H.R. Huebel
History
Texas A & I University (0)
Kingsville 78363

Fred Erisman
English
Texas Christian University (6)
Fort Worth 76129

Frank H. Smyrl
Dean, Humanities and Social Sciences
Texas Eastern University (1)
Tyler 75701

Gary Carr
Theatre/Cinema
Texas Southern University (3)
Houston 77004

Margurite Davenport
English
Trinity University (3)
San Antonio 78284

Joan Chandler
School of Arts and Humanities
Univ. of Texas at Dallas (7)
Richardson 75080

Carol Billman
English
University of Texas at San Antonio (5)
San Antonio 78285

Theodore D. Freidell
Dean, Arts and Sciences
West Texas State University (1)
Canyon 79016

William Martin
Sociology
Rice University (6)
Houston 77001

James W. Byrd
Literature and Language
East Texas State University (12)
Commerce 75428

Utah (14)
David Lee
English
Southern Utah State College (0)
Cedar City 84720

Tom Sobchack
English
University of Utah (4)
Salt Lake City 84112

Jack Scherting
English
Utah State University (3)
Logan 84322

Tad Z. Danielewski
Film/TV
Brigham Young University (7)
Provo 84602

Vermont (22)
Rush Welter
History
Bennington College (0)
Bennington 05201

Patricia Austin
English
College of St. Joseph the Provider (2)
Rutland 05701

Richard M. Judd
American Studies
Marlboro College (0)
Marlboro 05344

Kennech C. Smith
Assistant Dean
Norwich University (0)
Northfield 05663

Norbert A. Kuntz
History/American Studies
St. Michael's College (0)
Winooski 05404

Lee Thompson
English
University of Vermont (20)
Burlington 05401

Virginia (25)
Robert Pielke
Philosophy/Religion
George Mason University (4)
Fairfax 22030

William H. Young
American Studies
Lynchburg College (5)
Lynchburg 24501

Robert M. Nelson
English
University of Richmond
Richmond 23123

Larryetta Schall
English
Hampton Institute (1)
Hampton 23668

John K. Jennings
Journalism and Comm.
Washington and Lee Univ. (6)
Lexington 24450

Lynn Z. Bloom
English
College of William and Mary (4)
Williamsburg 23185

Washington (27)
Gary B. Wilson
Communication Arts
Pacific Lutheran Univ. (5)
Tacoma 98447

Patricia Kolk Connor
Fine Arts
Washington State Univ. (14)
Pullman 991643

C.A. Schwantes
History
Walla Walla College (4)
College Place 99324

Gordon Beck
Cinema/Art History
The Evergreen State College (4)
Olympia 98505

West Virginia (20)
Larry E. Grimes
English
Bethany College (4)
Bethany 26032

Guy E. Lometti
Speech Communications
West Virginia University (6)
Morgantown 26506

I.M. Taplin
Sociology
West Virginia Wesleyan College (0)
Buchhan 26201

David C. Brooks
Office of Academic Dean
West Liberty State College (10)
West Liberty 26074

Wisconsin (44)
Carl G. Balson
Performing Arts
Beloit College (1)
Beloit 53511

James W. Arnold
Journalism
Marquette University (6)
Milwaukee 53233

Albert E. Krahn
English
Milwaukee Area Tech. College (2)
Milwaukee 53203

David Allen
English
Northland College (1)
Ashland 54806

Douglas Pearson
English
Univ. of Wisconsin, Eau Claire (2)
Eau Claire 54701

James DeMuth
English
Univ. of Wisconsin, River Falls (2)
River Falls 54022

William C. Davidson, Comm.
Richard Doxtator, English
Univ. of Wisconsin, Stevens Point (12)
Stevens Point 54481

Egal Feldman
History
Univ. of Wisconsin, Superior (6)
Superior 54880

Mark S. Dorn
American Studies/History
Univ. of Wisconsin, Whitewater (12)
Whitewater 53190

Peter A. Fritzell
English
Lawrence University (0)
Appleton 54911

District of Columbia (27)
Trenton Batson
American Studies
Gallaudet College
Washington 20002

Kay Mussell
American Studies
The American University (7)
Washington 20016

Cynthia W. Chard
American Civilization
George Washington University (19)
Washington 20002

Virgin Islands
Dennis E. Parker
Humanities
College of the Virgin Islands (0)
St. Thomas, U.S.V.I. 00801

Appendix C:
Survey Questionnaire

Dear Colleague:

You have been selected from a list of college professors interested in the study of popular culture to contribute to an important new study in education at the college and university level.

The Popular Culture Association, using the resources of the Center for the Study of Popular Culture at Bowling Green State University, is undertaking a project to determine how many courses in popular culture are being offered at four-year colleges and universities in this country and what subjects are being taught in these courses.

Apparently, hundreds of schools offer courses such as "Science Fiction," "Mass Media," "Popular Religions," and "Popular Music and Society." The Popular Culture Association has reached a membership of about 2500 persons from all areas of the country; several hundred more belong to Regional PCA's. Despite the rapid increase in course offerings and despite increasing scholarly interest in popular culture, no recent attempt has been made to assess the state of popular culture studies in United States' higher education.

Because we feel it is necessary to obtain this information and because it will be a great benefit to interested persons at other institutions, we are creating a catalogue of popular culture courses offered in the United States. We hope the impact of this project will, among other things, enhance the communication between scholars mutually interested in various areas of Popular Culture. The goal of the project is a monograph listing the courses presently offered throughout the United States and an essay discussing trends, developments, strengths and failures of courses in popular culture.

Enclosed with this letter is the questionnaire for the project described above. Please complete the questionnaire at your earliest convenience and return it in the enclosed envelope.

The published outcome of the survey will include your name as a primary source. And for your assistance, we will be happy to provide you with a copy of the entire published survey at publication cost when it is available in the Fall of 1979.

Since you are the only faculty member of your school to whom this survey is being sent, if for any reason you cannot complete it, please pass it on to a competent colleague who is qualified and will do it.

If you have any questions we will be glad to answer them. Call at (419) 372-2981.

Sincerely,

Jack Nachbar
PCA Educational Programs Co-ordinator

Mark A. Gordon
Project Co-ordinator

PLEASE RETURN BY JANUARY 15, 1979

Instructions:
This research project is important to the developing field of Popular Culture and to all those who teach and work in this area. Please take some time out of your daily activities to complete the questionnaire in reasonable detail.

Since we are asking you to speak for your entire college/university, you may have to do some minor "research" yourself (e.g. consulting college bulletins). Please, do not limit your response to the particular department you are in. **It is necessary that we find out about courses offered throughout the entire college or university.**

We realize some of the questions might request information you simply cannot provide. Also, the second question asks for one-sentence course descriptions. We do not expect you to spend time describing each. **Simple course titles will suffice whenever the title is self-explanatory.**

We are concerned ONLY with Popular Culture courses. Do not include courses which use popular culture materials as supplementary parts of a traditional course (e.g. an introductory poetry course which uses some rock lyrics). Include only those courses which place their *central emphasis* on the study of popular artifacts, audiences, entertainments, formulas, social groups, etc. We intend to follow up on special cases or if some answers are ambiguous; so feel free to submit a course if you think that it is a Popular Culture course.

Most of the courses we are seeking will not be designated "Popular Culture" specifically. But even though there are few formal Popular Culture programs in the United States, many departments offer courses dealing with popular culture. The following are a few course examples to use as guidelines:

DEPT.	POPULAR CULTURE	NOT POPULAR CULTURE

English	Science Fiction
	Dime Novels
	Detective Fiction
	Literature of the Occult
		Media and Literature in
		  the Teaching of English
		Film as Literature
		  *Here the content is still
		  basically English, not P.C.

Radio, TV, and Film	Soap Opera in Television
	Theories of Popular Film
	The Western Genre
	Popular Art in Advertising
		Writing for Radio and
		  Television Filmmaking
		  or Film Production
		Advertising in Radio
		Radio Broadcasting
		  *These are not cultural
		  studies, but production (i.e.
		  "how to") courses.

Industrial Education &
  & Technology
	Man and Technology — The
	study of technology as shaper
	of the man-made world, human roles,
	and the future.
		Manufacturing
		Technology: Materials
		Processing
		  *Many technology courses
		  courses are primarily
		  vocational and therefore
		  not Popular Culture

Sociology	Love and Death in Modern
	  America
	i.e. if the emphasis is on
	the study of mass produced
	materials
		Sociology of the American
		  Family
		  *i.e. if the emphasis is
		  on fundamental
		  sociological principles
		  instead of mass trends,
		  popular values, etc.

POPULAR CULTURE STUDIES:
The State of the Discipline in Four-Year Colleges and
Universities in the United States

Please return to:

Dr. John G. Nachbar
Center for the Study of Popular Culture
Bowling Green State University
Bowling Green, OH 43403

_____   _____

(name)   (position or affiliation)

_____   _____

(department)   (institution)

_____   _____

(city, state, zip code)   (telephone)

Enrollment at your institution:

                              Undergraduate _____
                              Graduate _____

1. Are there any courses offered at your college/university which could be
classified as popular culture studies?

(circle one)   YES   NO

If NO, please move to question #3.

2. On the attached sheets at the back of the questionnaire please list the course(s)
and, if possible, offer:

a) a brief description of each, including graduate level or undergraduate;
experimental course; etc.
b) approximate number of students enrolled in each per year.
c) the year that each course was first offered.
d) the frequency of the course offering; i.e. how many times per academic
year is each course offered? Has it been offered only once?

3. Do you have knowledge of courses relating to popular culture that are planned
for the future at your college/university?

                    YES   NO

4. If YES, could you specify these and/or provide a general idea of what the
courses might concern:

Form for question #2

If more space is required for your response, you may supply additional sheets

MASS COMMUNICATIONS

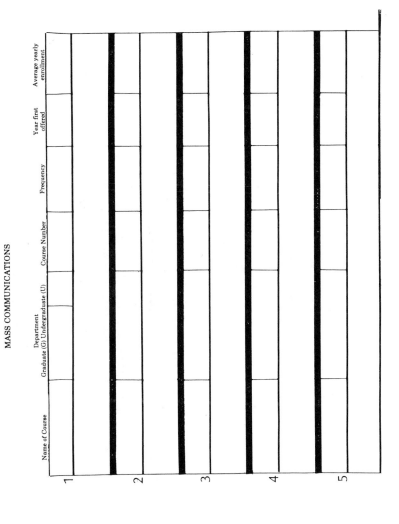

	Name of Course	Department Graduate (G) Undergraduate (U)	Course Number	Frequency	Year first offered	Average yearly enrollment
1						
2						
3						
4						
5						

Form for question #2

If more space is required for your response, you may supply additional sheets

PHYSICAL EDUCATION; FOREIGN LANGUAGE; SUB—CULTURE (e.g. Ethnic Studies); ETC.

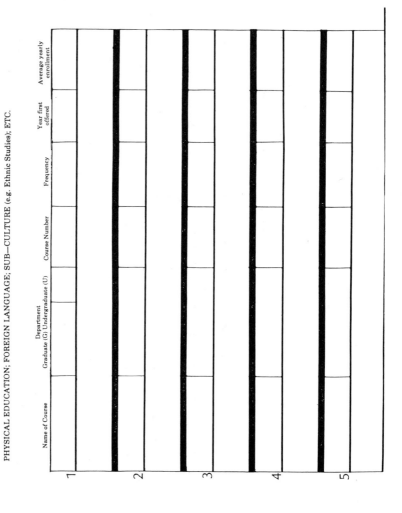

Name of Course	Department Graduate (G) Undergraduate (U)	Course Number	Frequency	Year first offered	Average yearly enrollment
1					
2					
3					
4					
5